UNDERSTANDING AUDIENCES
AND THE FILM INDUSTRY

Roy Stafford

Series Editor: Dr Stacey Abbott

Publisher's Note

The moving image is an integral part of our daily lives, representing an increasing share of our cultural activity. New generations of students know the moving image more intimately and more intensely than their predecessors, but are not always well served in relating this experience to the academic study of film and television.

'Understanding the Moving Image' is a series of short texts designed to orient the student new to the formal study of screen media. Each book introduces an important topic or theme within the subject. All the books are written at an accessible level, with no assumption of prior academic knowledge, by authors with teaching experience and a passion for their subject.

The series represents the BFI's commitment to making the appreciation and enjoyment of film and television and other screen media accessible to wider audiences. In particular, it is useful for the following readers:

- Students of film and media studies at post-16 level;
- Course leaders and teachers of film and media studies in schools, colleges and universities (first year);
- The general reader wanting an accessible introduction to the topic.

In *Understanding Audiences and the Film Industry*, Roy Stafford has produced a clearly structured and insightful account of a complex but fascinating topic. We hope you enjoy reading this book and that it helps you as you get to grips with the subject and develop your study of it. If you have any comments please do get in touch by emailing **publishing@bfi.org.uk**

With thanks to Stacey Abbott, for her help in the early stages of the development of this book.

First published in 2007 by the
British Film Institute,
21 Stephen Street,
London W1T 1LN

There is more to discover about film and television through the BFI. Our world-renowned archive, cinemas, festivals, films, publications and learning resources are here to inspire you. www.bfi.org.uk

Copyright © Roy Stafford, 2007

Typeset in the UK by Fakenham Photosetting Limited, Fakenham, Norfolk
Cover design: Paul Wright
Cover images: *Hero/Ying Xiong* (Beijing New Picture Film Co./Elite Group Enterprises, 2002); *Donnie Darko* (Pandora Cinema/Flower Films, 2001)

Printed in the UK by Cromwell Press, Trowbridge, Wiltshire

British Library Cataloguing-in-Publication Data
A catalogue record for this book is available from the British Library

ISBN 978–1–84457–141–3

UNDERSTANDING AUDIENCES AND THE FILM INDUSTRY

Preface

This is a book written by someone the UK film industry would describe as a 'frequent cinemagoer' (once a month or more). I have visited a wide range of cinemas on a regular basis for many years and I still watch a film in a cinema, with an audience, around once a week. I do not go to the cinema as often as some of my colleagues and nowadays I certainly visit arthouses more often than multiplexes, but I think I have a sense at least of what cinema audiences have been like and how they are changing. I also acquire large numbers of DVDs and record films from television, even though I do not actually like watching films on a video monitor.

My cinema habit is shared by a significant number of people (a quarter of the UK population are described as frequent cinemagoers) and rather more watch films regularly on television. Film (as viewed in cinemas) is not a mass medium in the same way as television, radio, the print press, or the internet. Much of the population sees only a handful of blockbusters in the cinema each year and a significant number of people never go to the cinema at all. There is also a small group of people (mostly reviewers, but also fans of various kinds) who experience cinema in all its varied forms on a very regular basis – but perhaps not in the same way as the rest of us. What is important is that we recognise that there is no single definitive cinema audience. Instead, there are many different audience groups with different expectations of cinema and many more audiences who watch films on DVD or broadcast television. Understanding this is fundamental to any formal analysis of audiences in film and media studies.

I think writers on film should watch films with a cinema audience, at least for some of the films they discuss. Quite often, film theory appears to come from academic writers who seem to have very little experience of sitting with an audience. Similarly, many film studies courses rely primarily on watching DVDs projected in a lecture theatre, and film reviewers routinely watch films with other reviewers in preview theatres on workday mornings. Distributors and exhibitors often have to make judgments based on screenings at tradeshows/festivals or from badly dubbed tapes or DVDs. There are good reasons why all of these professionals have to experience film in this way and most of them are well aware that the only way to get a clear understanding of how films work in cinemas is to sit in an auditorium with a paying audience, watching and listening to the audience and its reaction to the film.

In preparing for this book, I have reflected on both my recent and past experience of cinema going. There may be too much history here for some tastes, but I think it is necessary. Film history reveals that although things change, they often return to where they have been before, and this is certainly true of distribution and exhibition. For instance, the idea that local cinemas with digital projectors might be used to show live sports events (as in the 2006 football World Cup) is often discussed as an innovation. But there were similar experiments with television projected in cinemas in the early 1950s (see Gomery, 1985). I have included many historical references in the book precisely because the increasing use of the multiplex, by both younger and older audiences (often at different times), recalls aspects of cinema going from the 1950s and early 1960s when cinema was indeed a mass entertainment form.

There are several, sometimes quite detailed, analyses of films in the book. I have chosen these films because they seem to me to offer useful examples of the points I want to make. I am also conscious that they in some way reflect my taste in movies. I am not happy about commenting on films I do not fully understand, so I have left those out deliberately. Film teachers tend to divide films into two types – those they feel they need to see and those they want to see. Either way it is a matter of taste and judgment and I hope I have provided a wide range of examples, but the recognition that there are different audiences with different ideas about what they want to see is central to audience work. I make no assumptions about the cultural value film viewers assign to the films they watch – I simply record what they say about them and, where possible, include box-office figures that demonstrate how widely the films have been seen.

The UK and Ireland is currently the third largest cinema market (behind North America and Japan) by value and, because the market for DVDs has grown so quickly, it is now the second largest film market overall after North America. It is over 20 years since the dark days of 1984 when British Film Year was launched in a last desperate attempt to save cinema as an entertainment experience in the UK. Somehow we struggled into a brighter future, though there are always doom-mongers pronouncing film as 'finished'. I, for one, hope to spend many more years sitting comfortably in the dark anticipating a film screening. Now, on with the main feature.

Reference

Gomery, Douglas (1985), 'Theatre Television: The Missing Link of Technological Change in the U.S. Motion Picture Industry', *Velvet Light Trap*, no. 21, Spring

Contents

Preface	v
Acknowledgments	viii
Introduction	1
1: Agenda Setting	7
2: How the Film Industry Perceives Audiences	31
3: Distribution, Exhibition and Critical Commentary	56
4: How Do Audiences Read Films?	78
5: The Attraction of Stars and Genres	104
6: Theorising Audience Behaviour	117
7: Researching Audiences and the Film Market	134
8: The Culture of Film Viewing	147
Endpiece	175
Glossary	176
Resources	186
Index	188

Acknowledgments

This book would not have been possible without the help of colleagues in cinemas as well as the film teachers and students with whom I've worked over the years. Special thanks are due to Pat Bennett, Gill Branston, Paul Dewhirst, Chris Fell, Christine Geraghty, Nick Lacey, Bill Lawrence and Julia Short for help with specific questions I raised.

I'm also grateful to Wendy Earle for sensible advice and patience as an understanding editor.

Introduction

'Everybody loves the movies': it is an easy assumption to make, but in the century since the first film programmes were presented to a paying public, its veracity has been demonstrated all over the world. Film as a medium and as an entertainment form has proved to be genuinely universal. The circumstances in which people have watched films and the experience of watching them have changed significantly over time, but interest in stories delivered as sound and moving images has remained constant. The worldwide cinema audience at the start of the 21st century may be only a small fraction of what it was between the 1950s and the 1970s (particularly in the then massive markets of China and the Soviet Union), but those missing audiences still hunger for films watched on VHS, VCD and DVD and on television systems, both terrestrial and cable/satellite.

The film industry makes films and it needs audiences to pay to watch them. A straightforward statement that you might expect would be taken for granted as the basis for an understanding of films and film culture by filmmakers, audiences and scholars alike. But it is more complicated than that. Ask most people to select the best films or even the most successful films and they will tend to use a range of criteria in making their choices. How important will pleasing the audience or challenging the audience be in their selection? Most of us are really only aware of *ourselves* as the audience. Ask a filmmaker the same question about the best films and the response is likely to refer to artistic merit, technical skill and perhaps the importance of the story.

Consider the Academy Award ceremony for a moment, the filmmakers' own awards night. What are the criteria for deciding on the Best Picture? They are never properly spelled out, but it is interesting that it is the producer, not the director, who receives the award for Best Picture, so perhaps it is primarily about managing an industrial process? Is the Academy Award an award for selling the most cinema tickets? It is rare for a 'crowd pleaser' to win Best Picture. Wins for comedy films, for instance, are almost unheard of. Academy Awards are awarded by The Academy of Motion Picture Arts and Sciences, composed of industry personnel, which likes a serious and sometimes worthy drama that reflects well on its members, rather than a film that celebrates success in selling 'bums on seats'.

Film scholars have been studying films and film culture in a formal way since at least the 1920s, but film studies as a distinct academic discipline became established only in the 1960s. For much of its relatively short life, the new discipline has confined study of industry and audience to the margins, preferring to focus more acutely on formal questions about the filmic image, issues of narrative (how films tell their stories) and representation (how films re-present the peoples, places and ideas in the world around them). This has often involved imagining an audience who might read films rather than asking actual audiences what they thought of the films they had seen. When attention has focused on real audiences, it has tended to be from a position of lofty objectivity, from which researchers hope to establish the influence (usually malign) of films on susceptible populations. Fortunately, such work is less central to contemporary film studies and has been replaced by more interesting attempts to understand audiences in their great variety.

Work on the film industry as such has again been limited to specific aspects of the production process, with an understandable interest in how films are made, and to a lesser extent on exhibition practices – the culture of cinema going. There are also studies from a media economy approach that ask questions about the concentration of power among certain producers, about the impact of merchandising (the sale of goods related to characters in successful films) and the convergence of different media focused on film production (music, video games, TV, books etc.). What is much less common, at least within film studies, is any analysis of the business practices of the film industry, especially in the crucial process of distribution – getting the film to the audience (and vice versa), without which the film itself is meaningless.

The preponderance of certain kinds of film study in contemporary colleges and universities perhaps has something to do with the academic disciplines from which film scholars have been drawn. Film studies, like many of the other new fields of academic endeavour that developed in the 1960s, is multi-disciplinary, drawing on ideas and methodologies from English, linguistics, art history, sociology, philosophy, psychology etc. It shares interests with both media studies and cultural studies (both of which are perhaps more deeply rooted in social sciences), but it remains distinct. The approach adopted in this book will indeed be multi-disciplinary, including a pragmatic method informed by freelance work in cinema-based film education (i.e. teaching that requires consideration of which films are available to screen in public cinemas and often what might be attractive to a general public audience).

One of the major problems in researching film audiences is the sheer diversity of audience experiences at any one time. Much of the audience work in media studies has been related to television, which, until the arrival of multi-channel broadcasting, provided large audiences watching the same programme at the same time. By comparison, film audiences are much smaller, but may build over a long period. This raises a variety of questions. Does it make a difference, for instance, to see a film in its first week of release in a full cinema compared to experiencing the same film at the end of its run in a half-empty cinema? If there is a major news story (such as a terrorist attack, a murder trial etc.) during the run of a film with a similar theme, will it have an impact on audiences? We intend to answer some of these questions, at least partially, but there is plenty of research yet to be done.

The book also discusses research methodologies, acknowledging that all research has its drawbacks. The approach here is to draw on previously published research, augmented by a very small-scale primary research exercise, but also to make use of new forms of audience commentary provided via the internet. The different modes of internet commentary will be discussed in some detail. There are obvious problems with this material as a source, not least because of differences in accessing computers and in inclinations to participate in discussion about films. But as one element of a range of sources on audience experiences, internet commentary has definitely helped to expand our understanding.

The book's title, *Understanding Audiences and the Film Industry*, has been deliberately chosen to focus on the relationship between film producers, distributors and exhibitors and their audiences. In terms of academic film studies, it is therefore a book about 'Institutions' and 'Audiences': linking these two directly should prove useful for students, who often find the two concepts quite difficult. The discussion of the relationship between industry and audience should also be helpful for would-be filmmakers and those who want to work in other areas of the film industry, where the way in which decisions are made often appears quite bewildering. It is the case in many industries that its employees often forget (or are perhaps never introduced to) the basic function of their organisation – which in this case is nearly always to make films for paying audiences. The discussion of industry practices here might help to explain why decisions are made and create an appropriate focus for work on addressing the audience.

The book is written from a UK perspective, with a recognition that cinema going still has a local flavour despite the long-standing internationalisation of a film market dominated in most parts of the world by Hollywood. While there is not enough space to consider in much detail how the relationship between the film industry and its audiences might be different in Africa and Latin America, the book does include examples from outside UK, Europe and North America, especially from South Asia and East Asia, where audiences are largest. It is also important to recognise that the biggest audience of all is in India (over 3 billion) and that two-thirds of all the cinema audiences in the world are found in Asia.

How the book is organised

In one sense, this book deals with three separate stories – the industry story, the scholar's story and the audience's story. The first two can be studied through analysis of their practices and the publications they produce, but the audience's story is much less easily told. It will be an achievement if we can lay out at least some of the ways in which audiences engage with films. What should emerge from the book is a sense in which these three stories come together. Inevitably, there will be overlaps between the stories, with slightly different perspectives on the same experiences. I have tried to limit these overlaps and make cross-references wherever possible.

The book is organised as a guide. It is not a textbook and there is no set way to go through it. It does not claim to get you through any specific exam syllabus. Instead, it attempts to answer your questions, to explain how aspects of the film business work and to point you towards both useful reference works and theoretical writings that can extend your studies. Film studies offers a mixture of film history, cultural studies and a conceptual core comprising film language, narrative and genre, and representation, as well as audience and institution. It is impossible to write about the last two without reference to the other three. It is also difficult to explain why film scholars approach questions in a particular way without reference to how film studies itself has developed. As a consequence, I have included plenty of contextual material, along with, I hope, appropriate references that you can pursue. Some introductions and explanations are quite condensed, but you should be able to relate them to your other work on film.

Chapter 1 considers six examples from the range of films released in the UK in the last few years and the different ways in which these films have been distributed and exhibited to specific audiences. Reading through this chapter first should give you some ideas about the kinds of audience issues that are explored in more detail in each of the subsequent chapters. If you return to Chapter 1 after working through the other chapters, you should find that with your enhanced perspective on audiences, the examples give you even more insight.

Most of the other chapters can be read in any order. **Chapter 2** is designed to give you background on the film industry, especially in terms of production decisions. It takes you through an explanation of the production process and how this is influenced by a general industry approach to identifying audiences and creating films that they wish to watch.

Chapter 3 continues the exploration of the production process, concentrating on the distribution and exhibition of films. Distribution is often neglected in film studies, but it has a crucial role in determining which films audiences get to see and the circumstances in which they see them. The chapter includes a detailed study of the distribution of a recent British film, *Bullet Boy* (UK, 2004).

Chapter 4 considers film theory and its attempts to understand the ways in which audiences actually make sense of films. The chapter traces a shift in film studies from textual analysis, or the detailed study of individual films, towards ideas about how films have been read differently by real audiences in different viewing contexts. It includes a detailed analysis of how audiences have approached and responded to a recent film, *Brokeback Mountain* (USA, 2005). The shift from theories of **spectatorship** involving an imagined or implied spectator to theories of **reception** dealing with real audiences in cinemas marks an important development in film studies and its relationship to media studies and cultural studies.

Chapter 5 considers stardom and genre: two aspects of film studies that are generally recognised as important for audiences in selecting films to watch and in generally discussing their enjoyment of cinema. Two examples of recent films are considered. This chapter is really an extension of Chapter 4.

Chapter 6 explores ideas taken from film history and developments in media studies in exploring audience theories to discuss how audiences behave when offered films for consumption. These are mostly theoretical concepts used by external commentators as well as film theorists.

Chapter 7 focuses on the mechanics of audience research, both in terms of measuring audience numbers and eliciting ideas about behaviour. Where do we get our data from? What kinds of research and data are useful? There are examples of some small-scale research projects focusing on local cinemas. This chapter offers background to most of the rest of the book.

Chapter 8 explores the range of social practices related to film culture: going to the cinema, buying DVDs, watching films on television and discussing films in general. It considers why we choose some cinemas rather than others and what the consequences might be of switching our viewing to DVD and other media.

Further work

All of the sources consulted in the book should be clearly referenced. They are included both to give validity to the statements made, and second to provide you with a means of extending your studies. It is inevitable that some quite complex theoretical ideas will be introduced but not explained in detail – they should figure in other parts of your course or in more advanced studies at a later stage. The concern here is that audience studies are placed in context and that the references provide that context. The book employs two forms of specialised terms: academic/theoretical terms and those used by industry personnel. When such terms are first used in a chapter, they are given in bold, and are also explained in more detail in the Glossary. References are given at the end of each chapter and there is a list of useful general resources at the end of the book.

1. Agenda Setting

This chapter explores several short case studies of relatively recent films in order to establish a range of key questions about the film industry and audiences. There are six case studies in all, each chosen to represent a different relationship between producer, film and audience. This includes consideration of stars, budgets, recognisable genre elements and whether they are shown in **mainstream** *or specialised cinemas.*

Throughout this book, there is a conscious attempt to explore the relationships between producers, distributors and exhibitors, and audiences – all of which are linked via the films themselves. It seems logical to start with some relatively well-known films and to use them to sketch out what the main concerns of the book will be.

The film business is highly volatile. The process of making, distributing and exhibiting films is dynamic. Unlike some other forms of economic activity, it is difficult to predict trends in production and consumption. The industry nearly always appears to be in a state of boom or slump, and there is a general air of anxiety (and occasionally euphoria) among industry personnel. There is no certainty about the success of products that cost millions of dollars to make, but which may die in just a few days in cinemas. In an industry (filmed entertainment: cinema, DVD, television) with an international turnover predicted to rise to $104.5 billion by 2010 (*Screen International*, 22 June 2006), this lack of certainty can have various consequences, not all of them obvious at first sight. For instance, anxiety about failure can mean that producers are reluctant to try anything new and instead turn to projects that depend on proven properties, such as a best-selling book, a franchise title or a straight sequel. On the other hand, producers will often be happier spending a great deal of money on a production that could be made for less, simply because they feel more comfortable with big budgets.

Hollywood films are routinely called 'blockbusters', but the actual meaning of this term is not clear. Some suggest that it refers to the enormous bombs dropped on Germany in 1945, others that it refers to the city-centre blocks around which audiences queued for the cinema. In the 1970s, it began to be applied to films like *Jaws* (1975) that opened on the same day in cinemas across North America. (Current distribution practices are less than 30 years old.)

The task of film industry professionals is, at least in part, to be aware of audiences and their changing tastes. A glance through the trade press at various times of year reveals the concerns over territories with shrinking audiences. At the same time, there are likely to be some territories where admissions are rising. Modern industry practice depends heavily on a handful of major blockbusters – or '**tentpole**' movies. This helps to fuel anxiety, as the presence of one or two bankers, such as a *Harry Potter* or *Lord of the Rings*, can lift the overall box office one year, while the absence of such bankers in the next year almost guarantees that admissions will be down. In this rather febrile climate, it is possible to discern some clearly differentiated approaches to specific films and their assumed audiences.

Between the 1930s and 1960s, when cinema was a mass medium in most of the developed world, and before the triumph of television, releasing films was a more standardised process, partly because major studios made films to be shown in their own cinemas. Although there were clearly some films that made more money than others, the difference between the most successful and least successful films was much less than it is now. Contemporary cinema can be roughly divided into three separate categories:

- high-budget tentpoles;
- mainstream movies on wide release;
- specialised films that require a more selective and considered release.

These categories sometimes overlap and the films that fall somewhere between any two of these institutional categories can be the most interesting to study, because they ask more questions of both producer/distributor and audience. The six case studies here include examples from all three categories and also an example of a completely different system that lies outside the Hollywood-dominated international industry.

1. The 'tentpole': *Ice Age 2: The Meltdown* – The release of a Hollywood blockbuster

Tentpole movies have also been called 'ultra-high budget movies' (see Wyatt, 1994) and 'event movies'. To some extent, the high production cost is a contributing factor to the event. Some audiences may watch such a film simply to find out where the money has gone. Others go to a screening to be part of the event, and to be able to discuss it with everyone else. This was most evident with the release of *The Da Vinci Code* in 2006 – a film universally panned by critics that nonetheless achieved very high admission numbers and clearly became a social event for some audiences. Tentpole movies hope to achieve a box office worldwide of $500 million or more. Given production budgets and marketing costs that can total $200 million, anything under $500 million will mean that the film loses money in cinemas (see Chapter 2 for an explanation of the economics of production and distribution). The theatrical box office and profile will help to launch the DVD release (now the main source of revenue). To put this into perspective, the number of people who see any one of these films exceeds over 100 million worldwide. In the UK, over 10 million saw *Shrek 2* in 2004. (Estimate from <lumiere.obs.coe.int>.) This is no more than might see a popular television show, although the DVD release of the film will have more than doubled the total UK audience. The eventual free-to-air TV broadcast will further boost the figures. The audience will be large, but a significant proportion will visit the cinema only once or twice a year. The distributor must attract these occasional cinemagoers in large numbers. Tentpoles are about maximising numbers – and the numbers need to be very large to make profits.

> David Bordwell's book *The Way Hollywood Tells It: Story and Style in Modern Movies* (2006) has an appendix that gives useful information on the annual performance of the North American box office in the last decade.

> It is much more difficult to find out about the rentals/sales figures for films on DVD than for box office admissions. Figures from the MPAA reveal US consumer spending on DVDs in 2005 at over $23 billion. Cinema box office in US was around $9 billion.

1.1 Commercial tie-ins for *Ice Age: The Meltdown* presented on the Kellogg's website.

Tentpoles work best when they appeal to what is referred to as a **four quadrants** audience – i.e. every sector, including children, young adults, parents, male and female etc.

The 'trade association' of the Hollywood studio majors, the **MPAA**, publishes budget averages each year. The average cost to make and market an MPAA film was $96.2 million in 2005. This includes $60 million in negative costs and $36.2 million in marketing costs (from <www.mpaa.org/researchStatistics.asp>).

The most successful films (in box-office terms) are usually those targeting a family audience, and recently that has meant animated films designed to cater for both children and adults alike. The first *Ice Age* film was released by 20th Century-Fox on 15 March 2002 in North America and a week later in the UK and many other **territories**. This was a **wide release**, opening simultaneously in a cinema in every major town and city in each territory. It went on to gross $382 million worldwide.

The next title in what Fox hope will become a **franchise** was released on 2 April 2006 – just in time to build a family audience for the Easter holidays. The second time around, Fox increased the number of prints, hoping to fully exploit the buzz factor surrounding the wide opening. More prints (over 1,000 in Germany) meant an even greater outlay and therefore even more pressure to get audiences into the cinema in the first week. With a production budget of $75 million, the expectation would be that a further $30 million plus would be spent on promotion in North America.

Skwigly animation magazine (<www.biganimation.com>) reported that Fox raised an estimated $100 million in promotional support for the release. In North America, this involved considerable **synergistic** promotional activity – i.e. on Fox television channels – as well as partnerships with food retailers such as Kellogg's, Burger King, Wal-Mart, Safeway etc. (See Fig 1.1) These are familiar partners on family films, utilising the **pester power** of children, who demand cereal packets carrying *Ice Age*-related toys etc. However, it is important that the appeal is made to as wide an audience as possible, so some of the TV tie-ins, and a major promotion via the *Ice Age* Playstation 2 video game, target the important 15–35 age group. In the UK, one of the soft drink tie-ins with the German company WILD involved Capri-Sun and a puzzle game, with prizes of a PS2 game.

The promotions seem to have worked, with *Ice Age: The Meltdown* raising $427 million at the box office worldwide after just four weeks. Fox continued to monitor the performance of the film over the ensuing weeks, noting which territories had done particularly good box-office business and which may need further support or a different strategy for a third film (or indeed a different franchise using similar elements). The release will also have been analysed in terms of the time of year and how it performed against potential competitors. As an Easter opening, this film avoided most of the big blockbusters that launch in the 'holiday season', starting at the beginning of May in North America.

All the major studios have tentpole films each year. In 2006, the list for the first nine months of the year looked like this (US release date in brackets):

Disney:	*Cars (9 June), Pirates of the Caribbean: Dead Man's Chest (7 July)*
Paramount:	*M:i:III (5 May)*
Sony:	*The Da Vinci Code (19 May)*
Fox:	*Ice Age 2: The Meltdown (15 March), X-Men: The Last Stand (26 May)*
Universal:	*Miami Vice (28 July)*
Warner Bros:	*Poseidon (12 May), Superman Returns (28 June)*

Of the six majors, Paramount appears to be least concerned with the blockbuster strategy, generally spending less on its annual **slate** of films than the other studios. All the other majors regularly spend over $100 million on a single film in the hope of establishing or maintaining a franchise. The nine films in the above list are all, with the exception of *Cars*, either sequels/instalments in franchises or successful properties from other media (TV/novel). *Cars* is heavily identified with similar animation films from Pixar, the makers of *Toy Story* (1995) and *The Incredibles* (2004). In terms of release strategies, none of the titles clashed during the first week of release, although four titles were released on successive weekends in May at the start of the summer season.

The six major studios are all components of larger media corporations, which affords the possibility of using partner companies to promote the films and related products. In summer 2006, Fox introduced a new element, announcing that MySpace.com, recently acquired by the Fox parent, News Corporation, would become an outlet for promotional material for Fox releases. At the same time, Warner Bros. were contemplating the further decline of AOL as an internet service provider. AOL-Time Warner was founded in a highly publicised merger in 2001, with AOL as a senior partner. In just five years AOL's value had fallen dramatically and its name was dropped from the Time Warner company title. The changing fortunes of AOL and MySpace serve to show that nothing is assured in relation to new technologies. However, the one constant in the film industry is the enduring status of the six major studios, which have each survived 80 years or more because they are able to release around 20 to 30 films (including some tentpoles) each year.

AUDIENCE ISSUE 1
The tentpole titles need to appeal to as wide an audience as possible and because they must appeal to both occasional and frequent cinemagoers, they must be supported by extensive and expensive promotion, driving audiences into cinemas on the opening weekend and mopping up over the next two or three on the back of perceived popularity.

RESEARCH SUGGESTION
Look back over any year and identify the tentpole pictures distributed by each of the major studios. Try to define them as 'successful' or 'unsuccessful' using the production budget and box office totals listed on www.the-numbers.com What conclusions do you draw from this exercise?

2. The genre cycle and the remake for the mainstream: *Ringu/The Ring* – Audiences and genre films

Outside the summer and Thanksgiving/Christmas holiday periods, Hollywood (and the exhibitors) need to keep the cash flowing with a regular, reliable stream of product. This is the category of the mainstream movie on wide release. From the distributor's perspective, there is on the surface not much difference between these films and the tentpoles. They go out wide to every city and the opening weekend is crucially important. However, unlike the tentpole, these are not films that will necessarily be seen as major events, with massive expectations built up over several months. They are less likely to attract the occasional cinemagoer and more reliant on frequent attenders and, in particular, core audiences of 12–29-year-olds. With less emphasis on the **property** itself and smaller budgets/less spectacle, these films rely more on stars and genre appeal to entice audiences. Chapter 5 focuses in detail on stars and genres, here the focus is on one interesting example. Because horror films target the core audience directly, horror has retained its popularity in a film industry that now usually focuses on very broad genre categories such as comedy or simply mixes familiar elements from different genres. The result is that horror films are far more likely to interest fans than most other forms of mainstream cinema.

> The key youth audience is defined differently in the USA and the UK, but 15–24 is certainly one of the most important audiences.

In 1998, a low-budget Japanese film *Ringu* (*The Ring*) scored a hit in its own domestic market. This should not have been too much of a surprise, as the original 1991 novel (one of a series) on which the film was based had already been adapted for television (twice) and had appeared in audio form, as a *manga* book and as a fairground 'experience' (see Branston and Stafford, 2006, Case Study: 'J-horror and The Ring Cycle'). The Japanese film industry was the world's biggest during the 1930s and again in the 1960s, but it suffered badly from disappearing audiences in the 1970s and has not since recovered its dominant status. Even so, ticket prices are so high in Japan that box-office revenue remains strong, taking second place only to North America in this respect. However, most Japanese audiences watch American films. Local production, apart from certain high-profile titles such as the animations from Studio Ghibli (*Spirited Away*, 2001; *Howl's Moving Castle, 2004* etc.), is mainly confined to low-budget production, little of which is seen in the West. *Ringu* proved to be a notable exception, and this 'urban myth' about a deadly video recording went on to become successful elsewhere in East Asia and in arthouse and DVD distribution in Europe. *Ringu* proved to be the first of a **cycle** of similar films that came to the attention of Hollywood producers and, in 2002, a remarkably faithful (by Hollywood standards) remake was released by DreamWorks in North America. *The Ring* proved to be enormously popular both at home and internationally (out grossing the original in Japan) and in turn introduced a cycle of Hollywood remakes of East Asian horror films.

1.2 Matsushima Nanako plays the TV reporter, Asakawa Reiko, in *Ringu*.

Ringu is interesting in terms of audiences for a number of reasons. First, the original story as written by Suzuki Kôji was deliberately altered by the filmmakers precisely to meet the expectations of the cinema audience. The novel offered a male investigator hero, but the film producers recognised that the predominantly young cinema audience would expect a young female protagonist, similar to those found in Hollywood films such as *Scream* (1996) – the so-called 'Last Girl' who defeats the monster. By the time the American film appeared, there was a complex interaction between American and Japanese filmic ideas about horror and gender representation.

A genre cycle typically begins with a relatively low-budget film that is a surprise hit, and which is then remade with a bigger budget. Subsequent films may be sequels or based on different stories, but with a similar mix of genre elements.

Ringu did have an effect on Hollywood horror, helping to shift the focus away from the self-referential and jokey tone of films like *Scream* back to more psychological horror. This in turn allowed the producers to get a lower audience certificate for the remake (PG-13 rather than R

The Ring had a production budget of $45–48 million, with a large promotional budget of $35 million in North America (<www.the-numbers.com>). The worldwide gross on the film was $229 million.

in the USA, 15 rather than 18 in the UK) from the MPAA and the **BBFC** and therefore to market the film more successfully to a wider audience demographic (including a larger percentage of young women – see *Screen International*, 8 April 2005). In order to survive a ratings decision that many horror 'fans' might see as an indication that the film was not 'scary', *The Ring* had to deliver an effective psychological narrative. Despite DreamWorks' decision not to release the Japanese film in North America, significant numbers of horror fans acquired copies on video and DVD from Europe and East Asia. Matt Hills (2005) has analysed the ways in which fans have discussed the differences between the Japanese and American versions the film. Not surprisingly perhaps, the fans who found the Japanese version first claim that it is the 'best' (i.e. scariest). But they also seem to feel that an American version is not totally without value if it introduces audiences to the original. They feel secure in this position, because they were themselves the original American audience, finding the film via the internet.

The existence of a large group of horror fans, now organised around various websites, mailing lists and internet fora such as the Ringworld <www.theringworld.com/>, means that fans do have an impact on future releases and production decisions. In an immediate sense, the existence of such a fan base has encouraged specialist DVD distributors like Tartan, Optimum and Premier Asia/Hong Kong Legends in the UK to release both DVDs and some theatrical titles. This in turn has prompted cinema bookers, festivals and book publishers to look for other East Asian material and to keep developing an interest in East Asian cinema. Although not easily quantifiable, this audience factor is a generally accepted part of what has become an important element in recent film culture. It is related to, but distinct from, a more producer-led parallel development in Hollywood/East Asian co-production (see the comments on *Crouching Tiger, Hidden Dragon* below).

AUDIENCE ISSUE 2

How do cycles develop in terms of audience interest and producers' commitment? What is the relationship between hardcore fans and the more general audience for genre films?

RESEARCH SUGGESTION

On a generalist film website such as the Internet Movie Database (IMDb.com), look at a range of 'User Comments' on a current horror film. Then search for comments on the same film on specialist horror fan websites. Is there any difference in the type of comments? To what extent do fans attempt to influence more general debates – or do they want to keep their enjoyment of the genre to themselves?

The Ring was the first of a cycle of remakes of East Asian horror films. Subsequent films in the cycle saw box-office returns declining from *The Ring*'s high point (*The Grudge*, 2004; *The Ring Two*, 2005; *Dark Water*, 2005; *Pulse*, 2006 etc.). The producers are likely to find themselves in a position of making a film for the cycle at a time when the general audience has clearly turned away. They then have various options, such as abandoning production, shelving the finished film or releasing straight to DVD. In 2006, this appeared to be the reality, with some audiences seemingly moving towards films like *Saw* (with two films released and a third due soon) featuring more graphic scenes.

3. The 'art' or specialised film: Hidden – *How do films appealing to 'minority tastes' find their audiences?*

> Even in a year when powerful, politically engaged movies abound among the mainstream awards nominations, there is one film everyone is talking about above all others. Despite being absent from the Baftas and Oscars, *Hidden* (*Caché*), directed by Michael Haneke, has become the topic of heated conversations around water coolers and over dinner tables across the country. It is on its way to becoming the defining film of a generation. (Jason Solomons, *The Observer*, Sunday 19 February, 2006)

As this quote indicates, *Hidden* was received, in the UK at least, as a very different kind of film from all of the others listed here. The reference to water-cooler culture and the discussion of art films across dinner tables suggests two particular audiences. The first is the broad white-collar audience of office workers who, each day, have a topic of conversation, often based on what was on television last night. Solomons is perhaps being a bit fanciful if he imagines this is a particularly large audience (who will, in any case, not have seen the film on the same night), but certainly *Hidden* might have been discussed in some London offices when the film opened and in other cities that showed the film. The dinner tables, however, refer to a more narrowly defined audience – educated, wealthy and accustomed to attending arts events, perhaps? *Hidden* might best be described as an **art film**, although many would argue that the term is no longer widely used and the **UK Film Council** would now describe it simply as **specialised cinema**.

For many audiences, the concept of an art film is probably linked to subtitles, and for many years the most widely distributed art films came from France – the largest European producer of films and the European country with the largest audience base (i.e. size multiplied by frequency of attendance). In the UK, French-language films are now second to Hindi-language Bollywood films in terms of the numbers in distribution in the UK, and their overall audience numbers are falling. The consequence of this is that apart from one or two exceptions (specifically the two Jean-Pierre Jeunet films, *Amélie*, 2001, and *A Very Long Engagement*, 2004), most French films are now restricted to limited releases and can expect a UK box-office take of less than £500,000. In 2004, 31 French language films were released and only one, *Look at Me*, achieved that target.

The traditional audience for French films in the UK is often French-speaking, having learned the language at school and university. With the decline of language teaching in the UK education system, this audience is not being replenished with sufficient younger members and, although still enthusiastic for films, is getting older. Significantly in 2004, *Look at Me* was topped at the box office by two Spanish-language films, two Mandarin films (see *Hero* and *House of Flying Daggers* below),

1.3 Daniel Auteuil and Juliette Binoche star as the bourgeois couple at the centre of *Hidden*.

four in Hindi and one in Japanese (*Zatoichi*). How then did *Hidden* reverse the trend and garner £1 million in only a few weeks?

Hidden was directed by Michael Haneke, a veteran Austrian/German director who emerged from a television career to make *Funny Games* (Austria 1997), a controversial film about violence, which was widely discussed by critics. In 2001 he produced *The Piano Teacher*, in French and starring Isabelle Hupert, well-known to arthouse audiences, as was Juliette Binoche who appeared for him in *Code Unknown* (France 2000) as well as *Hidden*. Both these films were high profile for specialised films. *The Piano Teacher* raised disturbing questions about sexual behaviour – just as *Funny Games* had challenged views about violence. Although *The Piano Teacher* received a limited release, it eventually did reasonably well at the box office, but this was spread over three years according to the LUMIERE database (DVD income figures have not been published but may also have been significant).

> Despite the concerns of 'moral watchdogs', films that deal directly with non-mainstream sexual behaviour are rarely big money-earners in UK cinemas – at least not since the 1970s and *Emmanuelle*.

Hidden won Haneke the Best Director prize at Cannes in 2005. Its subject matter is less overtly shocking (apart from a single incident of sudden violence) in terms of sex and violence than the previous films, but it remains a thriller predicated on surveillance, a topical theme, and its protagonist is a TV reviewer. Perhaps this struck a chord with reviewers of the film? When it opened in the UK in January 2006, it received very positive reviews – not just in the films section, but more widely in the arts pages of the quality press. For example, Mark Lawson in the *Guardian* (20 January 2006): 'it's my contention that *Hidden* is one of the first great movies of the 21st century'. As an influential figure who is also associated with BBC Radio 4's arts review programme *Front Row* and BBC2's *Late Review*, Lawson's recommendations are meaningful for a significant proportion of the target audience for *Hidden*.

The film's UK distributors, the well-established and experienced Artificial Eye team, were cautious in releasing the film on only 26 prints, but because of the initial response this was raised to 37 and then 40 prints by week four. How important was the positive critical reception for the film? This is a difficult question to answer. In the case of mainstream films, there have been several cases where, fearful of the critical reception, distributors have simply refused to offer preview screenings for critics and released the film directly to the public (e.g. *The Pink Panther* remake in 2006). Overall, it is difficult to draw any conclusions about the outcome of such action. In the case of *The Pink Panther*, audiences were in line with most industry expectations, but in other cases, such as *The Avengers* remake in 1998, audiences quickly decided that the producers were correct in thinking that they were responsible for a ($60 million) turkey.

Most mainstream audiences are not going to read the *Guardian*, or even watch Jonathan Ross on his BBC1 Film programme, and are unlikely to be deterred by bad reviews in these and similar publications. However, the much smaller arthouse audience is more open to persuasion. It might be worth exploring the interest in *Hidden* in terms of the popular business model described by Malcolm Gladwell in his book *The Tipping Point* (2002). The model suggests that certain consumer goods can sell reasonably well over a period time, but can then suddenly increase in popularity when knowledge about them (and positive reaction) reaches a **tipping point**. The idea has since been applied in a range of contexts: Gary Younge in the *Guardian* (27 June 2005) used the model to explore how ideas about the war in Iraq changed in terms of US public opinion. The tipping point need not be a single event or be influenced by a single cause. When *Hidden* was released, it was in a period when quality films are often launched in the UK – after the Christmas holiday season and leading up to the Awards period in February/March (which, since 2001, has included the British Film Awards from BAFTA as well as the Academy Awards). In this period, a well-reviewed film receives further publicity by association with similar quality films. *Hidden* was released at a time when the arthouse audience in the UK was already eager to see (and discuss) *Brokeback Mountain*, released just after Christmas, and was anticipating George Clooney's *Good Night, and Good Luck.*

It is worth remembering that many individuals in the cinema audience will visit the cinema only once or twice a year and if they have a good experience with one film, they might make their other visit based on a trailer they see in the cinema. It is also worth remembering that films with only a limited number of prints take some time to reach isolated art cinemas, and *Hidden* was still making money in April 2006, even though it dropped out of the list of top 15 films in late February.

How much can a good review drive the art audience in these circumstances? There are two cinemas at the National Media Museum in Bradford (excluding the

IMAX screen). Pictureville has 300 seats and the Cubby Broccoli Cinema has 100 seats. For the week of 17–23 February, 2006, the new films in the programme included both *Hidden* and *North Country* (USA, 2005). *Hidden* was placed in the smaller cinema and *North Country* in the larger. This must have seemed quite logical based on the previous performance of Michael Haneke films and the fact that Charlize Theron was being touted as an Academy Award nominee for best female actor for her role in *North Country*. In the event, *Hidden* attracted large audiences and *North Country* struggled. The two films were switched, and *Hidden* proved a big success in the larger cinema. Like many regional independent cinemas, Pictureville has a printed programme published in advance and it is difficult to retain films for an extra week (even if this was possible, given the demand for the limited number of prints in circulation). *Hidden* had to wait until late March to get another booking, by which time interest in the film in Bradford had to some extent dwindled.

Why was *Hidden* such a hit? Part of the answer probably concerns the controversial ending, which viewers would often refuse to reveal to their friends, enticing new audiences by word of mouth and setting up a real sense of excitement. But as to who was being excited, the Pictureville box office offers a clue. Many independent cinemas now collect data about their audiences. On a very obvious level, they know where their audiences live via credit card addresses and various membership discount schemes. They may also have asked audiences questions about their other arts consumption, including which newspapers they read. For instance, the Pictureville audience includes a very high percentage of *Guardian* and *Independent* readers – significantly higher than in the population as a whole. It might be that a combination of good reviews and press coverage generally, proximity to other films popular with the same audience and strong word of mouth was enough to push the film to the tipping point in a number of significant cinemas. (*Good Night, and Good Luck* also did well in Pictureville a few weeks later, selling out on its opening night.) Bill Lawrence, the experienced Head of Film at the museum, suggested that *Hidden* might have been seen as a 'human story' and that French films with strong stories have traditionally attracted the arthouse audience. He quotes much earlier examples such as the Claude Berri films from 1986, *Jean de Florette* and *Manon des sources*. Film scholars might be surprised to see *Hidden* bracketed with these films, but the suggestion matches the idea of a traditional audience, which, given some prompting, will go to see a successful French film.

Just like the audience for mainstream films, the audience for specialised films like *Hidden* actually

The poster for *Lemming* (France, 2006) included a quote from a *Guardian* columnist announcing the film as 'the best thing since *Hidden*', suggesting that *Hidden* has now become part of a pantheon of recent French cinema.

AUDIENCE ISSUE 3
How different is the audience for specialised cinema and does it require different methods of distribution and exhibition to cater for it? In particular, does it require different marketing techniques?

comprises several different groups. It will include the traditional middle-class art audience described here (which, as we have noted, does not necessarily visit the cinema often); the element of the mainstream audience which is attracted to anything successful and high profile; and the **cinephile** audience that seeks out films by a specific director deemed important in terms of cinema. The difference between the first and third of these audiences is that the first is perhaps more interested in content, while the third is more interested in style. The mainstream audience may simply be there to see what all

RESEARCH SUGGESTION
Analyse your own responses to the idea of specialised cinema. Do you visit cinemas that regularly play specialised films? Do you search out films that are not advertised on television or in the mainstream press? What do you think attracts some people and puts off others about the concept of a specialised film?

the fuss is about. The tipping point for *Hidden* was perhaps reached when two of these audience groups became big enough to prompt the attention of the third: then, in a combustion process, word of mouth and press commentary saw one group sparking another over a period of a few weeks.

4. The crossover subtitled film: *Crouching Tiger, Hidden Dragon/Hero/House of Flying Daggers* – Audience response to studio-backed films from non-English-speaking film cultures

The Holy Grail of many film distributors is the **crossover film** – the film made for one market that succeeds in selling to others. In particular, Hollywood distributors are interested in films made outside North America (and therefore less expensively) that can be promoted to a range of audiences in North America and other territories. Hollywood distributors have two options: either to make (finance) the films themselves through an overseas partner or to buy the **rights** to completed films. Both these options have figured over the history of Hollywood, but apart from English-language productions from the UK and Australia, all such films raise questions about subtitling or dubbing and about whether genres developed in other countries will work for American audiences.

The massive North American box office for *Crouching Tiger, Hidden Dragon* in 2000–1(see <www.the-numbers.com>) set a new record for a foreign-language film (i.e. shown subtitled in cinemas, but with a dubbed version available as an alternative on DVD), with $128 million gross. *Crouching Tiger* was a co-production between China, Hong Kong, Taiwan and Hollywood, with American and Chinese contributions to the screenplay and direction by Ang Lee, a Taiwanese director who trained in the USA and who has worked consistently on Hollywood productions. The box-office figures and user comments on various websites suggest that *Crouching Tiger* was generally seen as a Hollywood film. This appears to refer to the production values and to the handling of the narrative. Most North American audiences had little or no knowledge of the traditional Chinese genre of the *wu xia* or martial chivalry film, so *Crouching Tiger* was received as highly original. In East Asia, however, where *wu xia* has long been a popular genre (both as literature and

1.4 Maggie Cheung is Flying Snow, 'heroic swordswoman' and one of the four central characters in the *wu xia* film *Hero*.

film), *Crouching Tiger* was viewed as a rather academic/art film compared to more popular Hong Kong *wu xia* films. (On the other hand, some Taiwanese users on the IMDB praise *Crouching Tiger*, citing its attention to detail.) The final box-office total for *Crouching Tiger* shows a skew towards North America: $128 million, with $105 million from the international market.

This skew was reversed for *Hero* (2002), which took $53 million in North America and $124 million internationally, including over $30 million in China (*Screen International*, 19 August 2003). *Hero* is a Chinese film, co-written and directed by Zhang Yimou, one of a handful of internationally-known and celebrated Chinese directors who emerged in the 1980s as members of the 'Fifth Generation' of students from the Beijing Film Academy. Zhang has been quite clear in interviews that he was making a *wu xia* film, albeit with a much larger budget than most other Chinese films and some variations in the genre elements. He did not make the film for American audiences. *Hero* is officially a Chinese film, but it was picked up by Miramax for North American distribution and re-titled *Jet Li's Hero*, as Li has appeared in a number of mainstream Hollywood action films. *Hero* also received a wide release in the UK, where, as in North America, it was successful, but not on the same scale as *Crouching Tiger*. In many territories, *Hero* drew audiences attracted by rather differently conceptualised stars. The meeting of martial arts stars Jet Li and Donnie Yen attracted a certain kind of fan audience, while the presence of Maggie Cheung, Tony Leung and Zhang Yimou as director attracted an arthouse audience educated by Zhang's earlier films and those of

Wong Kar-Wai (e.g. *In the Mood for Love* Hong Kong/France/Thailand, 2000, also starring Maggie Cheung and Tony Leung).

The third international *wu xia* film was *House of Flying Daggers*, also directed by Zhang Yimou, but this time distributed in North America by Sony Classics. The box-office split was even further skewed towards the international market at $11 million:$81 million. Veering more towards romance, the film elevates Zhang Ziyi (a supporting player in both *Crouching Tiger* and *Hero*) to the principal role, supported by two more of the Hong Kong stars known to both popular and art house audiences in the West, Andy Lau and Takeshi Kaneshiro. The internet feedback on these three films, which are often directly compared, is revealing of the range of responses and the difficulties audiences have in moving from the familiar to the unknown, even when, in many ways, the three films might appear to share similar elements of content and form.

At a basic level, the three films share a genre. *Wu xia pian* is a 'martial chivalry film' that features trained warriors with super-powers related to swordplay. These warriors live according to a strict code and they generally battle with similarly trained warriors who have broken away from the code. Combats take place in magical environments away from the world of ordinary mortals. All three films push the *wu xia* towards romance (in a way that reminds us that the word 'romance' in European languages originally referred to the tales of knightly endeavour and courtly love). Although the historical time period is different in each film, it is not likely to appear so to many audiences. The stars of the three films represent the cream of Hong Kong, Chinese and Taiwanese talent, but, with the exception of Jet Li, were perhaps not widely known in North America when the films were released. This leaves the main difference between the films as the directorial presence of Ang Lee and Zhang Yimou (there is also a difference between the approach to the scripts, but as both directors had a strong influence on the scripts, we will take them as representative of two creative teams).

The crucial difference appears to be that Ang Lee approached the whole enterprise from his position of being trained within the American industry. Objectivity in considering the three films is arguably impossible, but let us try. *Crouching Tiger* has more plot than the other two films. It is slow-paced, but includes well-staged action sequences. Visually it is a beautiful film, displaying control in staging and little use of visible CGI work (i.e. traditional Hong Kong wire work is used instead). Zhang Yimou is only three years older than Lee, but has worked consistently in a very different industry to make more features, including several that have gained critical acclaim on the festival circuit. For cinephiles, Zhang's reputation would be much higher than Lee's when the two films were released. *Hero* and *House of Flying Daggers* could both display familiar Zhang traits, including the use of colour, the slow and deliberate staging of carefully choreographed ritual scenes – and the explosion of violent action. Zhang's cinema makes more use of symbolic imagery than is usually tolerated in Hollywood, and this has been one of the ways through which he has conducted a long struggle with Chinese censors. Both *Hero* and *House of Flying Daggers* are thin on plot, but, in the case of *Hero*, very strong on narrative, which audiences are challenged to work through. The reaction of American cinemagoers (which is mostly what is available via IMDb and other internet sources) suggests that the mainstream audience recognises Lee's command of the Hollywood narrative, but, without the background of Zhang's previous work, feels able to dismiss *House of Flying Daggers* and to place *Hero* as inferior to *Crouching Tiger*.

There are perhaps three distinct audience groupings that would have each taken a different stance on the three films. The mainstream audience rarely if ever watches subtitled films and therefore needs the assurance, whether directly recognised or more subconsciously felt, that they are watching a Hollywood film, even if it is being presented in another language. The martial arts fan audience compares all three films to a body of martial arts films, including both North American and East Asian productions. Although this audience may not necessarily know *wu xia*, it will be much more familiar with aspects of the story in all three films. Unlike the mainstream audience, the martial arts fans may be surprised to see such big-budget productions on the largest **multiplex** screen. (Zhang's two films were low budget for Hollywood, but big budget for East Asia.) The third audience knows Zhang and perhaps to a lesser extent Lee (although this will have changed since *Brokeback Mountain*) from the arthouse films of the 1980s and 1990s. They will be surprised by the action content and perhaps by the unfamiliar (to them) appearance of Hong Kong actors they recognise from rather different kinds of films. They will also be surprised to find these films at the multiplex – although in many cases they will wait until the film appears at an art/independent cinema. Overall, they are likely to be more tolerant of the differences between the three films.

It will be interesting to see what happens to similar recent or projected films by Chinese filmmakers with international reputations, such as Chen Kaige (*The Promise*, 2005) and John Woo (*The Battle of the Red Cliff*, proposed for 2008). What happens to these films will be tracked carefully by distributors and exhibitors in the USA and the UK, not necessarily because of any intrinsic interest in Chinese Cinema, but because the possibility of a third crossover hit to follow *Crouching Tiger* and *Amélie* (France, 2001) is eagerly awaited. The reluctance of mainstream audiences to read subtitles was overcome in both these films. They attracted new audiences to some

Dubbing is perhaps less disruptive in action films, both because there is less dialogue, and also possibly because audiences are more likely to accept the unreality of the voices. It is more of a problem in talk-based intimate dramas.

In Europe, nearly all films in Italian and German will be dubbed into the local language (so famous Hollywood stars are always dubbed and the voice artist becomes well known). In some countries, film listings carefully show which films are being presented in the original language – in France this is indicated by 'V.O.' or *version originale*. It would be helpful if this practice was introduced for UK television and cinema listings. It is slowly beginning in respect of Bollywood films – see below.

multiplexes and widened the experience of existing audiences – both good for the long-term business of the exhibition sector.

As a footnote to this case study, it is important to consider the dubbing issue. If the three Mandarin films discussed here had been dubbed into English for their cinema release, would they have succeeded on the same level? Certainly, they would not have attracted some elements of the audience. Dubbing is widely acceptable in some film industries and is essential in others. The UK stands out in Europe for mostly dropping dubbed films for mainstream release, when in the past (e.g. in the 1970s) they were quite common. Dubbing survives on television and DVD (where two or more audio tracks can be offered). Distributors face a quandary, well illustrated in the case of the work of director Miyazaki Hayao whose international animation success *Spirited Away* (Japan 2001) was shown in Japanese in specialised cinemas in the UK and dubbed on BBC2 (which up until recently regularly screened foreign language prints).

> **AUDIENCE ISSUE 4**
> How do mainstream audiences respond to popular films from other cultures? How do distributors present stars and genres in these films? Subtitle or dub?

> **RESEARCH SUGGESTION**
> Ask a range of people about their attitudes to subtitled and dubbed films. Do you think more people would watch popular films from other language cultures if they were routinely dubbed?

5. The 'cult film': *Donnie Darko* – How does a film become a 'cult' attraction?

Film studies, especially since the development of a more cultural studies approach, has struggled to deal with the concept of a **cult film**. The same is true for producers and distributors. By definition, a cult film will attract a small but devoted audience who will watch the same film more than once in the cinema and may buy one or more versions of the film on DVD. No one sets out to make a cult film – films tend to become cult objects because of what audiences find in them and sometimes because of the circumstances surrounding their distribution and reception. Once established, cult films can be successfully exploited by distributors in terms of re-releases, special cuts etc. On the other hand, a commercially successful cult film is something of an oxymoron. Once well known and celebrated, can the film remain a cult object? The danger for academic film studies is that because so much critical attention is paid to certain films, their importance in industry terms can be overestimated.

The release of *Donnie Darko* in the USA in 2001 and in the UK in 2002 raised many questions about audiences. It is a difficult film to categorise. In many ways a personal film for its writer/director Richard Kelly, it also draws on a range of popular genres, including the teen film/youth picture,

> When *Blade Runner* was released in 1982, it was a commercial flop. In the 1990s, it became celebrated in the industry for the innovative production design and art direction, and in universities as perhaps the most significant example of a postmodern film. It certainly changed perceptions of what a science-fiction film might be. A Director's Cut of the film did good business on video, but it is likely that overall the film still lost money.

1.5 Jake Gyllenhaal as *Donnie Darko* with Drew Barrymore as his 'progressive' English teacher.

science fiction and horror. The narrative structure of the film employs a time-slip device. Similar devices have been used in a range of independent films, but they might be seen as problematic in a mainstream film. Overall, *Donnie Darko* conforms to an industry definition of an independent film. It was produced by a group of independent companies. One of these, Flower Films, is associated with actress Drew Barrymore, and some of its other productions (e.g. *Charlie's Angels*, 2000, and *Fifty First Dates*, 2004) have been co-produced with major studios. However, there was no major studio involved in *Donnie Darko*, which was produced for just $4.5 million – definitely low budget.

The film was released by Newmarket Films in the USA. Newmarket has since been very successful with *The Passion of the Christ* (2004), but previously its releases had been limited in scope. *Donnie Darko* went out on only 58 prints in October 2001. In the second week, this was reduced to just 26 prints and after that, although the film survived in cinemas until March 2002, it was only on a handful of prints, and the US box-office gross finished at just over $500,000. One possible explanation of the failure of the film was that it included a crucial scene in which a jet engine falls from an aircraft in flight. In the weeks immediately following 9/11, it was argued that this risked accusations of bad taste. Perhaps the distributor restricted the release for this reason? Certainly there are suggestions that the American prints were re-edited to replace what was seen as an Arabic-style typeface for the **intertitles** that introduced each section of the narrative.

In the UK, *Donnie Darko* was released by Metrodome (also an independent distributor with experience of handling American independent productions) on 37 prints a year later in October 2002, widening quickly to 52 prints as the initial promotional campaign proved to be working.

Although this may appear to be only a limited release, it was carefully targeted at a youth audience and the eventual box-office gross of over £1 million was three times bigger than in the USA and represents a definite success. In the UK, the film came to be seen as a cult hit, with fans needing to see it more than once to disentangle the complex narrative and argue over meanings. In December 2003, *Donnie Darko* re-surfaced in the UK via the Christmas singles chart. A version of Tears for Fears' song 'Mad World' sung by the relatively unknown Gary Jules had featured in *Donnie Darko* and now it was released as a (very unusual) Christmas single. When the song went to No. 1, it both confirmed the strength of the fan market for the film and also introduced the movie to new audiences (and allowed the singer to promote an album in the UK). *Donnie Darko* was also successful as a DVD release in the UK, although its rapid appearance in the bargain bins suggested that perhaps the distributors might have become over-ambitious in the numbers pressed.

The UK reaction also helped the film in the USA where a similar cult status was developing. In 2004, Richard Kelly was able to re-cut the film for a re-release in American cinemas, which eventually more than doubled the theatrical box office. This in turn led to a Director's Cut DVD release, and this was able to exploit the developing cult audience's need to study the film in detail. According to a report in *USA Today* (14 February 2005), the 'home video' revenue on *Donnie Darko* is over $15 million, meaning that the film will finally have made a profit (and will remain a valuable library resource). The US DVD release of The Director's Cut came via Fox Video, i.e. a major studio.

Donnie Darko points to a number of industry/audience issues. Like *Ringu/The Ring*, it is a film that has been widely discussed on the internet and has remained in circulation partly because of fans' interest and support in the marketplace. It is also a film that targets adolescent cinemagoers with its mixture of genres and identification with a central character who experiences many of the anxieties common to that audience (and which have begun to interest cultural studies academics). Finally, the different success of the US and UK releases points to the element of luck in selecting dates, the possible

The initial release of *Donnie Darko* on DVD in the UK included examples of promotional material such as the work of graffiti artists, which ran as an exhibition in London. For a low-budget film, the DVD was unusually packed with bonus material appealing to the inquisitive fan.

AUDIENCE ISSUE 5
How do audiences make a film their own?

RESEARCH SUGGESTION
Consider your own favourite film. What is special about it? What have you done to enhance your enjoyment of repeated viewings of the film? Have you bought the DVD or any other 'tie- ins'? How do you justify your love for this film to your friends?

Richard Kelly's follow-up to *Donnie Darko*, *Southlands* (2006), received its premiere at Cannes – and the worst reviews of any film at the festival. At the time of writing, the film has not been released. It should be interesting to see how the distributor approaches a release, as the Cannes critics are unlikely to be representative of the cult audience for *Donnie Darko*.

effects of linkage to news events and the difference that a carefully targeted campaign can make.

6. The Hindi film in the UK: *Dil Se* – A 'parallel' film distribution system with its own audience in the UK

Hindi films now constitute an important market for UK exhibitors, with a number of multiplexes offering regular showings and a total of 15 cinema screens dedicated to 'Asian Cinema'. By 2006, the Hindi film distributors had settled into a pattern whereby a chain such as Cineworld shows Hindi films on two or three screens at selected cinemas across the UK, mirroring the dispersal of Hindi-speaking populations (or more correctly, people who can understand Hindi and who enjoy such films). When these screenings began in the late 1990s, only a few films were subtitled in English. In May 2006, Cineworld's main website advertised a total of six films, all subtitled, playing at various cinemas. There are now several distributors releasing Bollywood films at the rate of around one per week and with total prints for each film ranging from four or five up to 38. At least one Hindi film figures in the UK Top 15 most weeks. The move to subtitling reflects an attempt to reach out to a wider audience, but either distributors do not press-screen all titles or they are unable to persuade 'mainstream reviewers' on the national press to review Hindi films on a consistent basis – even *Sight and Sound* (despite making appropriate noises) fails on this score.

Hindi films remain confined to a largely Asian audience and therefore exist within a different social institution, which incorporates a different set of expectations about the film, the audience who experience it and the screening. Hindi films have traditionally been longer (180 mins and more, but this is now beginning to reduce) and regularly feature an intermission, something no longer possible for mainstream films. The screen advertising companies recognise that the audience profile for Bollywood films is different and Pearl and Dean offer advertisers a different 'package' for Bollywood screens (see <business.pearlanddean.com/planbuy/select.html>

Dil Se (India, 1998) was one of the first Hindi films to gain a high profile in the UK. It was preceded by a successful soundtrack CD in India, but despite featuring one of Bollywood's biggest stars, Shahrukh Khan, the film flopped in the Indian market, possibly because both the style and the content (a love story involving a radio reporter and a 'freedom fighter'/assassin) were somewhat removed from the conventional Bollywood film of the time. However, the film did very well in the UK and North America, prompting the release of more Hindi films and the recognition that major Bollywood movies could make nearly as much money from the NRI (Non-resident Indian) market in the West as from the massive market in

Intermissions during very long films were a feature of **roadshow** films in the UK up until the 1990s. Hollywood distributors now requires films to be shown without a break – although small independent cinemas sometimes ignore rental agreements.

1.6 One of the spectacular dance sequences in exotic locations which are an integral element in Hindi films such as *Dil Se*.

India itself (i.e. because of the big difference in ticket prices). This led to the practice of simultaneous releases for major films such as *Kabhi Kushie Kabhie Gham* (2001) in London, New York and Mumbai/New Delhi. Success with affluent NRI audiences in the West has to some extent moved attention away from the traditional overseas market for Bollywood films in less affluent markets in Africa and the Middle East. At home, too, Bollywood seeks to cater for a rapidly growing Indian middle class whose tastes may (and sometimes may not) equate with the NRIs.

Dil Se also pointed to another aspect of Indian Cinema and its overseas links. Director Mani Ratnam – and his colleagues, the celebrated cinematographer Santosh Sivan and music composer A. R. Rahman – come from South Indian regional cinemas in the states of Tamil Nadhu and Kerala. *Dil Se* was the first film Ratnam made in Hindi, the language widely understood in North India and by educated classes across the country. His other films, mainly made in Tamil, had sometimes been dubbed into Hindi and into Telegu (the language of the state of Andhra Pradesh). Bollywood is the dominant form of cinema in India in terms of budgets and stars in the national media, but more films are actually made in the South (and audiences there are, if anything, even more passionate). Bollywood films are enjoyed in the UK by a range of Asian audiences with differing attachments to Hindi as a preferred language. Speakers of Urdu, Punjabi, Bengali and Gujerati can all enjoy a Hindi film, but they might also like to see films made from their own cultural/regional perspective, and this is possible only very rarely (and then it is

The latest Indian figures for films produced in language groups in 2003 show 221 Hindi films, but 479 in the four main South Indian languages of Tamil, Telegu, Kannada and Malayalam. (Central Board of Film Classification: <www.cbfcindia.tn.nic.in>).

usually an 'art film' rather than a popular film). The largest group of South Indians in the UK (and across the world) is the Tamil diaspora, and although they might be able to see a limited number of films in Tamil in London, they are mostly served by DVD.

Hidden from the mainstream, specialist distributors may bring single copies of foreign-language films into the UK or USA in order to show them directly, without subtitles, to audiences from a specific language group. In March 2006, a Turkish film, *Babam Ve Oglum* (2005) was released in the UK on just two prints. Interest from the Turkish community was so great that the film scored the highest average box office per screen in the UK that week, taking double what any of the major Hollywood releases could manage. The distributor, Maxximum, is German-based and has begun to achieve success in Germany with that country's large Turkish population, much as Bollywood distributors have done in the UK. It is likely that these audiences will be served with imported DVDs as well. If the language market is large enough, it may well attract a UK based distributor and eventually the attention of the Hollywood studios. Back in the 1970s, Cantonese language films were shown in hired cinemas in London's West End outside normal mainstream opening hours. Now DVDs are easily available and more Hong Kong films are released in UK cinemas.

In August 2006, the thunderous opening of *Kabhi Alvida Naa Kehna (Never Say Goodbye)* (2006) served as an indication of the potential for Hindi film in the UK. Writer-director Karan Johar has now made three films, each starring Shahrukh Khan and each massive hits. *Kuch Kuch Hota Hai* (1998) and *Kabhi Kushi Kabhie Gham* (also starring Amitabh Bachchan and Hrithik Roshan, older and younger

1.7 The Cineworld multiplex in Bradford advertising two Bollywood releases for the holiday season, which in 2006 covered both Diwali and Eid celebrations in late October.

superstars of Hindi cinema) represent the high-budget Bollywood event film, focusing on family melodrama, but also tying in to current concerns of the NRI and middle-class Indian audience. *Kabhi Alvida Naa Kehna* marks a step towards what some reviewers have seen as a more realistic portrayal of marital relationships. The film has divided some audiences (notably on IMDb), but in its first week it broke records in the UK, North America and Australia. In the UK it opened on just 60 prints, but its screen average was five times higher than any Hollywood film in the first three days at over £12,000 per screen, giving it the No. 6 slot in the UK chart. In North America, 64 prints moved it to No. 17 in the Top 20 and a screen average of $21,000, again the highest in the chart. The commercial success of this film will undoubtedly prompt further discussion of the potential for Bollywood to cross over to non-Hindi audiences. For this to happen, *Screen International*'s Indian consulting editor Bhuvan Lall suggests that it will take the form of cinema that, like Indian food in the West, develops into something different than that consumed at home: 'Perhaps we are waiting for the tikka masala film' (*Screen International* 28 July 2006).

AUDIENCE ISSUE 6
Film is a universal medium and with the migration patterns of the last 40 years and the subsequent development of multicultural societies in all parts of the world, the importance of diaspora cinemas and the possibilities of hybrid cinema cultures raises questions for producers, distributors and audiences alike.

RESEARCH SUGGESTION
Make a list of films you have seen that display elements of hybridity. This could include the use of Asian martial arts in films like *The Matrix* (US 1999) or the Bollywood influences on *Moulin Rouge* (Australia/US 2001). If possible, watch a popular Bollywood film (many are now available on DVD in UK stores) and look for ideas that have beeen incorporated from Hollywood.

Summary

We have seen that there are different strategies for releasing mainstream, high-budget Hollywood films and smaller specialised films, but, in both cases, the distributors and exhibitors are searching for specific audiences. Even the most widely seen film discussed here (*Ice Age 2*) will appeal to only certain audiences.

The economics of the film industry mean that relatively inexpensive films can be very profitable. This explains the enormous industry attention paid to films such as *The Full Monty* (UK, 1997), which grossed over $250 million worldwide having cost only $7 million in terms of production budget and initial marketing. The 'rate of return' is the crucial factor, with each dollar spent investing in the film returning $30 or more in revenue and $15 in profit. The prospect of success like this encourages distributors to persist in trying to sell specialised films (which is what *The Full Monty* was as a 'low-budget' British picture). In this chapter, we have looked at issues arising from distributing foreign-language films and getting over the hurdle of subtitles, 're-making' foreign titles and creating (although not consciously) 'fan groups' for specific films. We have identified different kinds of audiences who are attracted to cinemas for different reasons, suggesting that strategies other than mass marketing and promotion may be influential. We have also noted that timing of release can be crucial in both avoiding competitors and building on audience awareness of connected films and ideas (as in the case of *Hidden*).

The remainder of the book will look in detail at each of the different agencies that determine how films are 'received': the producers, distributors, audiences and critics/commentators.

References

Bordwell, David (2006), *The Way Hollywood Tells It: Story and Style in Modern Movies* (Berkeley and London: University of California Press).

Branston, Gill and Roy Stafford (2006), *The Media Student's Book* (4th edition) (London: Routledge).

Gladwell, Malcolm (2002), *The Tipping Point: How Little Things Can Make a Big Difference* (London: Abacus).

Hills, Matt (2005), 'Ringing the Changes: Cult Distinctions and Cultural Differences in US Fans' Reading of Japanese Horror Cinema' in Jay McRoy (ed), *Japanese Horror Cinema* (Edinburgh: Edinburgh University Press).

Wyatt, Justin (1994), *High Concept: Movies and Marketing in Hollywood* (Austin: University of Texas Press).

2. How the Film Industry Perceives Audiences

This chapter focuses on how the film industry uses its knowledge about potential audiences in planning each stage of the process whereby a film is conceived, developed, produced and post-produced and then distributed and exhibited.

Media students quickly learn that what can be defined as a media text will always have a purpose and a target audience. This should be the case with films as well, but the assertion is not so clearly presented in some film studies courses. Films are expensive to make and the costs are justified only because there is an audience, at least notionally, prepared to watch them. This applies to art films as much as commercial films, even if the relationship between producer and audience may be rather different in each case. Whatever kind of film we wish to consider, it will arrive on a cinema screen having gone through a series of production stages that may take anything from a few months to several years.

From property to screening

1. The property or the idea

A film comes into existence as a **property** – an idea about what will make a successful film. The property might be something quite substantial, such as a best-selling novel for which a producer has purchased the film rights, or it might be simply an idea, perhaps based on a newspaper story or something someone said in the pub last night. The latter, of course, is quite difficult to copyright. Studios may also look to make sequels of previously successful films for which they hold rights, or they may decide to option an idea pitched to them by a freelance scriptwriter or an independent company.

2. Development

The first stage of development is to begin considering how the script will be written (assuming it doesn't already exist) and thinking about how the film will be made – what kind of casting decisions, locations, use of SFX etc. The crucial issue for producers will be to consider the various kinds of budget is being suggested and whether the film would attract the kind of audience to make such a film profitable, given production and marketing costs and envisaged rental revenue. A decision to move forward and actually prepare the film for production should only be taken if the numbers add up at this stage.

We can think about audiences and their relationship with producers in several different ways:

- The expected audience size may influence the production budget.
- Audience knowledge of genres, stars etc. may prompt filmmakers into certain production decisions, including casting, scripting etc.
- Concerns about alienating audiences may constrain producers in terms of both style and content.

The six major Hollywood studios (Disney, Paramount, Sony, 20th Century-Fox, Universal, Warner Bros.) do not actually produce many films themselves, mostly relying on financing smaller independent producers to do the work. Even so, the major studio will distribute the film and will be concerned with audience issues from the beginning.

The first of these is a major concern for studios. They only feel secure when they can match audience and budget. Often they prefer a larger budget and the freedom to push the project towards an equally large audience. Only 'name' directors/independent producers can hope to put together a large budget for a film with seemingly limited audience appeal. A 'star director' can make marketing and promotion more effective, but such films will also need quite careful distribution. Sometimes, studios may invest in films that they do not necessarily expect to be profitable, if there is a long-term gain in terms of prestige/status and the opportunity to work with the same director on more commercial properties in the future. (The career of a director like Martin Scorsese is interesting in this respect.) The second consideration involves a minefield of decision-making, trying to meld different audience concerns over genres, stars etc, while the third factor again appeals to the innate conservatism of the studios. On this score, however, we might note that the European perspective on such production decisions is quite different to the climate within the USA, where the East Coast/West Coast culture espoused by many Hollywood personnel is at odds with the ultra conservatism of some of the 'red states' (i.e. Bush-supporting in the South and Mid-west). *Brokeback Mountain*, a film that took several years to move into production, would be an interesting case study for these three points.

At the time of its release, the promotional material for *Brokeback Mountain* tried to steer audiences away from thinking of it as a 'gay cowboy movie'. See the case study in Chapter 4.

Development costs money (perhaps $2 or $3 million or much more in Hollywood), but it does not guarantee that the film will be made. At some point, the production will either be **greenlighted** or put into **turnaround**. In the former case, the film will move into preparation/pre-production and in the latter it will sit on a shelf until another studio comes along, prepared to buy the property (and effectively pay for the development money already spent).

In the UK, development is a rather different process, as it will involve looking for funding from a number of sources, including **soft money** and deals with distributors and possibly broadcasters and sales agents (each of whom will have to be convinced of potential audience interest and will take a fee or a percentage of future box office).

> The Scottish writer/director of two well-received independent films (*Ratcatcher*, 1997, and *Morvern Callar*, 2002), Lynne Ramsay, spent two years working on a possible adaptation of the novel *Lovely Bones*, only to see the project passed to Peter Jackson when the novel became established as a bestseller. Ramsay moved on to the similarly themed *We Need to Talk About Kevin* by Lionel Shriver (*Guardian* 6 June 2006).

In his book on genre theory, Rick Altman (1999) refers to what he calls 'The Producer's Game' as a potential model to explain how genres develop over time. Altman suggests that producers are constantly looking at what is successful at the box office, identifying what they see as key elements in successful films and then trying to incorporate similar elements in their own films. This could mean that certain stars or scriptwriters become sought after or that new types of characters, locations or themes are seen as particularly attractive to audiences and may be incorporated in scripts conceived much earlier. In this case, properties in turnaround could be re-activated. The process of putting together a script, director, heads of technical departments and stars is called '**packaging the project**'. (The best explanation of the whole production process, in a UK context, can be found on Skillset's website: <www.skillset.org/film/business>).

Altman's work refers primarily to commercial, industrial filmmaking, but it could equally be applied to more personal films. It may be the case that some producer-directors have quite clear ideas about what kinds of films they want to make. But they still face the problem of raising funding for their script ideas and this means meeting some of the expectations of studio executives or controllers of soft-money sources, all of whom may be playing a version of Altman's game.

The practical problems associated with Altman's game largely derive from time lags. Producers scanning the industry figures and market research for current box-office films are unlikely to see the fruits of any decisions they make until 18 months or two years down the line. What seemed a good idea in July may seem much less attractive in December. As a consequence, some projects may be aborted or significantly altered during production.

Universal audiences?

During the 1990s, a significant shift in Hollywood perceptions saw the increase in importance of the international market. Traditionally, Hollywood concentrated on the domestic market in the USA and Canada. Success in international markets was a bonus – to be a hit, a film had to prosper in North America. Gradually, it has become apparent that the international market (i.e. everywhere else outside North America) is growing faster in value terms. The potential audience for Hollywood films (which dominate box offices in virtually every territory) has always been bigger than the 320 million people in North America, and now it is beginning to be prepared to pay more to visit new multiplexes (and to visit them more often). In 2005, major growth was predicted in Eastern Europe, where Russia in particular appeared to be recovering from the massive slump in admissions in the 1980s.

Because of difficulties in collecting box-office data in countries such as India and China, the international market is difficult to track in terms of overall income, and attention has focused mainly on Hollywood films and exports from Japan and South Korea. A *Screen International* report in 2006 suggested that the international market might actually be worth 50% more than North America (18 August 2006).

But do audiences in Moscow, Tokyo and Rio de Janeiro have the same tastes as those in New York and Omaha? In the last few years, industry observers have begun to log data in the international market (*Screen International* began its International Chart of showing the weekly Top 50 films outside North America in 2004) and it is already apparent that there can be significant differences between the overall figures for international box office and North America, and between different international territories. Hollywood films, particularly more action-orientated films, strive for universal appeal, with characters and stories that can be easily appreciated in different markets. However, if the characters and themes are too American, they may not succeed outside the USA. Conversely, some American films are better appreciated abroad.

Several websites post figures comparing the box-office grosses of mainstream Hollywood films in North America and the international market. The Worldwide Chart at Box Office Mojo <boxofficemojo.com> gives easy access to the percentage split between the two major market divisions. As the international market now usually grosses more than North America overall, the split for a film that plays everywhere might be 40–45% North America and 55–60% international. The 2005 chart suggests that this is indeed the case, but there are some titles that confound expectations. At the top of the chart, there are obvious exceptions such as the two animated hits, *Howl's Moving Castle* and *Wallace and Gromit: The Curse of the Were-Rabbit*. Animation should, with dubbing, be, to a certain extent, universal, but both films present American audiences with culturally specific material (*Howl's Moving Castle* is a Japanese animated film from Miyazaki Hayao, but it is an adaptation of a British story for children). Despite being distributed by Buena Vista and DreamWorks, the films' North

American share was 2% and 30% respectively – showing a major 'skew' towards the 'home markets' of Japan and the UK.

Weddings are also universal experiences, but attitudes towards them differ in many parts of the world. Perhaps we should not be surprised that a US comedy entitled *Wedding Crashers* took 73% of its $285 million box office in North America and only 27% in the rest of the world. Is this a function of the particular sub-genre of comedy explored in the film, targeting an American youth audience? Why should an audience in Hong Kong or Seoul want to watch a wedding comedy from the USA when their own industry serves up competent home product? Big stars might be one reason, but such films have less international appeal than action films, where Hollywood studio money is more clearly evident on screen and where local producers find it difficult to match Hollywood production values. But the failure of the film overseas might also be partly a function of the independent studio distribution by New Line in North America. New Line is a brand of Time Warner, but its films are not usually released in all territories overseas through Warner Bros. This need not be a problem in the international market (*Lord of the Rings* was a New Line film) but it does mean that the American studio may be selling the film to a range of local partners overseas who may be less successful at marketing the film in a coherent way.

Another American weakness is sports-orientated films. *The Longest Yard* (2005) a comedy about American football, did very good business for Paramount in North America but failed to interest audiences abroad to the same extent (17% share for international). Two action/SFX films from 2005, *The Island* and *Kingdom of Heaven,* were both saved by the international market, with a 77% share after flopping in North America. These two films are interesting, because they offer producers two different lessons. First, action films with stars and a non-culturally specific premise will travel (*The Island*). Second, international audiences do not have the same problems with historical subject matter as those in North America. It was noticeable in 2004 that Oliver Stone's *Alexander* was laughed out of North America as a major flop, but found significant audiences overseas ($30:$130 million split).

Where studios and independents have taken time and care to present their films in different markets, they have managed to find audiences. *Brokeback Mountain* is surely one of the recent films to be most rooted in American culture. Yet, with its Taiwanese director and high profile among both arthouse and gay audiences worldwide, the results for *Brokeback Mountain* so far look like falling within the 40–60 split for worldwide box office.

Japan is a significant market for Hollywood films (partly because of very high ticket prices) and it is interesting to note that the *Harry Potter* films, with their English school backgrounds work well, but that the *Lord of the Rings* films are significantly less popular. This may be because there are strong local traditions of science fiction, fantasy and horror in Japan. The *Lord of the Rings* films had some difficulty registering with Japanese fans of these genres, but other Hollywood films that are more clearly geared to Japanese genre expectations have done well. The Hollywood version of *The Ring* was more successful than the very widely known Japanese original *Ringu* and in a different generic context, *The Last Samurai* (2003) was a big attraction in Japan, helping to boost its international box office to $345 million (74% of the worldwide total).

In France, the American independent hit *Broken Flowers* (2005), starring Bill Murray, fared much better than it did in the UK. Perhaps this was associated with a long-standing French passion for certain kinds of American performers, such as Woody Allen, Dean Martin and Jerry Lewis, since the 1950s. When such artists are taken up in French culture, they can be very well supported, even when their work in Hollywood may be losing popularity. It may also be the case that a film like *Broken Flowers* is similar in some ways to more personal French **auteur** films.

3. Preparation or pre-production

There is plenty of work to do before shooting (principal photography) takes place, including full casting, location research, storyboarding, production design, special effects planning etc. Some decisions made at this stage may have an audience link. For instance, there may be a decision to include in the production schedule time for shooting a making-of documentary to enhance a future DVD. Promotional activities may also be planned to coincide with the shoot, including ideas about how to control the flow of information to specific internet sites, blogs etc.

4. The shoot

The shortest and most intense part of the process will have little time for audience consideration – unless it has been carefully planned in advance. In some cases, cast and crew may give interviews to selected media outlets. A pioneering website was set up by Revolution Films (Andrew Eaton and Michael Winterbottom) for the shoot of *Kingdom Come* (the title was later changed to *The Claim*) in Canada in 1999. This posted a diary of the shoot, with various interviews and other material, updated on a daily basis. In 2005/6, Peter Jackson and Bryan Singer produced accounts of the shoots for *King Kong* (2005) and *Superman Returns* and Danny Boyle for *Sunshine* <www.sunshinedna.com/>.

5. Post-production

Editing a film involves sound, image and special effects and may take several months. It is only at this time that the original ideas about target audiences can be assessed. At the rough cut stage, it will begin to become apparent whether the original ideas have worked. Is this the film that was expected?

6. Distribution

Post-production overlaps with the work of distribution. Until test screenings with real preview audiences have taken place, marketing people may not know how exactly they should attempt to sell the film. Previews may convince everybody that a new approach is necessary or that changes should be made to the edit. If the film has not been pre-sold to all territories, sales agents may be used at this point, travelling to **film markets** (often attached to film festivals) to make deals.

Distributors need to decide how best to create a buzz about their film, which may include taking it to festivals, organising various promotional events (including using new media outlets) and scheduling advertising. All of this will depend on the decisions taken about potential audiences.

7. Exhibition

The final stage involves finding exhibitors who will rent the film and organising a release date and a distribution pattern to suit the film and the audience. Distribution and exhibition are so important that the whole of Chapter 3 is devoted to exploring the process in detail. In this chapter, we will simply explore some of the basic points about audience demographics and how the industry thinks about the audience in general terms.

8. Ancillary markets and windows

The process does not stop in the cinema. Indeed, few films ever make any profit purely from cinema distribution. The real profits come from DVD sales and rental and television screenings. The cinema release creates a profile for a film and ensures that marketing the DVD is much more focused and effective. Overheads for DVD distribution are comparatively low and profits can be large. Films that failed in the cinema can also find new audiences on DVD, where immediate impact is not always essential (i.e. the film will stay on the shelves of the DVD store longer than on cinema screens and may eventually be found by an appropriate audience).

(For more on the production process, see Branston and Stafford, 2006: Industries chapter).

Knowing the audience and making a profit

Any entrepreneur looking at the film business as an outside observer would spot very quickly that the industry currently fails to maximise revenue, simply because it does not make films for all its potential audiences. Hollywood recognises two principal markets – the family market of parents in the 30–45 age group and their children aged 5–12, and the youth audience of 13–29-year-olds. As the population profile gets older (i.e. the proportion of the population over the age of 45 increases), the target audience for most films is actually shrinking. This is particularly important in European markets such as Germany and in the second largest market (by value), Japan. If age is a problem, so is gender, ethnicity and sexual orientation – a problem in the sense that Hollywood does not make enough films that target audiences in ways that reflect the make-up of the population.

Part of the problem here is that the filmmakers themselves come from a specific **demographic** – a section of the overall population profile. If there were more African-American and Hispanic women making films, would they want to make different kinds of movies? They might, but they would still need to seek funding from the same sources that had ignored them as an audience in the past. There are important institutional questions about film funding here.

Who funds films and what do they think about audiences?

A fundamental difference between Hollywood and almost every other film industry is the extent to which funding is dependent on market forces or public resources. This is often expressed via the concepts of **hard** and **soft** money. Hard money is money invested directly by a risk-taking capital holder. Hollywood success is supposedly built on hard money decisions. The major studios stay in business by taking new investment decisions when they greenlight a film project. Every new film is a risk, but the major studios are to some extent covered when there is a constant revenue stream coming in from previous film releases.

Soft money refers to a vast array of government schemes in different countries (including, at a local level, in the USA). These schemes provide tax relief or other forms of support (grants, loans etc.) designed to encourage film production in specific locations. Every year, *Screen International* provides a survey of such soft-money schemes across the world. These schemes are frighteningly complex in operation and, in many cases, producers will take a specialist financing company as a partner in a production in order to maximise benefits.

Is hard or soft money likely to have more impact on the kinds of films made and the audiences served? Supporters of free-market economics would always argue that the market will make the best decisions. If there are audiences out there who are not served, market mechanisms will operate to make sure that they will be in future. In practice, this is not happening – or at least not to the extent of balancing supply and demand that the free marketeers predict.

Does soft money offer a better option? There have been attempts by agencies such as the UK Film Council to promote diversity policies that encourage both the employment of personnel from a wider range of backgrounds and also the development of new audiences. But there is also plenty of evidence that such policies are constrained by a need to present the spending of public money as being conducted in a business like manner. Soft money that is spent promoting the production of films that then prove difficult to distribute/exhibit can become the focus for attacks by sections of the media. Much of the time, the tax relief schemes and location grants are used in a straightforward attempt to entice major Hollywood productions to make films in regions that will benefit economically from short-term projects.

Who is the audience?

Films are popular, but in cinemas not that popular. In the UK, at the height of the industry's appeal in 1946, British audiences recorded admissions of over 30 million per week. In 2006, weekly admissions were only around 3.2 million. If you consider that there are 3,200 cinema screens, that equates to an average of 1,000 admissions per screen each week. Cinema auditoria vary in size and perhaps the average has around 200 seats. Given that the average mainstream cinema shows a feature three or four times a day, seven days a week, there must be a lot of empty seats in many screenings. Most cinemas rely on a decent 'house' on Friday, Saturday and Sunday evenings and whatever audience they can entice in during the rest of the week. (Baker, Inglis and Voss, 2002, suggest that 15-20% seat occupancy is average for the UK.)

The film industry, at least in North America and other significant markets, is a highly organised and sophisticated business operation. We might expect that there will be a clear sense of who is buying the product. There is indeed a wealth of information available about audiences, collected via various forms of marketing surveys and simple number-crunching based on computerised ticketing systems. Since the 1990s, the size of the audience for particular films has become the focus for reports in the popular media (press and television) and it is now widely understood that, for Hollywood, the success of a mainstream feature depends on the opening three-day weekend of its release. If a film opens on a Friday, the distributor will have a clear idea by Saturday if it is going to be a hit. In some cases, it will also be possible to estimate not only the size of the audience, but also its make up. Distributors are particularly interested in gender splits, for instance. **Counter-booking** a film expected to attract women in their twenties and thirties against a major action film release aimed at the 15–24 male market is a common practice.

Sports events like the football World Cup or European Championship offer opportunities for counter-programming of a different kind, competing for attention with a worldwide game that Hollywood does not really understand. It is always worthwhile looking at which films get released during the World Cup to see what assumptions about who watches football are being applied by distributors.

Given the investment in data-gathering and monitoring of box office, it is perhaps surprising that producers and distributors frequently get it wrong, spending large sums on production and marketing and then failing to find an audience. There are many reasons why we should not be surprised at what seems to be a consistent misreading of the data.

Information is expensive. There is a great deal of information collected about the box office performance of films and the audiences who watch them, but much of it is only available at a high price, restricting analysis to the distributors themselves. It is difficult for a casual commentator to gain access to this data and to assess how well the studios use it in their planning. The expense also means that only the most important (i.e. biggest box office) films are tracked in detail. Smaller films are generally ignored, meaning that for distribution of specialised films, the independent distributors have to build up their own local knowledge.

Ae Fond Kiss registered nearly 1.4 million admissions in 2004/5, with over 400,000 in France and only 101,000 in the UK.

Audience data is not consistent. Although the film industry is effectively global in its operation, there are wide variations in local practices. For instance, the freely published box-office figures for North America and the UK quote the value of box-office takings (in US dollars and in sterling), but in France, box office is usually measured by the number of admissions. Comparing Britain and France involves making assumptions about average ticket prices in both countries. Because the European Union is supportive of the European AV industry, there are good statistics on admissions available via <lumiere.obs.coe.int/web/search/>. This searchable database gives the admission figures for all films released in both the EU (25 nations) and the wider Europe (36 nations) since 1995. These figures are revealing and extremely useful, especially in tracking audiences for smaller films that are not recorded in local Top Tens etc. Some of the data is quite startling. It has been a long-standing assumption that Ken Loach films do better in Europe, for example, but the extent of this is remarkable. *Sweet Sixteen (2002)* and *Ae Fond Kiss (2004)*, both had more admissions in each of France, Italy, Spain and Germany than in the UK.

The **LUMIERE** database also gives US admission figures, but these are only estimates (as are the UK figures) based on average ticket prices.

The gross box-office revenue figure as a measure of a film's popularity is flawed in many ways. First, it overstates the income coming back to the distributor – the profit on the film. It would be more helpful to know the rental income from each film – the net figure after the exhibitor has kept back a share of the box office. Unfortunately, the kinds of deals that distributors and exhibitors make include variable rates for the split between distributor and exhibitor according to the profile of the film, the length of run etc. In general, only about 40–50% of the box office goes back to the distributor (less in the UK). Given the high costs of marketing many films, the distributor's actual profit on a seemingly popular film may be quite small.

The other major problem with the gross box-office measure of popularity is that it underplays the importance of films that attract a family audience. If children only pay half-price for a ticket, the overall box-office gross for films like *Monsters Inc.* or *Shrek* (both 2001) will be deflated in comparison with films rated 15 (or PG-13 in the USA) for which full price tickets will be the norm. Added to this is the regional factor and other ticketing price differences in the UK. Together these can produce significant differences between admissions and box-office gross.

In 2002, the average cost of a cinema ticket in the UK was £4.29 <www.bfi.org.uk/filmtvinfo/stats/boxoffice/breakdown-02.html>. But this masks significant differences between prices in London (and especially the West End) and those in other parts of the UK. *Screen International* recognises the London factor (a greater cinema going habit) with a separate London chart on its website. (London had 4.1 visits per head in 2004, compared to 2.32 in the south-west). If a film does proportionally better business in London, its box office will be significantly higher than a film that attracts a higher proportion of its audience in other parts of the country where ticket prices are lower, even though the overall number of admissions may be the same. (*Bride and Prejudice*, 2004, attracted 44% of its audience in London alone according to UK Film Council figures.)

Box office will also be affected by very long-established habits in cinema going. Traditionally in the UK, Friday and Saturday are the busiest times of the week in cinemas, while Monday is the quietest. New releases in the UK come out on Fridays in anticipation of a weekend audience of younger cinemagoers looking for the excitement of a film opening. Cinemas attempt to attract audiences to shows in the slack periods through a variety of reduced-price screening deals on Mondays and Tuesdays. 'Orange Wednesdays' is another form of promotion and some cinemas host Senior Citizen matinees or morning screenings, often on Tuesday, Wednesday or Thursday. These screenings may attract significant admissions but at lower prices. As the industry analysts are fixated on the three-day box-office figures, they can sometimes miss the emergence of films that attract older audiences, who might avoid busy cinemas at the weekend and opt for midweek screenings instead. In 2005, this was highlighted by reports on the midweek business achieved by films such as *Vera Drake* (2005). Similar comments followed the release of *Brokeback Mountain* in early 2006. Films like this do

2.1 Reese Witherspoon and Joaquin Phoenix portray June Carter and Johnny Cash in *Walk the Line*, a film which did excellent business in Ireland, where Cash is a legendary figure.

A good example of the UK/Ireland divide was the release of *Walk the Line*, a high-profile release in 2006. As a biopic of country singer Johnny Cash, a legendary figure in Ireland, it is not surprising that the film took 50% of UK/Ireland business in Ireland, especially given the antipathy towards country music shown in urban England. The usual UK:Ireland ratio is 10:1. In June 2006, *The Wind That Shakes the Barley*, a Ken Loach film about Irish history, opened on over 100 screens in the UK/Ireland – half of these were in Ireland, and half the box-office total was achieved in Ireland. The film went on to do significantly better business in Ireland than in the UK.

particularly good midweek business in specialised cinemas, which tend to have slightly different attendance patterns to multiplexes.

A further inconsistency emerges in the reporting of audience figures across the territory of the UK and Ireland. Whenever figures are discussed in the trade press it is not clear if they refer to the whole territory or to the UK and Ireland separately. Does it matter? Yes, because Ireland (both North and South) has traditionally been a strong cinema territory, with a frequency of cinema going higher than in most regions in England, Scotland and Wales. These differences in frequencies are even more pronounced when audience numbers are compared across Europe and worldwide (North America, Australia and Iceland having rates of five visits per head per year and over, while parts of Europe struggle to make two visits per head per year).

Demographics and audience profiles

There is never a single audience for a film at the cinema or on television/DVD. There are many different audiences, watching in different circumstances and with different personal characteristics. At the simplest level, audiences can be recognised by reference to differences of sex, age and class. You may not be conscious of this if you always see the same kinds of film in the same venue, and it is a useful exercise to check on different audiences in different cinemas at different times of the day.

Demographics vary over time and across territories. In the UK, cinema has been at various times a more middle-class or a more working-class medium. At various times, it has also been skewed towards men or women and to older or younger groups. Alterations in the overall population structure will have an effect (e.g. with changes in the birth and death rates), but so will changes in social trends, such as access to other leisure facilities (see Chapter 8 on the culture of cinema going).

In 2005, **CAVIAR** (Cinema and Audio visual Industry Audience Research) represented the cinema attendance patterns of the UK population over 7 years of age as shown in Fig. 2.2. The UK film industry faces a number of issues associated with an ageing population. The audience that attends most frequently (15–24 year-olds in Fig. 2.2) is shrinking as a proportion of the overall population. This young audience is also the most mobile and tends to congregate in student cities and London in particular. By contrast, the largest proportion of the audience (and which is growing as a proportion) is the over-35 group – the least frequent attendees. As we have already noted, this is also true of the demographics of other Western European countries, but not of North America or parts of South America or Asia, where the average age is much lower. Although Hollywood is aware of

	Age 7–14% of population	Age 15–24% of population	Age 25–34% of population	Age 35+% of population
% of age group who go to the cinema > once per year	93	91	85	61
% of age group who go to the cinema > once per month	36	47	36	16
% of audience for Top 20 films	22	25	17	37
% of the audience for Top 20 UK films	20	23	16	41
% of total population in the age group	11	14	14	61

Fig 2.2 Cinema attendance by age group in the UK in 2005 (UK Film Council/CAVIAR).

the issue and does make films specifically for older audiences, it is still seen as primarily concerned with younger audiences, and this makes sense given the North American population profile. Hollywood product in much of Europe, however, dominates film screens but may not be attractive to a significant proportion of the potential audience.

The American view of the cinema audience as dominated by older male teenagers is well caught in this presentation from Alan Betrock's 1986 book, *The I Was a Teenage Juvenile Delinquent Rock'N'Roll Horror Beach Party Movie Book: A Complete Guide to the Teen Exploitation Film, 1954–1969*. He explains the exploitation film producers' maxim in the 1960s as follows:

> The younger teenager will watch anything the 19 year-old will watch.
> But the 19 year-old will not watch what the younger teenager will watch.
> Girls will watch anything that boys watch.
> But boys won't watch what girls will watch.
> So, make films for 19 year-old males.

There was a certain logic in this thinking and you may come across arguments that suggest it still makes sense today. However, if it did apply to low-budget exploitation pictures, it does not now apply in the same way to big-budget mainstream films. Hollywood is seemingly influenced by occasional dramatic box-office outcomes: so, for instance, the industry was convulsed by the success of *Titanic* in 1997, and it was generally accepted that one of the main factors in building its huge audience numbers was repeated viewings by teenage girls. Commenting on *Titanic*'s success, *US Today* listed several ways in which the film confounded assumptions inherent in Hollywood formulae. Among these were

1.   'Men rule the box office.'
2.   'The teen audience isn't what it used to be.'
3.   'Young moviegoers will not go to a period drama'. (as quoted in Studio Briefing on IMDb, 10 February 1998).

How much weight studios give to these observations is difficult to assess, but it is worth researching why certain films have been so influential on future thinking about audiences. Two good examples might be *Easy Rider* (USA, 1969) and *The Blair Witch Project* (USA, 1999).

You need to think about the implications of the figures in Fig. 2.2 carefully, as they can be misinterpreted. For instance, in the fourth edition of his well-respected book, *Film as Social Practice* (2006), Graeme Turner writes: 'the majority of those who attend movies in the USA, the UK and Australia are between 12 and 24 years of age'. It is difficult to know how he would be able to tell this from published figures as the UK measures 7–14 and 15–24, while the USA measures 12–29. The 2005 US Admissions report from the MPAA <www.mpaa.org> states: 'Moviegoers between 12 and 29 years of age represent nearly half of annual theatrical admissions.' In Fig. 2.2 we can see that for the Top 20 films, the 7–24 population provides 45 million admissions, but the over 25s produce 54.5 million. When we go outside the Top 20, it becomes more problematic, but it would be reasonable to argue that certain genres (horror films, for example, will have a much higher proportion of 15–24-year-olds). Certainly, the 7–24 age group is crucial to the overall success of the industry and, because they pay higher prices and have more disposable income and the independence to be able to spend it, the 15–24 age group is the single most important audience. But, as the figures clearly show, the over 25s (not, of course, a homogenous group) are equally as important, and neglecting them may be damaging in the long term to the industry's economic viability.

Monitoring the figures in Fig. 2.2 is an important exercise, as this gives the best overall view of the UK audience. Figures can shift quite dramatically. For instance, in 2003, the audience of 7–14-year-olds for the Top 20 films halved to 11 million – demonstrating the importance of big Hollywood films for children. It is also noticeable that there is a big difference between the older audience and the children's audience when it comes to home-grown films. Children do not watch UK films – partly because UK producers do not have the resources to make large-scale animations (except in conjunction with Hollywood, as with *Wallace and Gromit*). In one sense, the best course for British filmmakers would be to make films for older audiences, leaving Hollywood to cater for younger markets.

However, would that younger audience move towards UK films as it got older or would it want to stay with Hollywood? Overall, persuading the older audience to visit the cinema just one more time per year would increase total audiences more than trying to persuade younger audiences to visit more frequently. A good example of the kind of film that might do this is *Ladies in Lavender* (UK, 2004). Starring the two grand dames of UK film and theatre, Judi Dench and Maggie Smith, and directed by Charles Dance, still possibly best known as a romantic lead actor by older female audiences, this film went barely noticed by film journalists, but returned very good box-office figures in the UK and North America (nearly $20 million worldwide).

> Exhibitors tend to think about audiences in relation to film certification categories (U, PG,12, 12A, 15, 18):
> - Children (5-12 years old)
> - Family groups
> - Teenagers / Young couples / students
> - Adults
>
> This is a form of **audience segmentation**. See Baker, Inglis and Voss (2002)

CAVIAR also profiles individual films in terms of gender, age and social class (see Chapter 7 for more background on this). Here are a few examples of the headline findings of these research profiles for 2004:

> *Bridget Jones: Edge of Reason* split 68%:32% female:male and 53% of the audience was aged 35+
>
> *Resident Evil: Apocalypse* split 25%:75% female:male and 59% of the audience was aged 15–24

Audience divisions by social class are of interest to the industry, partly because advertising space on cinema screens is becoming more important as a source of income for exhibitors, even if it has only a small share of the advertising market compared with TV, the press and the internet. Advertisers classify media (i.e. specific newspaper titles or TV programmes as well as the medium itself) according to social class divisions. Film producers and definitely distributors also need to be aware of what kinds of audience they are targeting. In 2004, the total UK population was classified as ABC1 (professional, managerial, white collar, higher skilled manual): 48% and C2DE (lower-skilled manual, semi- and unskilled manual): 52% (descriptions from UK Film Council). However, the audience profile for the Top 20 films suggests ABC1: 59%, C2DE: 41%.

An example of the skewing of the audience on social class lines can be found with *Wimbledon,* which had a 41% AB audience (AB = 21% of population).

In terms of ethnicity, the UK Film Council has published research conducted by TNS in 2004, which suggests that the 'non-white' (black, Asian, Chinese, mixed and other) population aged 12–74 makes up 7.9% of the total UK population, 12–74, but 12.5% of the cinema audience. The 'non-white' population attends screenings more frequently, but buys DVDs and pay-per-view films on TV less often (6.7% and 7.3% of total buyers) than the white population. Films that had an audience skewed in terms of ethnicity (i.e. appearing in the Top 10 for one ethnic grouping, but not others) included:

For black audiences: *The Passion of the Christ* (2004), *Kill Bill Vol 2* (2004)
For white audiences: *Love Actually* (2003), *Van Helsing* (2004)
For Indian and Pakistani audiences: *Kal Ho Naa Ho* (2003), *Bride and Prejudice* (2004).

As noted above, skewing is also identifiable in terms of regions, with some films performing better in particular parts of the UK and overall some noticeable differences between frequency of attendance in different regions. These kind of skew patterns could be used to inform future marketing decisions. It is also useful to get a sense of how audiences have changed over time – and how they might change again.

Audiences now aged 55 and over were themselves frequent cinemagoers in their youth (audiences in the 1960s were significantly bigger than current audiences – see Fig. 2.3), and many of them could be persuaded back. They also have more leisure time and in many cases more disposable income than younger audiences. By contrast, current 35–45-year-olds belong to the generation with the least ingrained cinema going habit (i.e. audiences fell to their lowest levels in the 1980s, when this generation were teenagers). This generation was the first to embrace video as the main medium for film.

Film and video

The relationship between cinema (film) and television (video) in terms of audiences is complex and dynamic, with a history of over 50 years. It is very easy to leap to conclusions and many industry personnel, academics and cultural commentators have done so at various times. Let us look at one of the most common assertions.

'*Cinema audiences declined as home television viewing increased in the 1950s.*' This is certainly true in the case of the UK if we focus on the period from 1955-1959. In 1946, the UK had some of the highest cinema attendance figures ever seen (i.e. on a per capita basis). The frequency of attendance per person was around 40 visits per year. In practice, there were large numbers of people who went to the cinema two or three times a week (but there were also people who never went at all). They went 'to the pictures' (or 'the flicks') rather than to see a specific film. They didn't have television and even if they had been able to see programmes, they would not have been attracted to the rather staid programming of the BBC. In 1955, 'commercial television' (ITV) was launched in the UK, first in London and then gradually across the UK in the next few years. ITV offered entertainment that directly competed with the cinema, and the cinema audience was clearly affected.

In his study of the Gaumont cinema circuit in the UK, Allen Eyles (1996) reports on the experience of the Sheffield Gaumont cinema manager in late 1956 when ITV reached Sheffield and on a Rank Organisation (owners of both Gaumont and

Odeon cinemas at the time) report in 1958. The analysis concluded that the cinema was more affected by television than other out-of-the-house leisure activities such as dancing (which actually increased in popularity with younger people) and theatre. Cinema could still compete with television in terms of high-quality product, but not on a weekly basis. Some audiences presumably decided that staying in to watch what they perceived as relatively poor-quality television was acceptable if the cinema was not much better – they lost the habit of cinema going.

Two good examples of the older working-class viewer can be seen in the famous **New Wave** British films *Saturday Night and Sunday Morning* (1960) and *A Kind of Loving* (1962). The anti-heroes of both films, played by Albert Finney and Alan Bates respectively, are equally scathing in their criticism of an older generation attracted to television Westerns and game shows. In this way, they represent the view of leftish, middle-class film directors putting down television as 'mindless entertainment'.

The audiences who stayed in the cinemas were in the younger age bands, for whom the cinema still meant an escape from a home environment and a social activity. It was generally the older working-class audiences who switched over to ITV. (The higher socio-economic groups, as the Rank report put it, were also now missing from the cinema audience and had been, perhaps, earlier adopters of television when it was 'BBC only'.)

But this was not the whole story. Audiences began to decline in the late 1940s, and the late 1950s saw an acceleration of decline, not a beginning. Peacetime brought a gradual increase in affluence and slowly a new housing stock – making the home a more attractive place to spend time. Other social attractions also developed. As cinemas closed, some of them moved over to bingo, and later others

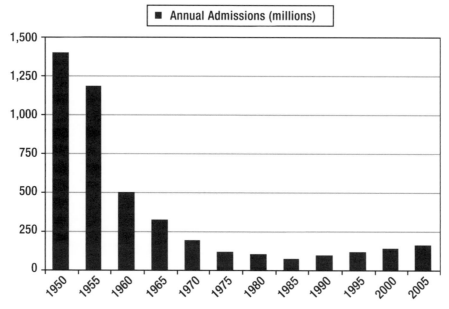

Fig 2.3 UK Cinema admissions 1950–2005

became clubs. Popular music became a focus for the first generation of teenagers, and studios attempted to attract audiences to cinemas with films featuring music stars.

After the sharp decline in the late 1950s, attendance levels fell each year, but in a less dramatic fashion. The audience gradually drifted away, as cinema going moved from a regular habit towards a special occasion for much of the population. Some critics have argued that during this period the UK cinema industry more or less accepted its fate and did little to entice audiences back. There were some new cinemas in the 1960s, but many smaller cinemas had remained unaltered since the 1930s and were beginning to show serious signs of wear and tear. By the late 1970s, cinema seemed to be on the way out for the mass audience.

What was television in the UK doing about film in this period? Here again there are a number of assertions to address. One concerns the quality of BBC/ITV programming. The late 1960s and through the 1970s is sometimes referred to as a Golden Age of television drama (as well as light entertainment, current affairs, documentary etc.). Such a view is, of course, subjective, but what is noticeable is that in this period, large audiences watched single plays (increasingly shot on film) directed by some of the well-known names from British cinema and later Hollywood, including Ken Loach, Stephen Frears, Michael Apted and Mike Newell. By large audiences we mean audiences measured in millions. *The Wednesday Play* (1964–70) and *Play for Today* (1970–84) were broadcast on BBC 1, and although it is difficult now to get

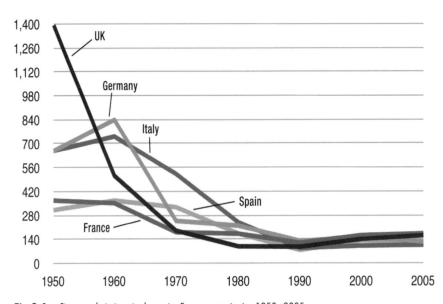

Fig 2.4   Cinema admissions in the major European territories 1950–2005

audience figures for these programmes, it is reasonable to suggest that most of them will have been seen by at least 2 or 3 million people and some by many more. By contrast, most British cinema films today fail to reach an audience of half a million. Although most plays were shot on videotape in the 1960s, 16mm film gradually became the main medium for these programmes and several had a form of 'afterlife' as 16mm prints for educational use. Even larger audiences watched Hollywood-made drama series, shot on film. In effect, UK television offered something of the range of material available at local cinemas in the 1950s. How important was this in luring audiences away from cinemas? In other European countries, where television services were perhaps less well developed at this time, cinema attendances held up longer (see Fig. 2.4), before similarly declining (but in France never as much as in the UK).

The number of cinema films appearing on the UK's three channels during 1965–79 was far fewer than in today's multi-channel environment. A study of cinema and TV audiences in Nottingham from 1956 onwards reports that while films were rarely available on television (fewer than one per week) in 1956, by the 1970s there were around 15 per week across three channels (see Jancovich et al., 2003), However, when a film was shown, it was likely to get a much larger audience than most films attract now in the fragmenting audience environment of contemporary television. It could be argued that audiences in this period did not lose their interest in films as such – they simply found them more difficult to access. Partly this was because film distributors were still wary of allowing their films to be sold to television. Initially, Hollywood was reluctant to allow any film libraries to be made available to television, and it was not until RKO, the only major studio to collapse in the decline period, released its library in 1956 that films became available.

When films were made available, there was usually a long window between the cinema release and the first appearance on television (around five years) with, as yet, no video release in between. Films stayed current after a cinema release only through distribution on 16mm, the format used for film societies, air and sea travel, schools etc.

In the 1960s, American television companies began to capitalise on the public's appetite for films by creating the 'made for television' feature film, some of which were seen in the UK in cinemas (e.g. *The Killers*, Don Siegel, 1964; *Duel*, Steven Spielberg, 1972; *Jericho Mile*, Michael Mann, 1978). For a period in the USA, it even looked like the TV networks might compete with the studios as producers of feature films (the TV network ABC established a film production company in the late 1960s, with *Cabaret*, 1972, perhaps its best-known production). Films shown on American television in the 1970s could attract very large audiences, so despite the seeming decline of the Hollywood studios, the popularity

> So anti television was Hollywood that in the early 1950s, smaller British film studios were able to sell 'made for television' films to the American TV networks.

The Granada cinema chain, mostly based in the south of England, successfully bid in 1954 to win the ITV franchise for weekdays across Lancashire and Yorkshire.

Television series were traded internationally on film because of the difficulties of converting video signals designed for the different broadcasting systems, NTSC (US) and PAL (UK).

of film itself was less in doubt. From the 1980s onwards, Hollywood gradually reasserted its privileged status as provider of television programme material and films for the cinema. Crucial to this was its gradual acceptance of video as a commercial format (see below).

It took some time for companies associated with cinema to properly come to terms with films on television – whether made for the medium or providing an outlet for features originally made for theatrical distribution. This was despite the fact that in North America and in Europe, the same companies had interests in both media. In the UK in the 1950s, ABPC (Associated British Pictures Corporation) owned film studios at Elstree and the ABC cinema circuit when it formed ABC Television to take a lucrative ITV franchise for weekend programming in the Midlands and the north.

The new ITV franchise holders believed they knew their audiences from their cinema experience and they did indeed attract new audiences to television. But as their initial move into television was a defensive strategy aimed at compensating for an audience lost to cinemas, they were not thinking in what now might be termed synergistic ways. In the main, television programmes were made in-house by the BBC and the larger ITV companies or imported on film from the Hollywood television companies. Only one major UK producer, ITC, later absorbed by the ITV company ATV, made UK television series on film that could be exported. These were sold worldwide and featured stars like the young Roger Moore (*The Saint*, 1962–9).

UK television and films for the cinema

The Hollywood experience of films made for television being released to cinemas and cinema films being made for cinema release by television companies did not happen in the UK until the 1980s. The BBC did not consider the potential of its plays/films as theatrical product. They did sometimes screen in cinemas abroad, but contractual difficulties (e.g. union agreements) made it difficult to get films into UK cinemas. The emergence of Channel 4 in 1982 changed all this when films it had commissioned were given a cinema release. It is not an exaggeration to suggest that Channel 4, with later help from BBC and ITV companies such as Granada, saved British cinema as a production base in the late 1980s. In the last ten years, Channel 4 Films and BBC Films have maintained a significant share of UK film production, releasing titles theatrically and then on DVD, with a short window before television broadcasts.

Investment by television companies in film production is a common practice in Europe. So is co-production, and certain smaller UK film producers have prospered by making long-term partnerships with European television companies and distributors. These European companies know their own local markets well and are prepared to put up money (to buy rights before production) for filmmakers they know. Ken Loach, for instance, has consistently been supported by production partners in France, Italy, Germany and Spain, enabling him to shoot films that could not be made using only UK funding. One of the issues for UK funding is how well do the people who hold the purse strings know the UK audience for the kinds of films that are submitted for production? In the UK, the relationship between film and television is not always valued as it should be. The phrase 'made for TV' is often used as a negative comment about how British films look, even if

> Channel 4's investment in film production, either directly for *Film on Four*, or as a partner in co-productions, amounts to an interest in hundreds of film titles since 1982. It is difficult to be precise, because of the different names used such as FilmFour, Channel 4 Films etc. In 2003, Channel 4 perhaps overreached itself after expanding into the distribution of big-budget American films, and had to cut back. But in 2006, it was still active.

they were made primarily for cinema. This sometimes refers not only to the visual qualities of a film, but also to themes about social issues. The implication is that television material is of less cultural value, and these kinds of negative ideas are communicated to audiences. Ironically, one of the main criticisms of UK film production refers to the poor quality of scripts – often seen as a strength of UK television production.

One of the bonuses for UK audiences from Channel 4's involvement in cinema releases was the channel's statutory obligation to provide programming not seen elsewhere on UK television. (Sadly, this means something very different in the contemporary environment.) This was most evident in relation to black and Asian cinema and gay cinema. Channel 4 was involved in funding both **avant-garde** and relatively mainstream films: for example, Derek Jarman's *The Garden* (1990) and Stephen Frears' film of Hanif Kureishi's script, *My Beautiful Laundrette* (1985). Channel 4 screened seasons of films from Africa and Latin America, introduced Hindi cinema to the wider UK audience and invested in productions such as *Salaam Bombay* (UK/India/France, 1988) and *Bandit Queen* (India/UK, 1994), which appeared in cinemas and on television in the UK.

Technical differences and audience appreciation

By the 1970s, it was clear to everyone that most people's experience of watching films had moved from cinema to television. In the UK the audience for (older) films on television could be counted as anything over 200 million per quarter-year (assuming an average audience of 1 million for some 200 films), whereas for cinema, it was barely 200 million admissions for a whole year – see Fig. 2.3 above). But what did they actually see on a TV screen? The standard TV set in the 1970s had a screen shape or aspect ratio of 4:3 and it received a colour signal (although there were still many 'black and white only' sets being used) with mono sound. For films made in black and white before 1953, the TV set gave a perfectly adequate picture and sound. The old 'Academy' aspect ratio in the cinema before 1953 was

1:1.33, the same as the 4:3 television screen, but cinema films made after this date used one of several different 'widescreen' ratios, with the widest in normal use being CinemaScope, at first 1:2.55, later 1:2.35. The widest Scope format was designed for stereo sound, and from the mid-1950s onwards, films were increasingly made in various colour processes. All of the changes made by Hollywood in the early 1950s (and subsequently adopted in other film industries across the world) were, of course, designed to make cinema as different as possible from television.

Widescreen films did not fit on the television screen and the only options for the television broadcaster were to **letterbox** the full image, losing half the screen area to black, or to **pan and scan**. This process selected the action in any scene and presented it inside a 4:3 frame, thereby destroying the original composition of the image. If the film's director had used the whole width of the frame, characters and other significant objects might be cut out altogether in the pan-and-scan version. Some films became virtually unintelligible on television. Even so, pan and scan was favoured, as it was believed that most TV viewers would not accept letterboxing. Stereo sound was not possible on TV sets at this time. This became a big issue once cinemas began to re-equip with Dolby Stereo in the late 1970s (the popularity of *Star Wars* in Dolby-equipped cinemas is usually quoted as the impetus for this change). Colour was a different matter. The standard broadcast TV picture was (and still is) a relatively **low-resolution** image and is incapable of carrying sufficient data to properly represent the range of shades in a cinematic image. To compound this problem, TV sets in the 1970s did not have computerised default settings, and engineers reported that many TV viewers simply turned up the colour controls to 'full', distorting any kind of balance that the film graders would have sought for a cinema release.

Television audiences in the 1970s were used to poor-quality image and sound, but in the declining film exhibition market, especially in the UK, they were not necessarily guaranteed a better experience in run down, cheaply twinned circuit cinemas. In this sense, the arrival of the multiplex was a definite improvement. Hollywood's response to the domination of television by the 1970s was to reduce the number of CinemaScope features and also to instruct directors to use a guide in the film camera's viewfinder in order to confine the action to a 4:3 **safe area**. This meant that the film was pan-and-scan ready for TV. A useful account of this complex history can be found in Neale (1998), and in the same collection, Warren Buckland analyses Steven Spielberg's approach to filming *Raiders of the Lost Ark* in 1981, making several interesting comments about the relationship between Spielberg's television background and the way he adopted certain strategies that would work well on both the cinema and television screen. For instance, television is not suited to

Grading is the process that allows technicians to adjust colours to produce a final positive print for cinema projection that meets the wishes of the production crew as closely as possible. Many films use distinctive colour palettes, which are easily lost if TV sets are badly tuned.

long shots and sequences staged in depth. Montage and fast-cutting with close-ups is preferable.

Do these issues really affect audiences beyond a small coterie of film scholars and technicians? Possibly not, but it could be argued that during the 1970s and 1980s, the audience learned to accept an impoverished image, compared to the quality films of the 1940s–60s. The compensation was the greater use of graphics, fast-cutting, aerial shots, popular music etc. to ensure that the television image remained exciting and busy. One outcome of this was to emphasise for certain producers and directors that they could distinguish their work as 'cinematic' simply by staging events for a widescreen camera. Buckland refers to a suggestion by Henry Jenkins that Hollywood directors like Spielberg were conscious of trying to develop a recognisable style that would increase their market value. Neale points to Ridley Scott's film *Blade Runner* and notes that although action is largely confined to the 4:3 safe area, the edges of the widescreen frame are filled with the elements of set design that help to develop the film's thematic. *Blade Runner* would later become one of the most important cult films of the 1990s and Scott would establish himself as a name director, with a large fan base seeking out his films in cinemas before a video release. We can see here the development of films that are suited to the multiplex experience and also the roots of the kudos attached to the more recent independent widescreen films of directors such as Wes Anderson (*Rushmore*, 1999) and Alexander Payne (*Election*, 1999). The whole issue of aspect ratios returned to the forefront of industry concerns with the advent of widescreen TVs and DVDs in the late 1990s. These are considered in the video section below.

> Filmmakers are well aware that different markets require films in different screen formats. The producers of the South African film *Tsotsi* prepared for 'about nine different versions' of the film including a 1:2.35 cinema print and both 16x9 (1:1.78) and 4:3 digital versions for DVD and television. (Bosley 2006: 39).

> Widescreen definitions: Hollywood cinema still uses the 1:2.35 ratio for selected films, but the 'standard' or 'modern' widescreen ratio is 1:1.85. In parts of Europe, the standard ratio is still 1:1.66. The television widescreen ratio is 16:9, which converts to approximately 1:1.78. This is not suitable for any standard film format. So unless viewers select letterboxing, they will usually be watching the wrong aspect ratio.

Hollywood and video

Hollywood finally learned to live with video and indeed to exploit it. At first reluctant to consider the VCR at all, by the 1980s Hollywood had not only agreed to its films being released on videocassettes, but had also been rewarded by new streams of revenue for rental and later retail that soon overtook theatrical box office. Video (and the new cable and satellite pay TV channels) completely changed the economics of the film business (see Gomery, 1988: 83). For the studios, and for other American producers/distributors, video stabilised the industry and pushed it into growth. Several bonuses were evident. First, it was noticeable that films that did not perform on initial release could still produce a profit from a successful life in the different context of domestic video/television. Second, successful titles could be

In the 1970s, the porn industry in the USA also switched to video. It became well-established as a profitable industry with claimed sales of over $4 billion in 1999 (*Observer* 12 September 1999).

RESEARCH SUGGESTION
List the main differences between watching a film in the cinema and watching the same film as a television broadcast. Is the list the likely to be the same for all kinds of films? Is there very much difference between the ways in which different TV channels present films for viewing (e.g. in terms of the correct aspect ratio, editing for television, interruption by advertisements etc.)?

even bigger when the high profile from theatrical box office helped to promote the film on video. Third, library films – back catalogue – started to look like a valuable asset.

Video also had an unforeseen role in promoting the new American Independent cinema in the 1980s. Smaller distributors making money from video distribution were able to finance the films of directors such as John Sayles and Steven Soderbergh (see Pierson, 1996: 19). Unfortunately, these were often the same distributors who had previously distributed foreign-language films to US cinemas, and this aspect of their work suffered. It is worth noting here that the term 'Hollywood' is often used interchangeably with American cinema. But the major studios, the MPAA members, release only around half of the films available in the USA (190 out of 535 in 2005) each year (figures from <www.mpaa.org>). It is difficult to gauge the economic performance of the independent releases which make up the remainder, but it is more than likely that they have performed better on video than on theatrical release.

When DVD arrived during the late 1990s, Hollywood was quick to exploit the new format. DVD is considered in detail in Chapter 8.

References

Altman, Rick (1999), *Film/Genre* (London: BFI).

Baker, Robin, J. Ron Inglis, Julia Voss (2002), *At a Cinema Near You: Strategies for Sustainable Local Cinema Development* (BFI). Available for free download from: <www.bfi.org.uk/filmtvinfo/publications/practical/cinemanearyou.html>.

Betrock, Alan (1986), *The I Was a Teenage Juvenile Delinquent Rock'N'Roll Horror Beach Party Movie Book: A Complete Guide to the Teen Exploitation Film, 1954–1969* (New York: St Martin's Press).

Rachel K. Bosley (2006), 'An Angry Young Man', *American Cinematographer*, March.

Gill Branston and Roy Stafford (2006), *The Media Student's Book*, 4th edn, (London: Routledge).

Buckland, Warren (1998), 'Notes on Narrative Aspects of the New Hollywood Blockbuster' in Steve Neale and Murray Smith (eds), *Contemporary Hollywood Cinema* (London: Routledge).

Eyles, Allen (1996), *Gaumont British Cinemas* (London: Cinema Theatre Association/BFI).

Gomery, Douglas (1988), 'Hollywood's Hold on the New Television Technologies', *Screen*, Vol. 29, No. 2.

Jancovich, Mark and Lucy Faire, with Sarah Stubbings (2003), *The Place of the Audience: Cultural Geographies of Film Consumption* (London: BFI).

Neale, Steve (1998), 'Widescreen Composition in the Age of Television', in Steve Neale and Murray Smith (eds) *Contemporary Hollywood Cinema* (London: Routledge).

Pierson, John (1996) *Spike, Mike, Slackers & Dykes* (London: Faber & Faber).

3. Distribution, Exhibition and Critical Commentary

The film industry is over 100 years old, but for the first 20 years of presentations to paying audiences, it was largely a structure of separate cottage industries that took time to become institutionalised. At first, films were made and sold as individual products. A filmmaker made a film and then sold copies to exhibitors – effectively 'showmen' – who would show a print in different venues until it literally wore out.

How do films actually get to audiences? How do they learn about them? Where do they see them?

The modern industry began around the early 1910s with the establishment of film exchanges and the concept of renting a print of a film for a set period, after which the print was returned to the rental company – the 'distributor'. Gradually, the industry developed three distinct sectors:

- production
- distribution
- exhibition.

By 1930 in the USA, the Hollywood studio system had evolved into a vertically integrated operation dominated by five major studios (Paramount, MGM, Warner Bros., RKO and 20th Century-Fox). In **vertical integration,** each stage of production is brought under the control of a single body, and in the film industry this meant that the studios produced films themselves and distributed them primarily to their own cinemas. The whole system was designed to maximise profits with a 'stream' of 'A' and 'B' features, newsreels, cartoons etc. to feed the demands of the studios' own cinemas. Outside the Big Five group, the Little Three (Columbia, Universal and United Artists) made and distributed films to cinemas generally (i.e. they did not own any themselves), and the larger independent studios such as Disney made films that were distributed by the majors. The remainder of the industry concentrated on making lower budget films that struggled to find distribution deals and that often appeared in smaller and less prestigious cinemas.

In Europe and Japan, similar systems operated, although not with the market domination seen in the USA and with differences between national industries. From the 1920s onwards, Hollywood began to gain power in a range of overseas markets and film soon became an international business. The internationalisation of the market was resisted in some countries more than others, but the major Hollywood studios made their presence felt everywhere, sometimes directly through their own subsidiaries (as in the UK), sometimes through partnerships with local producers, distributors and exhibitors.

The American film industry changed after 1948 following the US Federal Court decision to force the major studios to sell their cinema chains. They did this gradually (and reluctantly) over the next few years – the cinemas had been the most profitable parts of the studio empires. At this time, the audience for cinema was starting to drift away in the USA as other leisure pursuits, including television and a variety of home-based activities, developed with increasing affluence. (The decline in the UK occurred at roughly the same time but was proportionally greater than in the USA; in other major film markets it came much later.) Apart from a technological response to this change – making films bigger and more colourful with CinemaScope and Technicolor – the studio response was also to invest in fewer films and to concentrate more on making profit from them.

Distribution became the principal function of the majors. Although they did still make a few pictures on studio lots (which would later be sold or turned over to television production), they increasingly relied on independent production companies to make most of the films they distributed. For the studio, the distribution rights were the key. They would effectively pay to have films made and then own the rights. The system that developed in the 1950s, as the studio system declined, still operates, with some new developments, 50 years later and it has been described as the **package production** system. Each film is now treated as a separate project, a separate entry on a studio **slate** for the year.

The majors remain 'major' because they are able to maintain an annual slate of around 20 big-budget features. Considerable investment (over $1 billion) in acquiring titles is then the basis for future wealth, which must be generated by different forms of rental income from these titles. **Rights** – i.e. the legal right to show a film to a paying audience – can be traded in a number of ways. First, rights can be recognised for different territories. At one time, Hollywood considered the overseas market to be a bonus and commercial success was judged on the basis of performance in the domestic market, which comprises the USA and Canada. In the last five years, it has become apparent that the international market has in fact exceeded its North American equivalent and the majors now take both markets very seriously. In value terms, the major film markets/territories are ranked in this order:

1. North America
2. Japan
3. UK and Ireland
4. France
5. Germany

(These are ranked as **theatrical** markets. The popularity of DVD in the UK makes the combined theatrical/DVD market No. 2 to North America.)

Within each **territory**, rights are available for different forms of distribution. Cinema releases (also known as **theatrical rights**) usually come first (i.e. the first to be seen by the public), followed by DVD rental and retail, Pay TV and finally free-to-air TV. The time lag between these different forms of distribution, termed a **window**, was at one time seen as crucial for effective commercial exploitation. However, changes in viewing technologies and the viewing habits of audiences have recently undermined such differences. In 2006, *The Road to Guantanamo,* from Revolution Films in the UK, became the first film to be screened on television, shown in cinemas and made available on DVD and as an internet download, all within a few days. A few weeks later, in Italy, *H2Odio,* a thriller by a respected filmmaker, Alex Infascelli, was released first as a DVD sold in newspaper kiosks alongside *La Repubblica,* a pioneer of newspaper DVD distribution. Changes from now on might come very quickly. However, Hollywood producer-director Steven Soderbergh's simultaneous cinema/DVD release of *Bubble* in 2006 was not particularly successful and was not well received by some exhibitors (*Screen International,* 15 March 2006).

Rights are often sold for only limited periods. The same rights may then be sold to a different distributor for a further period. This explains why DVDs go out of print or why films cannot be screened in cinemas – even though a physical print of a film may exist, the rights to show it may have expired. In the case of the major studios, previous releases have always been of interest. During the studio period, it was common practice to remake a successful film every ten years or so. When this happened, the old prints would be destroyed to avoid any damage to the market performance of the new release. This is now seen as a waste. Any film has value as a library resource that can be exploited through re-releases in different formats. A library of films is a major asset and these can be bought and sold like any other assets.

> It can be very confusing as film libraries are sometimes sold to a rival company. For example, the MGM film library up to the 1980s is now owned by Warner Bros., while many classic British films are now owned by the French company Studio Canal.

How film distribution works in the UK theatrical market

A distributor is faced with the need to exploit rights on a particular film within a set period. Their task is to organise the release of the film so that it reaches the biggest audience possible in order to achieve a profit. The Film Distributors' Association (FDA) in the UK publishes a detailed guide to distribution on its website at <www.launchingfilms.com/uk_film_distribution_guide/distribution_guide.pdf> which opens with this definition: 'Distribution is the dynamic, competitive business of launching and sustaining films.' The second part of this definition emphasises that distribution is more than just releasing a film. It also means tracking a film's performance and sometimes taking secondary action.

For the subsidiary of a major studio, there will be a notional target figure for **rentals**, perhaps based on previous American performance. As a rule of thumb, the UK market is around 10% in value of the North American market. This is explained by two factors: the population of the USA and Canada is around five times bigger, and the 'frequency of cinema going' in North America is nearly twice as high (over five visits per person each year compared with fewer than three in the UK). On this basis, a film that makes $100 million in North America should make around $10 million in the UK. Unless they are peculiarly American, most Hollywood films actually better the 1:10 ratio in the UK (but it is noticeable that the reverse very rarely happens – UK films do not go on to take ten times their UK box office in North America). For a UK independent distributor, acquiring rights is a straight financial calculation – the rights have been bought, the film must now be sold to the public.

Before a film can be screened to the paying public in the UK, it must be certificated. This is carried out by the British Board of Film Classification, an independent body set up by the UK film industry to give advice on the suitability of films for specific audiences. Film classification is a form of **self-regulation** that is carried out by the **BBFC** on behalf of local authorities who have the legal power to grant licences for cinema screenings to the public. It is not illegal to show an uncertificated film in a UK cinema, but an exhibitor could lose their licence. The enabling local authority has the legal power to control what is shown as public entertainment and they do sometimes ignore the advice from the BBFC and make their own decisions. Some cinemas are able to show uncertificated films as part of special events such as film festivals.

The classification of films for release on video formats such as DVD is different, as the BBFC is in this case a **statutory regulator**, charged with this task under the Video Recordings Act (1984). Once again, the BBFC is not a legal enforcer – the law is maintained by Trading Standards officers, as it is an offence to offer for sale video material that has not been classified (or to offer material classified as 15 or 18 to younger children etc.).

Classification/certification is a slightly different issue for the larger distributors as compared to smaller independents. The major Hollywood studios are keenly aware of what different classifications can mean in terms of audience expectations. As far as possible, they wish to maximise audiences. Age-based classification excludes younger children and the importance of this became apparent when pressure on the

BBFC led to the introduction of the 12A certificate in 2002. It is important for the distributors and exhibitors that major blockbusters do not exclude younger children, and the release of *Spider-Man* in 2001 led to some local councils allowing parents to bring younger children to screenings. The majors are very aware of how different countries' classification systems work and are able to edit films accordingly before submission to the BBFC and similar bodies worldwide.

A slightly different example of how certificates work is the recent surge of horror films with lower age limit classifications (see discussion of *The Ring* in Chapter 1), some of which are argued to have increased the female audience for horror films. Conversely, some films may seek an 18 certificate to certain audiences to prove that they contain strong material.

Attitudes towards classification vary between countries: e.g. in the work of **EIRIN**, the regulator in Japan, which has traditionally banned images of genitalia, requiring a 'fogging' of the screen or a digital mosaic.

Whereas the majors are quite prepared to edit and re-edit big-budget films to maximise audiences, more personal films from established directors (which will usually not be big-budget productions) may lead to sustained negotiation with classification agencies, as possible cuts might be seen as threatening the artistic integrity of the director. This happened a great deal in the 1970s. It is rare today, in the UK at least, with the BBFC prepared to pass a number of films 'uncut' that in earlier periods might have been denied a certificate. It is worth noting here that there is an almost unspoken recognition that arthouse audiences are less likely to be corrupted than the audiences for mainstream films. This tells us something about attitudes towards audiences, or possibly about the class background of regulators.

For smaller independent distributors, the process of classification is a more pragmatic issue. Distributors pay a flat fee to have a title classified. They may have a trailer that also needs classification. For a major studio releasing several hundred prints, the cost of classification is negligible (i.e. a small proportion of the total spend), but for a distributor with only ten prints – or even occasionally only one – the cost is much more significant. A standard feature film might cost £700 or more to classify plus VAT and administration time. This could be the equivalent of the cost of an extra print.

Assuming a straightforward classification decision is possible, the distributor can move forward to consider a releasing strategy. There are several different strategies for releasing a film, but in broad terms there are just two. The first, often termed a 'wide' release (in the UK sometimes referred to as a 'saturation' release), usually associated with the majors, involves spending a large sum and attracting a mass audience. The second, usually associated with smaller independents, involves spending very little and attempting to target a smaller, more specialised audience. In either case, the distributor needs to think about audiences and how to persuade them into cinemas.

The wide or 'blanket' release

The norm for a major studio picture is a simultaneous release in all major urban centres (in reality, all multiplexes and also selected independents). Following the US model, the focus for the release is the opening weekend. In fact, this now often includes a fourth night of 'previews' on the Thursday before a Friday opening. The opening is supported by extensive advertising on television and other media, promotional visits by stars and sponsorship tie-ins. This is an expensive process and further expense comes from the cost of prints. A 35mm film print costs around £1,000 and a wide release may require anything from 300 up to 1,000 prints for a *Harry Potter* film. UK box-office charts are confusing, in that they quote the number of *sites* at which a film is playing, rather than the number of *screens*. *Harry Potter* films and other blockbuster titles are likely to require two or three prints at the same multiplex site, so that they can play on different screens at the same time.

> Where more than one print goes to a multiplex, it is likely that there will be one screen playing an 'Audio Described' version of the film or one subtitled for those with hearing impairments – an important change in access for audiences, but also an extra expense that may deter smaller distributors.

The combined cost of **P & A** (Prints and Advertising) for a major studio release in the UK is in excess of £1 million. This compares with a North American figure of $25 million plus (or up to 50% of the production budget). Few UK independent distributors can afford this kind of spending on a regular basis, and this is one of the main reasons why British films need the support of a Hollywood studio if they are to reach large audiences in the UK.

A wide release requires extensive planning and careful preparation so that everything is in place for the opening weekend. Here are some of the factors to be considered:

- previews for exhibitors;
- trailers produced for cinema/TV/online (possibly 'teasers' long before actual release) plus other advertising and promotional material, including 'point of sale' for cinemas;
- advertising space bought in different media (TV, 'outdoor' (posters), radio, press);
- promotional activities coordinated (stars' appearances, TV and radio material, book/music publishing tie-ins etc.);
- merchandising and sponsorship tie-ins;
- preview screenings for regional press/broadcasting/monthly magazines (weeks in advance) and national press/broadcasting (week of release);
- prints produced and delivery to cinemas organised.

Typically, distributors have a small staff team coordinating an army of suppliers and sub-contractors, and the pressure is great to open the film on schedule. This can mean it is difficult to change dates at the last minute.

The major Hollywood studios, faced with a growing problem of piracy, now have a strategy of simultaneous global release for the biggest films on the slate. This began with *X-Men 2* in 2003 and by summer 2006 had evolved to see *M:i:III* released on 9,000 screens worldwide over 5–6 May.

Platform release

The term '**platform release**' refers to an initial release in only a handful of major cities at selected cinemas. These will be chosen as the most attractive cinemas for a select audience – often young middle-class professionals or possibly students. These are 'frequent cinemagoers' who will help to build word of mouth and perhaps to generate press and television coverage of the issues in the film/director/stars etc. Having created a 'profile' for the film, distributors can then decide how to exploit audience knowledge of the film title over the succeeding weeks. One strategy is to slowly expand the release until the film reaches all parts of the country – effectively a 'wide' release that started as a platform. This strategy has been quite successful with some famous film titles in North America (e.g. *American Beauty* in 1999, which spread from an initial 16 screens in September to 1,500 by November and was then re-released for the Academy Award nominations in February 2000, to reach 1,900 screens in April).

In the smaller, more concentrated, UK market, such campaigns are less common but one celebrated 'platform' release success was *Trainspotting* in 1996. This film, based on a best-selling book by Edinburgh writer Irvine Welsh, was initially targeted at 16–24-year-olds, the core market (despite an 18 certificate). It was released on 13 screens in London, 23 in Scotland and selected screens in Cambridge, Oxford and Dublin. The distributor PolyGram (at the time building up to an attempt to establish itself as a European major) took the unprecedented step of spending an initial £850,000 promoting a film that cost only £1.7 million (thus following Hollywood practice of a promotion budget matching 50% of production cost).

PolyGram also worked closely with a rival music company, EMI, to promote the soundtrack album, and with a print publisher for a tie-in edition of the original novel. Crucially, the film received plenty of press coverage that addressed both the controversial drug culture references and the links to contemporary music culture. The production team of the previously successful *Shallow Grave* (UK, 1995) also succeeded in emphasising, through interviews, that this was definitely not an 'art film'. Word of mouth from the platform opening was very strong and press coverage pointed to a sense of 'discovering what youth was up to', enabling subsequent

PolyGram was owned by the Dutch electronics company Philips. It was set up as the principal record label for Philips' long-standing music recording interests but in 1991 PolyGram Filmed Entertainment was established, based in the UK under the leadership of Michael Kuhn. The company was successful and by 1999 had got to the point of launching in the American market, only to be sold by its parent to Seagram, then owners of Universal. *Notting Hill* (UK/US 1999) began as a PolyGram film and was released as a Universal film. PolyGram was the last UK producer/distributor to have real clout.

marketing to push the film towards older audiences. Eventually widening to 175 sites, *Trainspotting* grossed over £10 million in the UK and went on to do good business worldwide (see Finney, 1996).

A different strategy, used primarily for foreign language arthouse releases, is to 'platform' on dedicated London arthouse screens (Curzon, Renoir etc.) and then tour a small number of prints (ten to 20) around the UK regions. London generates around 25% of all UK cinema admissions, and London openings benefit from limited promotion in specialist media. As the concept of 'art house' changes to encompass more American Independent and British cinema, a new distribution strategy has emerged that sees an immediate release of new titles to a group of independent cinemas (and selected multiplex screens), perhaps 60 in total. This seems to be a kind of failsafe position, in which the distributor decides that such films will only play successfully in these cinemas and therefore it is best to limit the expenditure on prints, but maximise the benefits of opening like the mainstream films. The drawback can be that a film that does particularly well might be unable to stay in cinemas or that there are not enough prints to meet demand.

These are not the only strategies and it may be worth considering several earlier models that have some contemporary relevance.

Circuit release

Film distribution changed significantly in the UK in the late 1980s when multiplexes began to appear in significant numbers. Before then, the exhibition sector was dominated by two large 'circuits', ABC and Odeon, which operated traditional high street cinemas in most UK towns and cities. These two circuits each took films from specific Hollywood distributors: e.g. Warner Bros. films went to ABC, and Universal supplied Odeon. Films generally opened first in London's West End, in the distributor's own 'showcase' cinema. They would then move to north London, then south London and then eventually to the rest of the UK. This was the 'first run'. Later these films would turn up in smaller independent 'second run' cinemas. A film would stay in a local cinema for just one week and then be replaced. All the major films would get a circuit release, meaning that around 150–200 films (i.e. a new double bill in each circuit cinema) showed everywhere across the country each year. The circuit release system was quite rigid compared to current practice in the multiplex, but it did mean that everyone got a chance to see the main films in a local cinema. The current system offers more choice and flexibility – at least, that is the claim made by the exhibitors. But with fewer cinemas and popular films 'held over' for weeks at a time, the choice might actually be more limited.

One big difference between audiences in 1956 and 2006 is that the disparity in rental income between a successful film and a box-office flop in 1956 was not very significant, but in 2006 it might be the difference between a film that made £20 million and one that made £100,000. In 1956, every 'circuit film' was seen by a reasonably large audience, but films could not be held in cinemas indefinitely. The disparity is partly explained by the fact that in the 1950s, audiences had far fewer options for entertainment and therefore turned up more or less every week to see whatever film was on. Now we pick and choose our films much more deliberately.

The practice of circuit releases has ended, but there is still some interest in the concept. The UK Film Council has discussed a virtual circuit of digital screens (the Digital Screen Network). These are digital screens funded initially by the Council (with certain conditions relating to playing specialised films) and sited in multiplexes and independent cinemas across the country. One possibility is that these screens could enable specialised films to get a form of circuit release. Digital prints will not have the same duplication costs as a physical film print, so it is conceivable that 200 digital screens could show a specific title in the same week with national advertising. Such a scheme could see a significant change in exhibition practice, but so far it has not happened.

Roadshow screenings

One of the ways in which cinema in the 1950s fought back against television was by making films 'bigger'. This was not just a matter of a wider screen, Technicolor and stereo sound. Attempts were also made to present films as events. Typically, long films, especially the epics based on historical narratives, were shown with an intermission and sometimes introduced by an overture (as in an opera performance). There might be a glossy programme to be purchased as well. Such presentations were limited to more prestigious cinemas and required a more expensive ticket. So-called '**roadshow**' films did not follow standard distribution patterns; instead they would play at selected cinemas for long periods – often several months. One example of this practice was the presentation of films in an ultra-widescreen ratio via Cinerama technology. The Cinerama corporation built some new cinemas and converted others around the world. A group of features was made using the new process, but eventually these cinemas turned to more familiar roadshow fare. For quite a long period, many of the roadshow cinemas screened films in 70mm and with stereo sound (i.e. before Dolby and other sound systems became a standard feature of the cinema experience) (See Hall, 2002: 12 on the 'Roadshow').

The gradual spread of IMAX screens, 50 years after Cinerama first appeared has to some extent brought the roadshow back. As well as films made specifically for the IMAX screen, the IMAX corporation has now invested in a new process that allows mainstream films made for 35mm presentation to be digitally processed for IMAX presentation. Typically, these prints play a few weeks after the initial release in mainstream cinemas. Projected on the giant IMAX screen, they command a higher ticket price, and takings can be comparable to the opening weeks on conventional screens. IMAX films are not distributed in the same way as 35mm features – for the shorter 'made for IMAX' films, exhibitors must pay an up-front fee to hold the print for several weeks and then attempt to recoup as much as possible from the rental (see discussion of distribution economics below).

Bullet Boy: A case study in releasing a film in the UK

Bullet Boy was released in the UK in April 2005. It was produced by BBC films and the UK Film Council (as part of its New Cinema Fund operation). In this sense, it was a product of soft-money funding. Writer/director Saul Dibb has a background in documentary filmmaking, including work for the BBC. Following other (documentary) work on London 'street culture', Dibb put together a proposal for a fiction film based around the problem of 'gun culture' and its impact on an African-Caribbean family in north-east London. The casting of the film included, as the leading character Ricky, the selection of Ashley Walters, a young actor known for his UK television appearances. Walters is also 'Asher D' a prominent member of 'urban music' group So Solid Crew, both popular and controversial. Other cast members either had experience in British film or television or were recruited through workshops in London.

A relatively new UK independent distributor, Verve Pictures (founded in 2003), acquired theatrical and DVD rights in the UK, with the knowledge that the BBC would eventually show the film on UK television (it was screened on BBC2 in a Saturday mid-evening slot in spring 2006). Verve announces itself on its website as 'an independent UK specialist film distributor, with particular emphasis on British and independent films'.

Who is the film for?

Verve initially recognised that there were two possible audiences for the film. As most independent (i.e. not Hollywood-financed) British films are seen as

3.1 Luke Fraser (left) as Curtis and Ashley Walters as Ricky in *Bullet Boy*, a family melodrama built around a gun crime incident.

specialised rather than mainstream, the 25–34 AB audience was one possibility. Within the film industry, this group is sometimes referred to as the 'Curzon crowd' (referring to the Curzon cinema in London's West End – a very successful art cinema). To some extent, this audience also exists outside London, where it is perhaps more skewed towards older audience members. Reaching this audience with a youth film like *Bullet Boy* is not impossible and Verve noted the success of the Brazilian film, *City of God* (2002), which performed very well with the 25–34 AB audience. The second target group was the youth audience of 15–24 (the film was given a 15 certificate), which might also be slightly skewed towards ABC1, but not as significantly as with the 25–34 group.

The material in this case study is based on research material provided by Verve Pictures, for which many thanks.

In both cases, the distributor would also have to consider how important the black audience would be and how much the distribution pattern for the film's release might be affected by this. Similarly, would the film's strong London community feel work in other UK regions? A little while after the initial release, it became apparent that *Bullet Boy* had been accepted as part of the black British film culture celebrated in the British Film Institute's 'Black World' festival that ran through the summer of 2005. (Writer/director Saul Dibb is a white filmmaker, but the focus on black culture and other creative inputs lead to its inclusion.) Part of Verve's research looked at a group of similar films and how they fared at the UK box office. These were all films focusing on 'black youth', some British and some American. At the top of the list was *Boyz N the Hood* (1991), which made over £900,000 in the UK. In contrast, British films such as *Young Soul Rebels* (1991) and *Babymother* (1998) made less than £100,000.

Small independent distributors do not have large amounts of money to spend on advertising and therefore 'promotion' becomes very important. *Bullet Boy* had Saul Dibb and Ashley Walters as two focus points for media attention, and both were willing to give interviews and support the film. Dibb was most comfortable with the broadsheet press and specialist journals and in discussing his film in terms attractive to the AB audience. Walters was equally comfortable in dealing with media such as the urban music press and Radio 1 Xtra that appealed more directly to the youth audience.

The release

Verve decided to release the film on 75 prints across the UK. This was a brave, positive decision and meant that it was important to attract a wide audience. A pattern has emerged in the UK where even Hollywood films with a focus on African-American culture (as distinct from genre films that just happen to feature a major star like Will Smith) are restricted to a release of around 30 to 40 prints, sometimes only in cities with a significant black population. Black British films have generally had even more limited releases. Verve's release was mostly into multiplexes across the UK, and on the first weekend (after a number of previews, some of which featured personal appearances by Ashley Walters), *Bullet Boy* took an impressive £140,000 to land at No. 12 in the UK box-office chart. In the second weekend, Verve maintained the 'wide' distribution of prints and the box office dropped at around the average for all titles that weekend, keeping *Bullet Boy* at No. 12. Apart from the child/family orientated *Valiant*, there were no other UK films in the Top 15 in the opening two weeks, and with a screen average of around £4,000 for the first ten days, *Bullet Boy* was certainly a success for a British film without stars.

The competition for audiences in this period saw *Bullet Boy* up against the spectacular arthouse success of *Downfall*, the German film about Hitler's last days and a number of major Hollywood releases, including horror films *The Ring Two* and *The Amityville Horror*, as well as the Will Smith starrer *Hitch*, all three of which might have attracted some of *Bullet Boy*'s potential audience.

Bullet Boy lasted on 'wide' release for five weeks (the number of prints falling to 26) and then remained in a handful of venues for a further six weeks. At the end of its theatrical run the film had made approximately £500,000. Verve were delighted with this and saw it as a definite success, especially compared with the previous 'black youth' films listed above. The timing of the release eventually worked out well, although, as is often the case, it was actually some six months later than planned (the film won an award before its release date at the British Independent Film Awards in March 2005). The DVD release was boosted by the cinema success, although a late-August release was probably not the best timing, as this is a slow period for retail sales. The theatrical success also no doubt helped the BBC2 screening and, now that the film has appeared on an exam syllabus, it may keep DVD sales 'ticking over' for a longer period.

Analysing the audience

Verve commissioned some exit polls on the film and this led to some interesting conclusions. In respect of the two possible audiences discussed above, it was clear that the 25–34 AB audience did not turn out, but that the youth audience certainly did. Various readings were made of this:

- The youth audience was attracted to the multiplex – in all parts of the country, not just London.
- The traditional art cinema audience were not attracted to the film (which got generally very good reviews) partly perhaps because of the negative views of Asher D (in relation to his conviction for possession of a firearm). Some of the broadsheet press also carried reviews by black journalists or community leaders which criticised the film for its 'typical' representations of black youth and gun crime.
- The audiences that did see the film were skewed slightly towards males, but arguably less so than might be expected for this type of film – validating, perhaps, co-writer Catherine Johnson's attempts to push the film more towards family melodrama and away from 'youth gangs'.

Perhaps inspired by Verve's success with *Bullet Boy*, Hollywood major distributor UIP decided in November 2005 to release *Hustle and Flow*, an African-American film starring Terrence Howard, one of the leads in *Crash* (USA/UK/Germany, 2004). UIP spent more than the average for an African-American film on advertising and promotions and released 41 prints (technically a wide release). However, the film did not take off and managed an average of only £1,457 per screen, leaving it well short of *Bullet Boy's* opening. (Unless a film makes more than £2,000 per screen on a wide opening, it is unlikely to succeed.)

Distributors and exhibitors

Distributors and exhibitors are both looking for audiences, but in the UK they are separate organisations with different priorities (in the UK in 2006, only Showcase of the major multiplex chains had a direct link to a Hollywood studio). A distributor might have three or four films on release at any one time, but a cinema manager is trying to fill six or more auditoria in a multiplex. Inevitably, there are going to be conflicts between distributors and exhibitors, and these may well have an impact on audiences.

The number of films being released to UK cinemas has risen for each of the last few years. In 2005, it rose above 500, averaging ten new (or re-released) films each week. Fewer than 200 of these films receive anything approaching a wide release. Films that do go wide are usually supported by a major studio that has plenty of muscles to flex in any negotiations with exhibitors. Conversely, smaller distributors will struggle to get their films into cinema chains, as they have little bargaining power.

The UK is increasingly being seen as 'under-screened' – there are not enough screens available to take ten new films each week. Note that this is an issue of films per screen, not a reflection of demand for more seats by audiences.

The UK has around 5.6 screens per 1,000 of the population. In North America, the ratio is over 12:1,000. Screens are not evenly distributed throughout the UK and it is noticeable that where the number of screens per head is highest (London and Northern Ireland), attendance is greater, and where it is lowest (north-east), it is far less (all figures from UK Film Council 2006).

It could be argued that the real problem is lack of flexibility. Ideally, cinema managers should be able to easily move films between screens in a multiplex, increasing showings for some films and dropping others as consumer demand changes. However, it is not as simple as that. The major distributors will demand that their prestige films are in the biggest auditoria. Their focus is on making their film available to the public. In practice, by the Monday after a film has opened, it will be clear to everybody – distributor and exhibitor alike – whether a film is either a success or a flop and negotiations will begin either to drop the film or extend for a second week. If the film is clearly a flop, it is likely to be put to death quietly without too much objection. Problems are more likely when a smaller film from an independent distributor is moderately successful, but is occupying a screen that is due to receive a heavily promoted blockbuster. Who do you think is likely to win out? On the other hand, smaller cinemas are often faced with problems trying to book films. They may know their audience well and wish to book a film for only two or three days rather than seven, but when the film is still 'new', the distributor may insist on a minimum of one week (and sometimes two).

The economics of distribution

The economics of the business are well laid out in the FDA guide. The distributor receives a rental fee for each film. In the UK, often quoted as a tough market for distribution, the distributor receives 30–40% of the box-office income (usually a flat 35% for specialised films). Each film involves a separate deal and rates can vary over the run of the film. The distributor has to pay for P & A, so overall profit may be small. Depending on the deal between the film's producers and the distributor, part of this profit may be shared with the producers, with the distributor effectively taking a fee for distribution plus a percentage. Most films do not make a profit on a theatrical release. This may seem surprising when box-office sums of £10 million or more are quoted for successful films. However, these films are returning only £3–4 million to the distributor, who may have spent this amount on P & A for a major film release. Cinemas keep not only a majority of the ticket money, but also all the profit from concessions. This can be considerable as these are products with very high margins. Cinemagoers spending on popcorn, soft drinks etc. delivers a profit of more than £1 per audience member – a total of £204 million in 2004. (*RSU Statistical Yearbook 2004-5*) Some commentators have argued that the function of commercial cinemas is really to sell popcorn and that what is screened is secondary. (Cafés and bars are also important sources of income for independent cinemas.)

See Gomery (1992) on the history of concessions in American cinemas.

We could extend this argument to suggest that what exhibitors are offering is an entertainment package, with the audience attracted by the ambience of the cinema as a social space, the promise of fast food etc. The film may be of secondary importance (see also discussion of cinemas in Chapter 8).

Despite the low profits on theatrical distribution, many films now return substantial earnings from DVD retail and rental and television rights. These are lower-cost operations involving greater audience numbers. Success on DVD release depends largely on the high profile gained via a cinema release (however, some films do much better on DVD, while others do worse than might be expected). This success in ancillary markets is fine if the same company has a stake in both theatrical and DVD rights (a major studio will often control both through separate subsidiary companies). Small companies that operate only in theatrical distribution are really up against it.

Concepts of mainstream and independent/alternative

It is difficult to discuss distribution and exhibition practices without reference to terms like 'mainstream', 'independent' etc. Throughout this book, mainstream refers to Hollywood films distributed by the major studios (Sony, Warner Bros., 20th Century-Fox, Universal, Disney and Paramount). Whenever cinema is discussed in public discourse, the likelihood is that reference will be made to the films released by these studios. Their films are what the majority of the cinema audience see, either in a multiplex or on DVD/pay-per-view etc.

The multiplex cinema is an important component in the 're-birth' of Hollywood entertainment worldwide since the 1980s. Having begun in North America, the 'multiplex revolution' has spread, first to Western Europe and now to Eastern Europe and South and East Asia. Multiplexes are designed to play Hollywood movies (e.g. with the drinks-holder built into the seat) – they offer modern facilities designed to enhance big-budget films on big screens with high fidelity sound. In some cases, the large foyer space is designed to display film posters alongside the concessions stands. A multiplex visit is a 'night out' and a chance to go out in a crowd (and, in some cases, choose what to watch when you arrive). It might be argued that some of the bigger multiplexes attempt to reproduce the sense of occasion that accompanied a trip to one of the '**super cinemas**' built in the 1930s (see Chapter 8). However, most of those buildings are still standing 70 years on – the first generation of multiplexes are already being torn down and replaced, with some lasting only ten years. There is little 'romance' in such 'sheds' (as cinema historians tend to describe them) but they are efficient in generating profit and in providing for the needs of the audience.

In the UK in 2006, there were approximately 3,400 cinema screens, of which well over 80% were mainstream multiplex screens. Around 900 cinemas are classed as 'traditional and mixed use'. These cinemas could be:

- Traditional cinemas built prior to 1980 with fewer than five screens, still used for mainstream films.
- Traditional or modern cinemas built for 'specialised' or art cinema screenings.
- Mixed-use buildings such as arts centres, showing a variety of films on a 'part-time' basis.

Although these cinemas attract a much smaller audience, they are important in terms of film culture and audience study, as their audiences will often have a significantly different relationship with them compared to the multiplex and its audience.

'Independent', 'specialised' and 'art'

These three terms have quite specific meanings within film and media studies, so it is important to try to use them precisely.

Independent is a loaded word, carrying connotations of romantic positioning 'against' a central power, of being rebellious, 'individual' etc. But take care, all film and media production is dependent on an industrial and institutional structure of some kind. Romance is hard to come by given the business practices of media industries (see Branston and Stafford, 2006, 239-41).

'Independent' really means 'not the majors'. In the film industry, any organisation that is not directly controlled by one of the six Hollywood majors is an independent. Of course, in the exhibition sector, the studios do not usually control cinemas directly. Instead, they work with the biggest multiplex chains in each country on the basis that there is a symbiotic relationship between the two – the majors need an outlet, the multiplexes need Hollywood product. Therefore, the multiplex chains are considered to be 'not independent'. A complicating factor in describing the films themselves is that over the last ten years, the major studios have each bought or set up their own 'independent brands'. This leads to some odd outcomes. The trade papers routinely list the box-office figures for 'Independent Films' separately, but the majority of the films in this chart are distributed by the independent 'brands' of the majors. In the UK, brands such as Miramax (Disney) and Focus Features (Universal) are sometimes distributed by their (major) parent companies, but films from New Line (owned by Time Warner) are usually released in the UK through the major UK independent, Entertainment Film Distributors. Thus, technically, the *Lord of the Rings* films were independent films released by an independent distributor – even though they made millions in multiplexes across the country. On the other hand, a film like *Crash* was produced independently in Los Angeles and distributed by independents in both North America and the UK – untouched by the major studios.

Perhaps because of the difficulties with 'independent' (and with 'arthouse', see below), the UK Film Council decided in 2002 to use the term **specialised** to refer to any film that was not considered 'mainstream' in terms of distribution. Rather than focus on ownership, the UK Film Council went for how the film might be perceived by distributors and audiences. Although a distinction between 'mainstream' and 'specialised' may seem straightforward, it does produce some strange results. All foreign-language films are automatically 'specialised'. Despite the success of a handful of crossover films such as *Amélie* (see Chapter 1), most foreign-language films will attract a limited audience, and distribution will require subtitling. But Hindi/Bollywood films are not considered 'specialised' – presumably because their relationship with a popular NRI audience is similar to that between Hollywood films and the mainstream UK audience. Under the heading 'Asian films', they are put into a separate category by the UK Film Council. (Whereas Chinese films will be classed as specialised). The real anomaly comes with English-language films. British, Australian and New Zealand films, for example, are often 'mainstream' if they are distributed by a Hollywood studio and 'specialised' if not. Most of the time, because Hollywood studios pick their films for distribution carefully, the distinction works smoothly, but occasionally, when an independent distributor spots a 'winner' (e.g. Helkon with *Bend it Like Beckham*), it can look confusing.

It is not just a matter of semantics. The UK Film Council has built several policies around the concept of specialised cinema. The diversity of films and the diversity of audiences attracted to watch them are key concerns for cultural policy – a remit given to the Council by the UK government. In order to develop the specialised cinema sector and increase the scope of cultural diversity, the UK Film Council has developed various strategies:

- After surveying the number of 'specialised cinema screens' in the UK (around 200 in 2005), the UK Film Council envisaged the new Digital Screen Network as a means of increasing the number of specialised cinema screenings. On this basis, mainstream cinemas were offered digital projection facilities on favourable terms.
- Each year, certain 'specialised films' will receive support from public funds in terms of investment in production and grants/loans towards distribution costs.

Art cinema and 'arthouse' are perhaps terms that should be dead and gone, but audiences, critics and journalists still use them. Within the UK Film Council and mainstream cinema, and within much of the specialised sector, people will avoid using the terms if possible. They are seen to refer to the distant past and are thought to be off putting for younger audiences. There are many definitions and histories of **art films** and 'art cinema', but in simple terms, we could see the beginnings of art cinema in two ways:

- In the 1910s, some of the more prestigious films were adaptations of classic novels, plays, operas etc., that dealt in some way with 'high art' content.
- In the 1920s, certain filmmakers became recognised as taking a more 'personal' approach to their work, akin to that of a fine artist. The films of these directors were often seen in specialist film clubs or film societies and discussed in intellectual journals.

In the 1950s, in what was the period of mass audiences in Europe, more cinemas were built to screen the work of 'art film' directors and the concept of 'art cinema' became quite clearly defined to include a range of European films (e.g. from Ingmar Bergman in Sweden to Federico Fellini in Italy) and also from selected filmmakers in Japan. What all these films had in common was a focus on characterisation and ideas – very often a 'humanist' or 'modernist' approach – and a refusal of what was seen as the formulaic cinema of Hollywood. At this time, the so-called 'quality cinema' of literary adaptations could still be screened within the mainstream of Hollywood and British cinema.

By the 1980s, the European idea of art cinema was barely sustainable and increasingly the cinemas were turning to 'American Independents', which were thought to be attractive to younger audiences. At the same time, the literary adaptations had retreated from the mainstream to what had now become the 'specialised sector'.

(A good example of such films is the series produced by Ishmael Merchant and James Ivory, such as *A Room with a View*, UK, 1985, and *Howards End*, UK/Japan, 1992) Art cinema, the art film, still survives in the work of certain *auteur* directors and, certainly for older audiences, the term 'art house' (to describe either the cinema or the film) still has meaning. In Chapter 1, we looked at the reception of *Hidden* and the work of directors such as Zhang Yimou. A significant part of the audience for these films still holds to

> Isaac Julien is a British filmmaker (trained in film and fine art) who produced several important British films during the 1980s and 1990s, but he became much more well known when he was nominated for the Turner prize in 2001.

the idea of 'film as art' and distributors have to decide how to sell films to this audience.

Finally, there is also a category of what has sometimes been known as 'artists' film' – the work of fine arts practitioners in film. Once seen as **avant-garde** work and screened in a limited number of specialist venues, this has now acquired a higher public profile through the work of conceptual artists working on video, the annual Turner prize and the interest in digital films, installation work etc.

As in all these categories, there are overlaps, so here the distinction between 'film' and 'artwork' has become blurred. In audience terms, we might expect a different kind of response to a film screened in a cinema and one seen in an exhibition space in an art gallery.

Critical commentary

Cinema is an industry and it is a social institution. As an industry it produces a product by means of an industrial system. As a social institution, it organises the ways in which people think about filmmaking and about films and how they are seen in cinemas. Within the institution, everyone has an idea about how to behave as a filmmaker, a distributor, an exhibitor or an audience member. There is an industrial production base that once produced films on a production line model (the studio system) and that now crafts films as individual products. The distribution and exhibition companies then present the film to an audience, offering an entertainment experience. The audience is a crucial element in this process. Without an audience, a film is merely some reels of celluloid in tin cans (or now perhaps a computer file). With an audience, it lives and has meaning. Of course, this could be said of many if not all consumer products to some extent, but cinema/film is still worth considering as a special kind of product, in which the role of the audience/customer is crucial.

But there is also a second group of people who, if not absolutely essential, are still important in the reception of the film by audiences. These are the community of 'commentators' on films. We can divide them into sub-groups:

- regular film reviewers across a range of media writing directly for cinema audiences;
- trade journalists writing about films and the film industry for professionals;
- critics/academics – more considered writing undertaken over a longer period for film scholars;

• non-specialist journalists/writers discussing specific aspects of a film's content.

We could perhaps add a fifth sub-group, increasingly important in the current media environment:

• audience members who comment on films in internet user groups, bulletin boards and increasingly in blogs and other forms of personal web-space, where a virtual community of unofficial writing has now become established.

Does anyone take much notice of film reviews in popular media? Certainly, readers use reviews as a source of information about new films. There is evidence to suggest that some media, such as regional newspapers, are very conscious of readers looking for information about films playing locally. This may come from listings, advertisements or promotions as well as actual reviews. But are readers concerned about the opinions of reviewers? The job of a reviewer is to provide both information and entertainment. National press reviewers will be aware that their readers have chosen a specific paper because of its apparent market position in terms of ideology, lifestyle etc. They will be expected to address this audience, and we might assume that their reviews will reveal questions of taste that match those of their readers in the main. It is unlikely that they would sway audiences if they adopted a very different stance over a significant number of films. How long would the *Daily Mail*'s film critic, Christopher Tookey, survive as the main reviewer in the *Guardian* or *Independent*? In Chapter 1, it was suggested that in the case of certain kinds of films and reviews in the quality press, there is the possibility that audiences will follow recommendations, but in terms of mainstream films, dependent on heavy advertising and promotion, reviewers are less likely to be influential.

The worldwide release of *The Da Vinci Code*, in May 2006 was widely reported as proving that film reviewers had little influence. Although panned by reviewers everywhere, audiences flocked to see the adaptation of a best-selling book. This does not mean the reviews had no effect – some audience members were certainly conscious of seeing for themselves whether the reviewers were right. If they agreed that, yes, it was a poor film, they still enjoyed the event and working through their own response and that of the reviewers. Would these individuals have gone to the film without all the fuss over the reviews?

More likely is the impact of specialist film publications. Film magazines cater for a niche audience, one that comprises both frequent cinemagoers and purchasers of DVDs, soundtracks, books and other film-related material. Magazines may be bought specifically for advice on the purchase of DVDs, especially of specialised films that do not appear at local cinemas. Coverage of films in longer, more substantial articles is also likely to increase interest. Since the late 1980s and the re-emergence of Hollywood as a commercial force, many new film magazines have been launched (followed by many subsequent closures after only a few issues). Much as the quality press addresses a specific readership, the specialist magazines also address what is a stratified market. At the top end of the market in the UK is the so-called 'magazine of record', *Sight and Sound*, published by the British Film Institute. The Institute's monthly journal has survived for some 70 years, shifting into the public marketplace more directly when it absorbed the *Monthly Film Bulletin* (which aims to review every film released in the UK, but in practice excludes most Hindi films). Alongside *Sight and Sound* are more specialised magazines such as *Vertigo* and also an array of imported magazines from North America, such as *Cineaste*, *Film Comment*, *Film Quarterly*, and *Cineaction*. All of these magazines are distinguished by their long, scholarly articles that serve to keep circulation confined to cinephiles and film scholars. Nevertheless, these magazines do reflect changes in fashion and popularity and they may collectively increase interest in certain kinds of films. More specialised still are the academic screen studies journals such as *Screen*, *Intellect*, and *Framework* in the UK. These rarely deal with films on release and have readerships confined largely to universities (and generally to practising academics and postgraduate students).

In the middle market are a number of film magazines that either specialise solely in film or that include film as a prominent element in a lifestyle approach. In the UK, the most established of these magazines is *Empire*, first published in 1989. *Empire* reviews most films, mainstream and specialist, but feature articles are devoted to mainstream films – or, rather, those that are likely to be most popular with its target readership:

> Empire readers are 16–35 year olds passionate about movies, with a male/female split of 70–30. They are early adopters and opinion formers that want to be the first in their peer group to be 'in-the-know' about all things cinema related. 75% of them go to the cinema at least twice a month in addition to consuming films and video, television and DVD. (<www.emapadvertising.com/magazines>, 11 May 2006)

The advertising industry is very interested in this demographic. As well as frequent cinemagoers, the *Empire* readership is also likely to be interested in alcohol, mobile phone technology etc., which provide the necessary advertising revenue alongside film-related promotions. *Empire* is joined in this market segment by *Total Film* and *Hotdog*. These three titles are all film-based, but *Uncut* features films and music together. The demographic for *Uncut* is slightly different, still male but older ('ABC1 males aged 25–45', according to <www.ipcadvertising.com/magazines/uncut/> 11 May 2006). This produces a magazine that often focuses on articles about cult heroes such as Sam Peckinpah and Martin Scorsese. *Empire* and *Uncut* have had varied success in exporting their approach to North America where a similar market segment is covered by *Premiere* and *Rolling Stone*.

The bottom end of the market comprises titles that focus solely on mainstream

A report in the *Guardian*, 15 May 2006, revealed that the proportion of women readers of music magazines has increased since digital downloading of music started. Perhaps these new readers will also influence the combined music/films titles?

films at a relatively superficial level. At one time, under the studio system, this market was huge, but it has now been almost completely overtaken by celebrity magazines on the one hand and the growth of promotional material (free magazines, usually distributed via cinemas) on the other, plus internet activity.

There are also specialist magazines that focus on cult cinema or on specific genres and which don't conform neatly to the other market categories. They may mix popular approaches with sometimes quite specialised and scholarly material (see Chapters 6 and 8 on fans and fan culture). These magazines are sometimes international in coverage and include horror, science fiction and martial arts among other genres. Titles such as *Fangoria*, *HorrorHound* and *SFX* are published in the USA and the UK. These magazines target fans and offer a much more specialised service, not only in terms of the films covered, but also of issues such as censorship, buying foreign DVDs etc. There is a magazine title for virtually every type of fan, so it is worth asking fans what they buy. Most magazines have either started a website to complement the print version or shifted to a virtual magazine format. In many ways, the various forms of internet commentary have now overtaken print journalism, certainly for younger audiences.

Internet commentary

The growth of internet usage has run parallel to the development of DVD and the current mode of Hollywood filmmaking. It is difficult to distinguish them as separate developments. We look for cinema listings online, we watch trailers online, we may even book tickets online. In the UK, the founder of easyJet, Stelios Haji-Ioannou, attempted to change cinema exhibition practice with discounts for tickets pre-booked online. He received little cooperation from UK distributors, who felt his business model threatened their business. In Belgium, the established cinema chain Kinepolis is embracing both digital cinema and discounts for tickets bought online (see <www.kinepolis.be>). When we get home, we can check what other people thought of the movie on the IMDb and post our response to various bulletin boards. We can buy or rent our DVDs online and soon we will be able to download legal copies of films. In these circumstances, it is inevitable that for audiences who use the internet to this extent, print media become much less appealing. The internet presence of print media may also feel strangely old-fashioned next to the DIY, interactive feel of YouTube and similar websites.

The world of film online is explored in various places throughout this book, but most of it is included in Chapter 8 on film culture. Here we will simply note that

RESEARCH SUGGESTION

Select two British films that have had some success at the UK box office. One should be a film that appeals mainly to younger audiences (e.g. *Alien Autopsy*, 2006) and one to older audiences (e.g. *The Queen*, 2006). Using the archive of box-office charts on <www.ukfilmcouncil.org.uk/cinemagoing/boxoffice> trace the distribution patterns of the two films. Note how many prints were in circulation for the opening weeks and how long the films lasted in cinemas. Analyse how the box office fell each week (sometimes it might go up). Refer back to the discussion of how younger and older audiences are perceived in Chapter 2. What conclusions do you draw?

having stumbled over the introduction of video, Hollywood has attempted to keep pace with internet developments. Following the enormous success of the independent promotion of *The Blair Witch Project* in 1999, which was widely interpreted as proof of the power of fan postings on the internet, in 2006 *Snakes on a Plane* was released by New Line (a Time Warner company) with marketing based primarily on an internet campaign. The hype worked extremely well, but didn't translate into quite the successful box office anticipated. Perhaps this showed that studios can't duplicate genuine fan interest – or perhaps it does matter that the film itself has to deserve the hype?

References

Finney, Angus (1996), *The State of European Cinema: A New Dose of Reality* (London: Cassell).

Hall, Sheldon (2002), 'Tall Revenue Features: The Genealogy of the Modern Blockbuster', in Steve Neale (ed,), *Genre and Contemporary Hollywood* (London: BFI).

Baker, Robin J., Ron Inglis, Julia Voss (2002), *At a Cinema Near You: Strategies for Sustainable Local Cinema Development* (BFI). Available for free download from: <www.bfi.org.uk/filmtvinfo/publications/practical/cinemanearyou.html>

4. How Do Audiences Read Films?

This chapter gives a brief outline of the development of theoretical approaches to analysing films and focuses on the changes that occurred after the 1980s, with consideration of actual audiences in cinemas as distinct to imagined or implied readers. It includes a detailed case study of readings of Brokeback Mountain *and analyses some of the ways in which the film might have been understood differently by various audiences.*

What is central to the concerns of film studies? Is it the 'text', the film itself, or is it the process of creating meaning when the film is screened to an audience? Or are these simply two different ways of approaching the same question? These are fundamental questions about the whole nature of film studies and we will not necessarily be able to answer them definitively. However, to understand the importance of the reading debate, we do need to explore how film studies itself has changed over the last 30 or 40 years and then recognise that quite different approaches to films and audiences still co-exist in the public discourse of film studies: e.g. in how the subject is handled on academic courses, in textbooks and journals, and at conferences and public events. As space is limited here, we can only introduce and outline the different positions and suggest some ways of following up the arguments.

To return to our opening question, a film itself has no real meaning (other than as a rather expensively produced object) until someone watches it. The problem arises when we try to consider what watching a film actually entails and how we can study the process. In practical terms, apart from the clearly impossible task of asking everyone who has watched a film to describe how it was for them, how do we develop methodologies for researching how a specific film or group of films is understood by audiences?

To put the argument at its simplest, there is a choice between two broadly opposed positions. In the first, we assume that a film has its own internal logic and that it will work in such a way that the majority of the audience will be amenable to making sense of the film in terms of the way in which it has been constructed. In other words, meaning is inscribed in the film and the audience somehow digs it out. Any reading other than that inscribed will be in some way aberrant or partial. This places the focus of film studies firmly onto the film itself and its formal properties, and on the ways in which it engages a spectator in terms of both what is shown and the ideas, emotions and values it explores. This focus is now often discussed in terms of **spectatorship** – the relationship between the film text and the individual viewer. This spectator is not a real person, but one constructed as ideal for the analysis.

The second option is to assume that audiences are composed of very different individuals and groups of people who, because of who they are and their personal circumstances, will generally approach films in different ways. The possibility of different readings in this case becomes a probability. A second factor here is the material conditions under which the watching takes place. In other words, how do real audiences watch films in real cinemas? This second approach moves the focus away from the film itself to the position of the film, and the audience, within film culture. This approach is discussed in film studies in relation to **reception theory**.

This broad opposition between spectatorship and reception is evident in much of the film studies practice of the last 30 years, but, of course, the debate is much more complex than the simple opposition suggests and it has a longer history. When scholars first began to take films seriously, they looked at films as art, relating them to the practices of painting, theatre, music and later photography. (There was also an early interest in the possible impact of films on vulnerable audiences. This

Avant-garde work is literally 'ahead of' anything else that is happening in a particular art form. **Expressionism** and **Surrealism** were related to similar trends in other art forms.

work was not really concerned with the qualities of individual films themselves and is not discussed here – but it is an important aspect of the debate about audience theories in Chapter 6.) The film scholars' work was most evident in relation to various European art film movements such as German Expressionism in the early 1920s and the **avant-garde** Surrealist films in France in the later 1920s.

In Britain, some of the early work in film studies came from scholars who had studied English literature and who brought to film some of the ideas they had developed about studying the canon of great works of literature. Gradually, the early theorists' attention shifted towards more popular films and, in France and the UK in particular, towards Hollywood films. This raised important questions about the industrial/commercial aspects of filmmaking (i.e. rather than films being the product of the artistic expression of a single filmmaker), but in the early 1960s, this still meant attention focused on a film author (an *auteur*), albeit one who worked within a commercial studio system and related to a concept of a genre production.

La novelle vague

Film scholarship across the world was heavily influenced by the writings (and the films) of the French critics of the 1950s, which led to the recognition of *La nouvelle vague* later in the decade. Drawing on European traditions of art cinema, critics such as François Truffaut argued for the 'personal vision' of the film director as similar to that of the novelist. This claim for authorship helped to produce a **New Wave** of French filmmakers that included Truffaut himself and rapidly spread outside France, so that New Waves appeared in the UK, Czechoslovakia, West Germany etc. Classification as New Wave helped filmmakers to be recognised by the industry and by audiences.

Film theory, like film production and its New Waves, often moves forward by reacting against what has gone before, and this is what lay behind the various sets of ideas that have sometimes been grouped together as **1970s theory** or, in the English-speaking world, *Screen* **theory** (after the UK magazine *Screen* which translated new work, mostly French, and introduced it to new readers). The objective of much of this new work, derived from **semiotics** and **structuralism**, was to be both more universal in developing ways of analysing any form of media text and to be more scientific in attempting to understand how meaning was produced.

Semiotics, structuralism and the cinema

There is not space here to go into 1970s theory in great detail. Instead, we will just pick out a few examples that will serve to indicate how these various approaches still tended to focus on texts rather than on audiences. For instance, semiotics, the study of sign systems, drew on much earlier work in linguistics to suggest that media texts could be studied in order to reveal their systematic use of particular signs. This work covered print images on posters and in magazines as well as moving images. It identified signs, not only in the content of an image (which included the possibility of a sound image), but also in the way in which that image was presented – the use of colour, lighting, camera angles, film stock etc. These ideas could be discussed in more general terms as the recognition of a specific film language, actually not that dissimilar to much earlier ideas of the grammar of film. Christian Metz's work suggested that if it was possible to define film language in terms of shots and sequences (i.e. the equivalent of words and sentences), it would be possible to discern the different ways in which films could be constructed. Metz went as far as analysing a specific film, *Adieu Philippine* (France, 1962), and breaking it down into a system of organised shots and sequences. By showing how this could be done, film semioticians hoped to change ideas about analysing films.

Previously, critics and scholars had assumed that so-called 'great films' contained important truths and unique perspectives on the world. The job of analysis was then to reveal these truths to a reader/viewer. Semiotics helped to show that film language, like every other form of language, is socially constructed – it creates meanings through its use. Texts do not have intrinsic meanings, only those that readers/viewers discern through their use of a language shared with the texts' producers. Whatever meanings were intended by a producer are **mediated** by the use of language in its social context.

In the 1960s and 1970s, a time of great political activity and questioning of traditional forms, the introduction of semiotics to film studies was very exciting. It helped to explain how meaning could be created almost transparently in a range of media using photorealistic technologies. A documentary film about soldiers on a battlefield was no longer a slice of reality or, as one famous phrase associated with the television programme *Panorama* had it, 'a window on the world'. Instead, it became a constructed image that could be read carefully, recognising the use of signs, some recurring conventionally in many other films, others being foregrounded through use of aspects of film language etc.

Semiotics was also part of a much wider movement in philosophy termed **structuralism**, which promised to enable analysis to discover the structural basis of communication, to reveal the range of systems operating in a society. Some of the well-known theorists associated with structuralist ideas include Claude Lévi-Strauss, Vladimir Propp and Tzvetan Todorov.

> Structuralism refers to a philosophical movement that promises a **grand theory** about how everything works. **Structural film** is something rather different and refers to a form of avant-garde film in which the filmmaker explores the physical qualities of film as a medium.

Lévi-Strauss was a social anthropologist whose work suggested the idea of **binary oppositions** as a structuring agent in narratives. In 1969, Jim Kitses analysed a number of film Westerns and came up with a set of oppositions, such as East–West, Garden–Desert, Civilised–Savage etc. that he saw as important in structuring the dramatic conflict in most Westerns. Propp worked on Russian folk tales and formulated a set of **character functions** and associated 'actions' that could be combined in different ways and used to describe virtually any folk tale. Todorov was credited with introducing ideas about narrative structure that explained how most entertainment narratives attempted to engage a reader as the story unravels. In the simplest terms, this suggests a way of thinking about narratives as beginning with a 'disruption' of some form of stability or 'equilibrium', followed by a gradual build-up of conflict that eventually explodes in a climax and is then 'resolved' in some way to produce a new (and probably different) equilibrium. All three of these theorists contributed ideas to the development of structuralism in film studies, and aspects

> Lévi-Strauss and Propp were not themselves interested directly in film and they produced their work in the 1960s and 1920s, respectively. Their basic ideas can be useful in thinking about a film's narrative, but they do not provide a formula for writing scripts.

of their work are still discernible in some of the academic studies that film students undertake today.

For an introduction to semiotics and structuralism in film and media studies, see Branston and Stafford (2006) or any other introductory textbook. For a more detailed introduction, see Bignell (2002) or Chandler (2004).

Psychoanalysis and film

Another related approach, which was imported into film studies in the 1970s, was psychoanalysis. This proved to be much more controversial. Psychoanalysis as a clinical practice had been introduced, in the USA in particular, from the 1930s onwards (having been developed by Sigmund Freud in the 1890s), and it had found its way into Hollywood dramas by the 1940s (e.g. in the Hitchcock thriller *Spellbound*, 1945, featuring Ingrid Bergman as Gregory Peck's analyst). In many ways, the basis of psychoanalysis – the gradual drawing out of a patient's repressed memories, often via an analysis of dreams, in order to confront and overcome fears (a process known as abreaction) – does seem to relate to the experience of watching a film. The spectator sits in a darkened auditorium, focusing intently on sounds and images that, not unlike dreams, invite identification and participation in a story. Filmmakers seem to collude with this idea, offering the spectator the pleasure of spying on characters – acting like a voyeur – and vicariously enjoying scenes of physical action, including sexual activity.

Martin Scorsese discussing *Taxi Driver* (US 1976), a film that elicited very strong reactions from audiences: "Much of *Taxi Driver* arose from my feeling that movies are really a kind of dream-state, or like taking dope. And the shock of walking out of the theatre into broad daylight can be terrifying." (Thompson and Christie, 1989: 54).

As Freud's work focused on the possible impact of infantile sexual activity and how this might affect adult life, readings of films have often referred to the creative use of symbolic sexual imagery and the Freudian concept of **fetish** objects. In Freudian terms, a fetish is a displacement of sexual desire that is directed towards a specific object or part of the body rather than a whole person. Thus, a foot or shoe fetish (e.g. in many of Luis Buñuel's films, such as *El*, Mexico, 1957), or one associated with stockings or gloves, is particularly well suited to a cinema screen, which offers directors, cinematographers and costume designers the chance to use close-ups, camera movements and editing to isolate images. Indeed, the promotion of film stars in classical Hollywood often seemed to be carried out through a fetishisation of parts of the body – Veronica Lake's hair, Marilyn Monroe's breasts, Cyd Charisse's legs etc. Although men's bodies also received this treatment, feminists in the 1970s were justified in seeing cinema as perhaps too concerned with 'the male **gaze**' focused on celluloid representations of the (fetishised) female body. The terminology of psychoanalysis soon entered film studies, with the spectator becoming a subject to be worked on by the film.

Freud was not the only psychoanalyst used as a resource. Carl Jung was referenced in some work, but the most important figure in linking structuralist linguistics and Freud's ideas was Jacques Lacan (1901–81) and associated thinkers such as Michel Foucault, Jacques Derrida and Louis Althusser. Through the 1970s and 1980s, psychoanalytic work in film theory was extended in several directions. One crucial change saw the initial feminist interest in the male gaze extended to consideration of the female gaze and a more complex set of ideas about gender differences in terms of spectatorship. However, the combination of semiotics, structuralism and psychoanalysis led film studies towards a position in which a spectator was clearly 'positioned' to watch a film, cinema becoming an institutional 'apparatus', a machine for creating meanings (sometimes referred to as **apparatus theory**). The context for this was a political will among the theorists to present the dominant mainstream films as operating ideologically – in simplistic terms to view cinema as creating meanings that supported the prevailing ideology.

1970s theory was important in introducing many new ideas and in helping to establish film studies as a legitimate and intellectually rigorous discipline. But this in turn produced film theory that many found was jargon-laden and obscurantist. Equally importantly, it did not engage with what was happening in contemporary cinema. (Much of the 1970s theoretical work used films produced in 1940s Hollywood as texts. Relatively few films from the 1970s got much attention.)

Re-thinking film studies

The theoretical ideas of the 1970s were challenged in several different ways and we will try to focus on those that had most impact on audience studies. Three collections of essays are useful in representing the various debates that developed. *Post-Theory: Reconstructing Film Studies* edited by David Bordwell and Noël Carroll, appeared in 1996, followed by *Reinventing Film Studies*, edited by Christine Gledhill and Linda Williams, in 2000. Both these collections include a range of responses to the need to re-think the subject and, in particular, to re-think the relationship between the film text and its audiences. *The Film Cultures Reader* (2002), edited by Graeme Turner, goes further, in the sense that its title refers to the way in which the new discipline of cultural studies has influenced film studies. Changes in approach are also clearly signalled in some of the textbooks for undergraduate study, such as *The Oxford Guide to Film Studies* (1998) edited by John Hill and Pamela Church Gibson. These four titles have all been used as background for writing this chapter and you can follow up ideas by referring to them.

One attack on 1970s theory came from the **postmodernist** perspectives that began to emerge in film studies in the 1980s. The various **post-theory** approaches (as in the book title above and in forms such as postmodernism, poststructuralism etc.) argued for the end of **grand theory** – the attempt to develop theories that would explain everything. Again, we have no space to explore the ideas here, but one aspect of postmodernism was the emphasis on **intertextuality** – the way in which a specific text, a single film, might require knowledge of several other films in order to grasp all of its meanings. In such films, images are seen not to be constructed in order to suggest fixed meanings, but are instead intended to allow the spectator to play with a range of meanings. This approach gave more attention to the spectator in suggesting that he or she might be sophisticated and cineliterate – aware of many films and their meanings and therefore able to engage with a film in a playful way, rather than being positioned as a subject.

Another challenge came from what has been called the **cognitive approach**, usually seen as derived from the work of David Bordwell and expounded in his influential textbook *Film Art: An Introduction* (latest edition 2005) written with Kristin Thompson. This approach sees the work of textual analysis of films as a problem-solving process, following clues and making causal links in narratives. Cognitive psychology suggests that this is how we make sense of experiences and learn from them. Bordwell and Thompson also stress the importance of empirical work, studying film styles over many years of production and rooting their approach in film history. The re-introduction of film history into film studies by a wide range of academics has been important in several ways, not least because it has addressed the changing circumstances in which audiences viewed films and producers thought about audiences. The cognitive approach helped to establish the idea of an active questioning audience who would effectively interrogate the text to elicit meanings – as distinct from being positioned by it.

The third challenge came from the developing academic discipline of cultural studies. Some of the leading film studies scholars of the 1970s and 1980s were unhappy with aspects of *Screen* theory and they drew on early cultural studies (see Chapter 6 on the foundation of cultural studies in the UK) in an attempt to shift the focus of film studies. It is noticeable that many of these scholars were women who felt that textual analysis of films seemed to ignore both the female audience and the kinds of films that these audiences might enjoy. This led to sustained work on neglected genres such as melodrama, the women's picture, costume pictures etc. (see the work of Pam Cook (1997), Christine Gledhill (1987), Sue Harper (1994) etc.) and also on the female audience and the pleasures it might enjoy in what had previously been assumed to be masculine genres. Yvonne Tasker (1993) on the action film, and Carol Clover (1992) on horror, offer examples of representation studies indicative of this shift. Pleasure as a concept was quite a new idea. When attention turned to real audiences, it seemed important to ask what kinds of pleasures audiences got from films, rather than what films set out to do.

Once the focus turned to real audiences, it was possible to discern two lines of enquiry, both of which would add a great deal to the traditional approach of analysing the film text. The first can be seen as related to the key concept of representation as it functions in both media studies and film studies and the second to consideration of the wider social context of viewing. The development of ideas about representation was part of the structuralist project, in the sense of developing skills in reading that enabled scholars to show the way in which texts were constructed. As in the example above, a documentary film about soldiers does not offer a transparent slice of reality, but instead *represents* soldiers. It 're-presents' images of soldiers through use of camera techniques and editing. It selects some soldiers as 'representatives' of others etc. The pioneering work of scholars such as Richard Dyer enabled a much wider and more complex analysis of films to develop. Part of this development was the recognition of the **typing** of both characters and other aspects of the film narrative. All forms of narrative at some time use types rather than well-rounded and complex characters. Popular films are more clearly structured using types, partly because they need economical devices for introducing easily recognisable characters. In a comedy or horror film, we do not need to know everything about a character who is going to slip on a banana skin or be attacked by a monster. It may increase our pleasure to recognise a character as the kind of person we expect/hope to be treated in this way, but equally we should be concerned if it is always the same type who is the victim (or the perpetrator), especially when audiences carry over that recognition/identification into everyday relationships outside the cinema.

At a time when personal politics was developing, links between popular movements supporting feminism, gay liberation, black consciousness etc. and film studies became an important site of struggle over questions of **identity**. How did audiences think about themselves as female, gay, African-Caribbean etc. when they started to watch a film? How did their sense of identity become part of the process of constructing meaning from the images they encountered on the screen, especially if recognisable types such as the 'dumb blonde' always seemed to be treated in the same way? It seems so obvious a question that it is perhaps surprising that relatively few people had asked it before. Simply asking the question immediately challenged the notion that a reading of a film could be produced for an ideal spectator. Clearly, readings might be different if the identity of some audience members was in conflict with that of the film's producers and creative personnel. This in turn raised the question of the importance of the identities of filmmakers. Why were so many filmmakers white heterosexual males? Would female audiences respond differently to films made by women?

These kinds of questions raised furious debates. Focus inevitably moved towards consideration of what were seen as negative images of groups in society, who often seemed to be typed as the bad guy or the victim and generally to reproduce the same undesirable character traits in each film. Some audiences argued for more positive images, placing an extra burden on new directors and writers to produce these images. This has been problematic for British black and Asian writers and directors, who have sometimes complained about what they feel is a 'burden of representation' – being expected to make films that do not criticise or denigrate what is

Work on issues of personal identity was fundamentally different to earlier ideas about identification – the psychological process by which spectators identify with, or imagine themselves as, characters in the narrative playing onscreen. Identity issues imply that the spectator is also thinking about his or her social role outside the cinema in relation to the representation of characters in the film.

perceived to be their cultural identity or being expected to act as a spokesperson for a cause. In Chapter 5, there is a brief discussion of the star image of Denzel Washington, a leading Hollywood player who has maintained a largely successful balance between what he sees as a commitment to his cultural identity and his personal right to play less than perfect characters if he so wishes.

Various writers have explored the question of representations and personal identity. Richard Dyer has written extensively about gay film culture and his own identity as a gay man. bell hooks provides a good example of how film studies embraced what might be called an identity- or issue-based approach:

> . . . I began to realise that my students learned more about race, sex and class from movies than from all the theoretical literature I was urging them to read . . . [movies] provide a shared experience, a common starting point from which diverse audiences can dialogue about these charged issues. Trying to teach complicated feminist theory to students who were hostile to the reading often led me to begin such discussions by talking about a particular film. Suddenly students would be engaged in animated discussion deploying the very theoretical concepts that they had previously claimed they just did not understand. (hooks, 1996: 2)

This approach in itself was by no means new. Films had long been used to stimulate discussion about all kinds of social issues. The difference now was that film studies could draw on the experience of 1970s theory and consider the context of production. But this raised another question that is important in terms of audience study. Unless film students have already developed some formal understanding about cinematic realism, they run some risk of leaping to conclusions in much the same way as the newspaper commentators who ignore films as films and treat them as presenting slices of real life. The bell hooks book is exemplary in showing how to avoid this danger. Nevertheless, there is a problem with the kind of popular discussions of films that appear in other media. In Chapter 6, there is discussion of **media effects models** – those studies that attempt to show that audiences demonstrate short- and long-term effects from watching certain kinds of films. Film and media scholars have shown that these studies are invalid as theoretical models. On the other hand, debates about identity politics and audiences suggest that, over time, filmic representations certainly do have effects on audiences (see the conclusions in Chapter 6). Also discussed in Chapter 6, and deriving from cultural studies, is the suggestion that, within audiences, individuals or groups may produce different readings of films based on their experience, political consciousness, current social relationships etc. So, within the same general audience of women watching a film such as *Erin Brockovich* (2000) (also discussed briefly in Chapter 5), there might be **dominant, negotiated** and **oppositional readings**.

Erin Brockovich is based on a true story about a working-class single mother who builds up a legal case against a large corporation accused of dangerous pollution of the water supply, while working part time at an LA legal firm. At the end of the film, after a famous court victory, she receives a large cash bonus. The dominant reading of the film may be that this is a feelgood film celebrating what an assertive woman can do in difficult circumstances. A negotiated reading may generally accept this view but want to argue with other aspects of the film, while an oppositional reading may see the feelgood ending as disguising many of the other important issues that are not resolved or explored (including what happened to the corporation's culpable managers etc.). The important point here is that all three readings are based on the same film and that the readings are constructed by the audience in the context of viewing. In the case of *Erin Brockovich,* there is also the interesting question of what happened to the real Erin Brockovich, whose personal story has been presented and mediated in various press and broadcast features.

The viewing context

The work that produced ideas about dominant and oppositional readings came from broader developments in cultural studies, and television studies. Television studies began by recognising a crucial difference compared to film studies in that viewers watch 'television' rather than specific programmes. This has now changed with multi-channel, time-shifting and personal video recorders, but generally we watch several programmes together. Film studies has tended to concentrate on the film and to ignore what precedes it on screen – the ads and trailers. But audiences enter a screening having come from doing something else and possibly follow a screening with another social activity. Once we begin to consider the social context of viewing, a wide range of factors that might influence a reading come into play. This is the basis for Chapter 8 and a discussion of film culture.

In his interesting and useful book written with Thomas Austin, *From Antz to Titanic: Reinventing Film Analysis* (2000), Martin Barker sets out to question what academic film studies actually does with films. He is sceptical about many of the approaches associated with 1970s theory, and although broadly supportive of Bordwell's cognitive approach, quizzes this as well. His overall conclusion is that film watching is a social role that audiences perform. In the cinema, we respond to what films offer in all kinds of ways, emotionally, sensually, aesthetically, intellectually, physically (we can get up and leave, stand up and wave our fist at the screen). We enter into games, quizzing the narrative, guessing ahead what will happen next. We take sides with characters, we fall in love with some and despise others. We do try to understand what the whole thing means. Or at least we do part of the time. Sometimes we fail to make sense of it, sometimes we refuse to play. What goes on when we

One of the advantages of being a film teacher is to show films that you know personally very well to a large audience in a public cinema. Because it is not necessary to watch the screen, it is possible to observe the audience and to notice how some groups of spectators will laugh while others remain silent, how some become engrossed and others distracted. Audiences do not all perform in the same way.

watch a film is partly concerned with how the film was constructed and partly with how we perform our role (and our performance will be affected by what is going on around us in the cinema or in a domestic context if we watch it on DVD). Finally, Barker makes the point that it does not matter what kind of film it is – art films are just like popular films in this context. In the spirit of Martin Barker's approach, what follows is a case study of one film, exploring different ways of making sense of the film and performing the role of viewer.

A Case study: *Brokeback Mountain*

Brokeback Mountain (USA, 2005) is a relatively low-budget ($14 million) independent film part financed by the classics arm of Universal Studios, Focus Features, which spent some $35 million on P & A. With a relatively high-profile director in Ang Lee and two fast-rising young stars in Heath Ledger and Jake Gyllenhaal, the film would automatically have received attention by both the critics and general film fans without a major studio promotion. The film is not difficult or demanding in terms of audience engagement, though it is clearly not a mainstream blockbuster. It sits on the dividing line in institutional terms between mainstream and specialised. The fact that it also won the Golden Lion Prize at the Venice Film Festival for Ang Lee in the autumn of 2005 and was then released in December with a campaign that carefully sidestepped the description 'gay cowboy movie', but obviously courted controversy and made appeals directly to gay audiences, guaranteed that it would be talked about. At the end of its initial theatrical release, the film had achieved a gross box office of $180 million worldwide.

Synopsis

If you have not seen the film, the following brief synopsis should help to explain some of the issues surrounding an audience response. (Spoiler ahead! In the best tradition of internet sites, you are warned that this synopsis gives away plot information that you may not want to know now if you intend to see the film.) Ennis Del Mar (Heath Ledger) and Jack Twist (Jake Gyllenhaal) are 19-year-olds in rural Wyoming who are employed on a summer job, looking after sheep on the high pasture up on Brokeback Mountain. It is 1963. Living together in this isolated place, they become very close and begin a sexual relationship. When the summer ends, they separate. Ennis marries and becomes a father in the same part of Wyoming. Jack tries to become a rodeo cowboy, but eventually marries into a relatively wealthy family in Texas. A few years later Jack contacts Ennis. He visits Wyoming and the intense affair is rekindled. Ennis denies that he is 'queer' and it is

Jack who is prepared to take the initiative in their sexual encounters. However, Ennis is the more aggressive and dominant partner.

When Ennis separates from his wife and family, Jack suggests that they set up home together but Ennis refuses (as he had earlier, telling Jack about a man beaten to death because he was thought to be gay). Over a 20-year period, Ennis and Jack maintain a long-distance affair, meeting for 'fishing trips' once or twice a year. As his two daughters grow up in their new family, Ennis has a succession of low-paid jobs and Jack (still married) seeks solace with a new (secret) partner in Texas. One day, Ennis learns about Jack's death after a roadside incident (which may have been an attack). When he visits Jack's parents, he learns about Jack's friend in Texas and finds the shirt he wore and lost on Brokeback Mountain in Jack's boyhood room. When his elder daughter arrives at his trailer to announce her marriage, Ennis breaks a habit and tells her he will be at the wedding even though he will lose work. The film ends with Ennis looking at the two shirts Jack and he wore 20 years before and at a postcard image of Brokeback Mountain.

Preparing the audience

A film like *Brokeback Mountain* doesn't come out of nowhere. It is increasingly the case now that the work of particular stars (actors, writers, directors etc.) will be reported via the internet on blogs, bulletin boards and websites (see Chapter 8). Fans want to know what Heath Ledger and Jake Gyllenhaal are doing next. Within the industry, as soon as a project is greenlit at a specific studio, there will be an interest in the production's development, but the main interest will come when either the shoot is the subject of a press/internet article or when the finished film is shown at film festivals. Winning a festival prize at one of the major events (Berlin, Cannes, Venice) grants a high profile that spreads out to a fan audience beyond the industry. Even so, the general cinema audience will not be particularly aware of a new film until studio marketing – advertising and publicity – starts to appear. This may well have particular resonance if the story or the property is already well known. In the case of *Brokeback Mountain*, this meant that a small potential audience would have been aware of the original short story by Annie Proulx, first published in *The New Yorker* in 1997 and then in a collection of Wyoming stories in 1999. Annie Proulx is a well-known writer and award-winner for *The Shipping News* (1993) – and again for the *Brokeback Mountain* short story.

Audience expectations

Film studies has several critical tools that might help to explain how audiences approach a new film. Although now largely discredited, the concept of the film *auteur* or author remains in general public discourse as a way of identifying or categorising films and it is perhaps relevant here. Some audiences may have built up expectations based on the director Ang Lee's previous films. As these have encompassed a variety of genres and source materials, ranging from *Sense and*

Sensibility (1995) to *Hulk* (2003), it is not clear what these expectations might be – except that Lee seems as adept at dealing with cultures he does not know first hand as with those he does (See Chapter 1 for comments on Ang Lee and *Crouching Tiger, Hidden Dragon*). Perhaps more important is the authorial presence of Annie Proulx, as original creator, and the screenwriting team of Diana Ossana and Larry McMurtry. We can say with some confidence that Proulx and McMurtry both have a high profile as novelists dealing in Americana and in McMurtry's case, with Western films and television. *Lonesome Dove* (1985), an epic novel by McMurtry, became what is generally recognised as one of the most successful TV mini-series to have appeared on American television, and audiences aware of his involvement would have had strong expectations of a certain kind of authenticity in the depiction of the cowboy lifestyle.

The adaptation of Annie Proulx's story is faithful in the sense that all the main events in the story are included in the screenplay and the additional material that is added is consistent with what the short story reveals about the characters. Even so, we should remember that a film is a different kind of text than a short story and will engage audiences in quite different ways (see Geraghty, 2008, on literary adaptations).

Film studies is well aware of stars and the importance attached to them by audiences. Heath Ledger and Jake Gyllenhaal would both have attracted audiences, Gyllenhaal being particularly hot after the release of *Jarhead* in November 2005, built on his cult status that dates from *Donnie Darko*. These two stars appealed particularly to younger audiences, but they wouldn't necessarily be well known to older audiences attracted by Lee, Proulx or McMurtry.

Genre is another critical tool that is also seen as an audience factor. Some audiences certainly have genre preferences and strong genre expectations (see Chapter 5). Audience questions about *Brokeback Mountain* will depend very much on whether the film was approached as a Western or as a romance. It is worth spending a little time on this.

What is a Western?

The Western is, in terms of the numbers produced in the USA (without adding any of the many Westerns made abroad), historically the most important American film genre. It has a second claim to importance in that it embodies the 'central narrative' of American history and its founding myth about a frontier society. The main problem with such assertions is that Westerns are no longer popular – at least not at the cinema.

An argument could be made that the concerns of the Western – questions about freedom and the law, honour and masculinity etc. – have been transposed to other genres, including science fiction, urban thrillers, action films etc. But what remains clear is that younger audiences have less knowledge of Westerns and therefore perhaps fewer expectations – or that their expectations are more limited.

Within the USA, Westerns have also had a problem in terms of value and status. Part of this is a function of location. In the last great period for Westerns in the 1960s, studios still thought that they were likely to make most of their money in Texas and the south-west. In more sophisticated cities like New York and Los Angeles, traditional Westerns had far less appeal. In his book on Sam Peckinpah, David Weddle uses studio distribution plans for the release of *The Wild Bunch* in 1969 to illustrate how the late, revisionist Westerns of the period reversed this view. *The Wild Bunch*, famously violent and seen by many as a critique of American military action in Vietnam, was released in the same week as the traditional John Wayne blockbuster Western, *True Grit*. The *Wild Bunch* easily out grossed *True Grit* in Los Angeles among the film buffs, but died in Texas (see Weddle, 1996: 368).

Westerns remain popular on American television, if not in the numbers of series shown in the 1950s (as many as 48 Western shows were aired in 1959 according to David Weddle, 1996: 133), as much as the 'quality'. In 2006, both the series *Deadwood* and the mini-series *Into the West* were Emmy-nominated.

Traditional Westerns, or 'shoot-em ups' as many fans called them, were often considered to have an audience skewed towards boys and men. Many were cheaply made with relatively simple narratives and fairly conservative values. The films of a handful of directors such as John Ford, Howard Hawks, Anthony Mann etc., which became important study objects for film studies scholars in the 1960s, were not necessarily representative of all Westerns. If *Brokeback Mountain* can be accepted as a Western, then it would fall into the category of the Twilight Western. As the term implies, these films deal with the end of the West and the end of 'the idea of the West'. There are three ways in which we could consider this 'end'. First, it could be the historical setting of the 1890s–1910s, the literal end of the frontier when the Wild West was tamed. *The Wild Bunch* fits this description. It also fits the second possibility – films made after the 1960s which are part of the twilight of the Western film genre itself. *Brokeback Mountain* is perhaps classifiable according to the third possibility – films set in the classic locations of the Western states of the Union, in this case Wyoming, after 1945. Such films might also be called 'contemporary Westerns', but what is important about them is that they are essentially narratives about disappointment, peopled by characters who cannot somehow come to terms with the loss of the cowboy life. In many of the twilight Westerns, there are two male characters, both originally committed to a cowboy life and its associated freedoms and obligations, and both faced with modernity that threatens their future. One of the two will eventually compromise and accept modernity; the other will remain with the cowboy life and suffer the consequences.

In his detailed review of *Brokeback Mountain*, Roy Grundmann sets out the case very well:

Clearly in evidence is [Larry] McMurtry's stature as the dean of twilight Westerns – a realist, demystifying subgenre that produced such classics as *The Lusty Men*

(1952), *The Misfits* (1961) and *Hud* (1963) and depicts the West as an orphaned, beat down territory passed over by the great societies heralded by Eisenhower, Kennedy, and Johnson. McMurtry's novels – most notably *Horsemen Pass By* (the basis for *Hud*), *The Last Picture Show* (adapted by McMurtry himself for Peter Bogdanovich's 1971 film), and *Lonesome Dove* (made into a popular TV miniseries in 1989) – have stamped their indelible mark on the twilight Western. The author understands how to expound the genre's latent capitalist critique, which he unrelentingly harnesses also to Proulx's story: the erotic rhythm of Ennis and Jack's cowboy romance, we realise, echoes the kind of transience and mobility that lastingly constituted frontier life as the archetype of American social formations straight into industrial capitalism. (Roy Grundmann, Review of *Brokeback Mountain*, *Cineaste*, Vol. XXXI, No. 2, 2006)

Here we have a good example of a detailed textual analysis of the film, utilising a number of theoretical ideas. There is little doubt that an audience steeped in genre knowledge of the Western and of what Grundmann calls this specific sub-genre would make a specific reading of the film. Let us just add one more point to this observation. One of the most affecting moments comes at the end of the film and it concerns the shirts the two young men wore on their last day on *Brokeback Mountain* in that first summer. Ennis finds the two shirts, one symbolically wrapped around the other, in Jack's closet in his parents' house. The bloodstains from their fight are still clearly visible and Ennis hugs the shirts as if to inhale the essence of Jack. In the last scene, Ennis notices that his daughter has left behind her cardigan, and when he opens his closet to hang it up he discovers the shirts again. This time it is Ennis' shirt on the outside and Jack's inside. Tears in his eyes, Ennis mutters, 'Jack Twist, I swear', and the final shot shows the shirts and a postcard of Brokeback Mountain taped to the back of the closet door.

We could take this to be a classic use of a significant object in the film's *mise en scène*. Clear narrative links are made via the shirts and the daughter's cardigan to the loss of the time that Jack and Ennis could have had together and to Ennis' new resolution not to make the same mistake and lose the happiness he has for his daughter's marriage. The importance of the shirts in narrative terms is that the first mention of the lost shirt in the early part of the film is a marker or a pre-echo of what will come later. This is a classical device often used by directors such as Alfred Hitchcock. When we first hear Ennis say, 'I can't believe I left my shirt up on the mountain', we note it but do not appreciate its significance. At the end of the film, we realise that Jack had taken the shirt and that he was deeply affected by his first encounter with Ennis. This kind of audience work is something associated with David Bordwell's cognitive approach to textual analysis. We could go further and link this to a general analysis of the importance of costume in the film. The cowboy's shirts, jeans, boots and hats are what have survived from the traditional West into modern life. They function in the film as symbols of what is timeless about the cowboy image. In this sense, they contrast with the changes in facial hair – moustache for Jack, sideburns for Ennis – which offer one of the few ways of marking the social transformations in American culture that have occured over 20 years.

Interestingly, referents such as costume and hair-styles have traditionally been seen as more important to women rather than to men (although gay men may disagree), and in the gendered roles of Hollywood production, costume designers have mostly been women. Stella Bruzzi (1997) produced one of the first studies of the importance of costume, in *Undressing Cinema: Clothing and Identity in the Movies.*

But there is another reading of the shirts incident. For many Western scholars and fans, one of the most important Westerns is John Ford's *The Searchers* (1956). In this film, John Wayne plays Ethan Edwards, an anti-hero, a man who at the end of the film is so bitter that he can no longer return to the community and must roam the range alone (the French title of the film translates as '*Prisoner of the Desert*'). The reason for his bitterness is that the woman he loved, his brother's wife, Martha, has been killed (and probably raped) by a Commanche raiding party. At the beginning of the film, when the Wayne character first appears, the deep emotional attachment between Ethan and Martha cannot be spoken about in dialogue (and nothing suggests that their love has ever been physical). Instead, it is suggested by the looks exchanged between the two characters, their positions in the frame and the use of camera and editing. When Ethan is about to leave to search for the Commanche (making the house vulnerable), Ford uses a deep-focus composition so that we see Ethan in the foreground framed with Martha, who then goes into a back room, where she picks up and caresses Ethan's coat before bringing it to him. This famous scene is a wonderful way of articulating in *mise en scène* what cannot be said in dialogue. It is particularly appropriate in a Western in which cowboys are taciturn at the best of times and virtually mute in terms of expressing their love. Is there a direct reference to *The Searchers* in *Brokeback Mountain*? The shirt incident is there in the original Annie Proulx story, and there is no suggestion that a reference was intended, but I cannot believe that I am the only person to have made the connection. It does not matter if there was no intention to make the reference – audiences will make a connection and, in this case, it imparts even more of an emotional overload to the ending of the film

The purpose of this long discussion about the Western is to make the point that for some audiences, specific genre knowledge makes for a rich text of a certain kind and places the story in a particular context. But this is certainly not the only reading, and it may indeed be a minority reading. Far more likely is a take on the film that derives from expectations of a romance.

A cowboy romance?

The term 'romance' has a long history and in its original meaning referred to adventure tales about medieval knights, first in oral form and eventually written in

Melodrama is a complex category and the term has been used differently by critics, producers and audiences over a long period. At one time, most Westerns were classed as melodramas because of their spectacular action sequences, but contemporary use refers to films about emotional relationships, often expressed via exaggerated use of *mise en scène*, camerawork, music etc. See Gledhill (1987), Neale (2000) and Altman (1999).

vernacular language (i.e. not Latin). Eventually, this romance fiction turned towards courtly love and then to the kind of popular romantic fiction about ordinary couples that is an important modern category. The film genres associated with romance are action-adventure/epic stories that refer to the original meaning and both romantic dramas and romantic comedies that refer to the more modern meaning of romantic love. Romantic drama often becomes a form of melodrama, with a strong emphasis on passion and emotion (as in the classic women's pictures of the 1940s in Hollywood).

Romance is often seen to be a genre for female audiences, as the reference to the 1940s melodramas above suggests. Of course, in many cases commercial film industries in Hollywood and abroad mixed elements from different genres to produce a film that appeals to both men and women. For example, *Casablanca* (1942) is a famous romantic picture, but also has enough elements of wartime intrigue to satisfy a male audience. There is currently a website that announces 'Romantic Fiction for men' (<www.romancenews.net>) set up by someone who, as a fan of Japanese romance *manga* and *anime*, wanted to search for English-language romantic fiction for men. The possibility of romantic fiction for men also poses the question of whether romance as a classification can refer to gay as well as heterosexual relationships.

After the publication of Roy Grundmann's review of *Brokeback Mountain*, *Cineaste* received a letter that raised several issues, to which Grundmann then replied. Part of his reply addressed the question of 'queer romance':

> Because romance carries so many heteronormative constraints, will it be possible to create a new genre called 'queer romance'? Are *Brokeback Mountain's* limitations ultimately an indication that queerness and romance are incompatible? Or are queers interested in and capable of creating their own romance genre out of, alongside, and away from Hollywood – a genre that honours their complex ethics and transgressive sexualities in all their full glory? (Letters, *Cineaste*, Vol. XXI, No. 3, Summer 2006)

Grundmann is pointing here to the way in which the romance genre is very often concerned with marriage as a form of narrative resolution. In many cases, after a series of narrative events that brings together two characters and then splits them up, the film will end with marriage (or in a narrative like *Romeo and Juliet*, the death of both partners). So how can romance be handled in Queer cinema?

Queering the Western

As well as genre, film studies has also appropriated a critical approach associated with identity politics as outlined above. At first associated with gender studies and ethnicity studies, identity politics (see page 86) has also included lesbian, gay, bisexual and transgender studies (LGBT). In simple terms, Queer Theory is concerned with a mode of textual analysis that searches for points of tension in texts around issues of gender identity. It is part of a concerted effort to resist easy distinctions between 'male' and 'female' and any notion of strict biological difference. For queer audiences, the pleasure of watching some films lies in the way in which rules are broken and identities confused.

As part of this refusal to categorise, Queer Studies focuses also on films about transgendered characters, bisexuality etc. Queer can also be used in relation to ethnicity and similar issues about easy distinctions and categorisations based on racial difference. Overall, queer is a term that could be used of any media text that does not conform to expectations of its conventions etc. Gay and lesbian texts often deal with narratives and representations of open gay and lesbian lifestyles. Queer narratives deal with what might have to be secret or unspoken identities. The term 'queer' is an example of taking back what was a term of abuse and brandishing it in the open.

See Alexander Doty's *Queering the Film Canon* (2000) for examples of queer readings of some well-known films.

Brokeback Mountain is, according to some gay and lesbian critics, a queer movie, as its two heroes are unable to be out, not just because of the conservative culture in which they find themselves, but also because they have not themselves faced up to their own sexual identity, remaining queer characters. So, when Grundmann discusses romance from a queer perspective, he recognises that new conventions would be needed to accommodate different forms of relationship.

The Western is a good site for exploration of the concept of queerness. Part of the narrative pleasure of Westerns is explained by the constraints they do place on characters in terms of gender relations. There is a tension in the classic Western between the freedom that men enjoy as cowboys on the range and the encroaching domesticity and family life associated with settlement (as played out in classic Westerns such as *My Darling Clementine*, 1946). In the period before domesticity in the real West, women were limited to roles as saloon girl or

4.1 Jake Gyllenhaal and Heath Ledger as Jack and Ennis, the two young men who fall in love in *Brokeback Mountain*.

schoolteachers, and men often found themselves in close friendships with other men. The release of *Brokeback Mountain* has seen several attempts to analyse earlier Westerns in terms of homoerotic relationships. For example, in *Sight and Sound*'s 'Western Special', Ed Buscombe pointed to relationships in both classic Westerns such as *My Darling Clementine* and twilight Westerns such as *Ride the High Country* (1962).

Often in these Westerns, characters would displace any homoerotic desire into physical action – usually a fistfight (similar to the fight that produces the blood on the shirt in *Brokeback Mountain*). Once the process of studying Westerns to find these moments of tension began, many other examples were recorded. In a famous scene from the John Wayne/Howard Hawks film *Red River* (1947), two cowboys ask to see each other's six-guns (which are fondled and admired in turn) before competing in a shooting competition. One of the two actors involved was Montgomery Clift, now recognised as one of Hollywood's leading closeted gay actors in a period when an out gay identity was impossible. These kinds of discoveries have led to a canon of LGBT or Queer Westerns. Another such film is *Johnny Guitar* (1954), in which Joan Crawford, a gay icon in the 1950s, plays a saloon owner threatened by a town mob.

4.2 Joel McCrea and Randolph Scott, ageing Western stars play ageing cowboys with a shared history in the 'Twilight Western' *Ride the High Country*.

The 2006 London Lesbian and Gay Film Festival programme notes described the film as 'a rule-defying Western'. This rule defiance is a feature of various late Westerns that also began to revise the traditional Western's values by giving more narrative voice and greater status to Native Americans as well as the freed slaves who became cowboys – this could also be seen as part of a queering process.

The audiences for Brokeback Mountain

In this case study, we have already suggested that there may be three audiences for the film. Firstly, there is an audience that knows and appreciates the Western genre and its twilight variation. This audience might be older and more likely to be male. Similarly, a romance audience might have expectations because of knowledge of the romance genre. This second audience may possibly be younger and female (although as Westerns have been out of favour for so long, it is possible that some older women may simply have forgotten about them and placed themselves in relation to the romance genre). Third, there is an LGBT audience who accept the film in its queering role.

Identifying these three audiences does not preclude other audiences and also does not preclude audience members who might be in two or more of the three audience groups. We should also note that a sense of other audiences might be disturbing, especially for some audience members who identify with Western or romance genres, and are faced with possible queer readings. What we have done is to demonstrate that textual analysis does help produce richer readings, that it draws on knowledge of other texts and that it also requires contextual consideration of the audience and how they identify themselves. Have we described most of the audience for the film? Probably not. For any film, especially a Hollywood film with a significant profile, there are many audiences. For instance:

- the literary audience who has read and enjoyed the original story and wants to see the adaptation;
- the fans of the star actors, who might not usually see a film like this;
- audiences attracted by the cinematography (the beautiful scenery of Alberta, standing in for Wyoming) or the music;
- film fans who go to see every film that wins an award (*Brokeback Mountain* had won several awards even before it opened);
- audiences who are most concerned with good stories and interesting characters rather than specific genres;
- the casual audience that saw the film because there was nothing else on at the multiplex that they fancied that day;
- and probably other groups as well.

Any screening of the film might have included all these groups. Some audiences will certainly have found the film disappointing or even irritating, and perhaps they will have left before the end. To some extent, we know that these groups exist, because we have the evidence of what they have said or published, in print and on the internet, about their reaction. Chapter 8 explores the various ways in which audiences discuss films using internet sites, blogs, bulletin boards etc. You could do an internet search now and see what kinds of responses you find.

Ideally, at this stage, it would be good to look at a range of audience responses in more detail in a formal manner. We can do this on a very small scale in relation to a sample of responses from cinemagoers who elected to attend two education events that I offered at specialised cinemas, dealing with *Brokeback Mountain* and the two concepts of the twilight Western and the Queering of the West. The events were held in May and July 2006 and the third session of each was a discussion of *Brokeback Mountain* itself after a short questionnaire in which anonymous responses were given to the following questions:

Q1. What initially drew you to the film? Choose as many answers as you think appropriate and give as much detail as you need to make your point clear:

- The film's publicity and promotional material.
- The press coverage suggesting that this was a controversial film.
- The previous work of Ang Lee, the director.
- The previous work of Annie Proulx, the writer of the short story.
- The stars of the film (say which one or more).
- The possible genre of the film (say which you assumed it would be).
- The scenery, camerawork – the beauty of the film.
- Good (or bad!) reviews of the film.
- The chance to discuss an 'event film' with friends.
- Anything else.

Q2. After you had seen the film, were you:

- pleased because it matched your expectations?
- excited because it turned out to be something else?
- disappointed because it failed to live up to expectations?

Fourteen questionnaires were received from these two self-selecting groups. Each person was self-categorised as 'Male' or 'Female' and as 'under 35' or 'over 35'. The overall group comprised one Male under 35, three Females under 35, six Males over 35 and four Females over 35. Noone was asked to divulge their sexual orientation, but some of the answers and the discussion suggested that this was a group with a range of gender identities.

I do not claim that this group represents the range of *Brokeback Mountain* audiences – as a comparison, the IMDB user ratings on the film reveal voters to be mostly under 30 and male – but even so, there were a range of responses. The distributors will be pleased to learn that publicity and promotional material was the most cited reason for seeing the film, followed by knowledge of Ang Lee's work. All the other reasons were also cited, but (and perhaps this is an indication of a UK arthouse audience) the least important reason was any sense of controversial press coverage. One person admitted that they only saw the film because they wanted to come to the event. Five people recognised the film as a kind of Western, one cited it as a Queer Western and three used 'gay' or 'queer' as a descriptor for the film. One person called it a 'love story'. As might be expected, the stars of the film were an attraction for the under-35s. Most respondents (9) were pleased that the film matched their expectations, but the other five all saw the film as prompting two or more of the responses suggested. Two people felt that they had had all three responses. In other words, it did what they expected and some more, but, overall, perhaps not as much as it might have done.

Evaluation

The objective of this small-scale research was to attempt to demonstrate that even within a relatively defined sector of the overall cinema audience, a range of responses and a range of reasons for seeing the film was likely to be recorded. This kind of research is discussed in Chapter 7 and could easily be applied on a wider scale (but do consider the problems with such an 'open' mode of collecting information – i.e. the difficulty of measuring responses and reporting them when so many different options can be chosen).

In the context of an education event, one of the objectives of the survey was also to prompt the group to think about their responses to the film and their reasons for seeing it initially, as well as to explore their readings of sequences in the film. In a sense, the whole exercise became a form of **qualitative research,** and the most interesting aspect of what followed was an insight into how individual members of an LGBT audience might have approached the film. Two points emerged from discussion that extend the analysis of the film's reception outlined above.

1. Preparing the LGBT audience

The promotion of the film was very carefully orchestrated to appeal to a straight audience as a romance. In the UK, Ang Lee appeared to dance around the description of the film as a gay cowboy movie, on the one hand saying that it should not be limited by such a phrase, but then also insisting that he was quite relaxed about how people approached the film. There was far less controversy in the UK than in parts of the USA, but Lee's ambivalence is also explained by the parallel campaign to promote the film directly to the LGBT audience. The *Brokeback Mountain* website (see 4.3 overleaf) set up a bulletin board on which people were invited to record their own *Brokeback*-style experiences. The website shows the two lead characters in medium shot next to each other but looking down in different directions. The landscape is visible in the background and the tag-line reads, '*Brokeback Mountain* – Love is a force of nature'. (This composition is actually representative of the film, in which the two characters often appear in close-up, near to the camera with the landscape in the background; they also appear in long shot in compositions that emphasise the importance of landscape. Ang Lee was influenced to some extent by the 'look' of

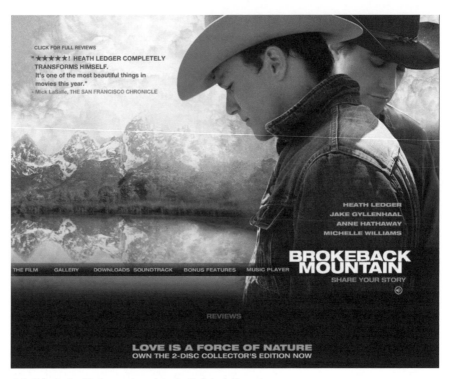

CLICK FOR FULL REVIEWS

"★★★★★! HEATH LEDGER COMPLETELY TRANSFORMS HIMSELF.
It's one of the most beautiful things in movies this year."
- Mick LaSalle, THE SAN FRANCISCO CHRONICLE

HEATH LEDGER
JAKE GYLLENHAAL
ANNE HATHAWAY
MICHELLE WILLIAMS

THE FILM   GALLERY   DOWNLOADS SOUNDTRACK   BONUS FEATURES   MUSIC PLAYER

BROKEBACK MOUNTAIN
SHARE YOUR STORY

REVIEWS

LOVE IS A FORCE OF NATURE
OWN THE 2-DISC COLLECTOR'S EDITION NOW

4.3 Gyllenhaal and Ledger on the website for *Brokeback Mountain*.

The Last Picture Show (1971), in which director Peter Bogdanovich used a similar arrangement of close-ups and deep-focus backgrounds.)

The stories submitted to the website reveal a range of positive responses, many clearly written before the film was released and expressing enormous anticipation of local screenings. The film was trailed in various gay publications in the USA and abroad. For instance, in the UK publication *Gay Times*, an article appeared in time for the film's December 2005 release entitled 'Homos on the Range', written by two American academics, Sean Griffin and Harry M. Benshoff, a writing partnership responsible for several film studies and cultural studies books. The illustrated piece is very detailed and traces the 'long, but some times dishonest' tradition of gay cowboys in Hollywood. Many of the references match those quoted by Ed Buscombe in *Sight and Sound*, but there is much more discussion about the history of Western imagery in gay pornography, the tradition of 'athletic physique films' featuring Western characters and about the only other occasion when a recognisably gay Western was released (albeit in a very limited way), in the form of Andy Warhol's *Lonesome Cowboy* (USA, 1968). The piece ends with the hope that *Brokeback Mountain* will 'set the record – if you'll pardon the expression – straight. Queer cowboys have always existed on the American frontier, despite the overtly heterosexual posturing of the Western film genre that seeks to write its history.'

2. A queer reading?

The opening of *Brokeback Mountain* provides a useful example of just how different readings of films can be. The first four minutes or so of the film have no dialogue – only music and sound effects/ambient sound. In an alternating pattern of long shots and close-ups, we see a truck driving across the plains just before daybreak, then stop and drop off Ennis after the sun comes up. Ennis walks to a hiring office, where he waits as a train goes past and then watches Jack arrive in a beat-up pick-up. Jack uses a wing mirror as a shaving aid and the camera captures Ennis framed in the mirror. Neither man speaks but Ennis furtively glances at Jack and then turns away. The dialogue only begins when the hiring agent arrives.

The beginning of the film does a great deal of work. It creates a mood and indicates that this film will be both beautiful to look at and slow to tell its story. Each image appears to have been carefully selected as if in a photographic exhibition about the West. The pick-up driving into shot mirrors the openings of two other Larry McMurtry adaptations, *Hud* and *The Last Picture Show,* and the appearance and stances of the two young men, especially Ennis, suggests every rebellious country rock star of the last 30 years. The only clear narrative marker is the framing of Ennis in the mirror being used by Jack. With knowledge of what happens, we can see on repeat viewings that Jack is looking at Ennis and perhaps thinking about what might be possible. As it is Jack who will make the first move, this seems like the clearest reading. Yet, one of the audience group described above suggested that for them it was Ennis whose body language and glances were those of someone looking and falling instantly into a state of desiring the person they see. This is a very different reading and, if pursued, would create a different set of narrative tensions to those set up by seeing Jack as the initiating partner.

Brokeback Mountain is a film that has provoked a range of responses, many positive, some dismissive. It has also generated considerable discussion within the film industry, with analyses of its box-office performance and attempts to discern how much of its success was attributable to its profile as a gay film and what this, in turn, might mean for the distribution of future films with similar themes. In 'The Other Side of the Mountain' (*Screen International* 16 June 2006) Peter Bowen used test screenings of *Boy Culture* (USA, 2006) to explore whether, post *Brokeback Mountain,* distributors would have more confidence in trying to sell gay-themed films to straight audiences. He found evidence of more industry interest in gay movies, but also wariness, with observations that *Brokeback Mountain* had stars and studio support. Also, it was not set in an out community, which straight audiences might find intimidating. There is a small but

RESEARCH SUGGESTION
Choose a film you have seen recently which you enjoyed and which for you had a clear set of meanings – that enabled you to make a reading that you could confidently support. Now look up the film on IMDb.com (or similar websites). Focus on the 'User comments' and 'User ratings' (see Chapter 8). Compare your response with users of the same age/gender (shown in the voting figures) and consider the range of other user comments. What conclusions do you draw about the range of audience responses?

profitable market for gay films that distributes to a restricted theatrical market as well as on specialist DVD labels, but which is quite distinct from the market targeted by *Brokeback Mountain* and other similar films such as *Capote* (USA, 2005).

Chapter 5 continues this focus on how audiences read films, using two further case studies – more mainstream films with A List stars and genre appeal. It would be useful to read that chapter next.

References

Barker, Martin, with Thomas Austin (2000), *From Antz to Titanic: Re-inventing Film Analysis* (London: Pluto Press).

Griffin, Sean and Harry M. Benshoff (2005), 'Homos on the range', *Gay Times*, December.

Bignell, Jonathan (2002), *Media Semiotics* (Manchester: Manchester University Press).

Bordwell, David and Kristin Thompson (2005), *Film Art: An Introduction* (7th edition) (New York and London: McGraw-Hill).

Bordwell, David and Noël Carroll (eds) (1996), *Post-theory: Reconstructing Film Studies* (Madison: University of Wisconsin Press).

Bruzzi, Stella (1997), *Undressing Cinema: Clothing and Identity in the Movies* (London: Routledge).

Branston, Gill and Roy Stafford (2006), *The Media Student's Book* (4th edition) (London: Routledge).

Buscombe, Edward (2006), 'Western Special: Man to Man', *Sight and Sound*, January.

Cook, Pam (ed.) (1997), *Gainsborough Pictures* (London: Cassell).

Chandler, Daniel (2004), *Semiotics: The Basics* (London: Routledge).

Clover, Carol (1992), *Men, Women and Chainsaws – Gender in the Modern Horror Film* (London: BFI).

Doty, Alexander (2000), *Queering the Film Canon* (London: Routledge).

Geraghty, Christine (2008), *Screen Adaptations: Transformations and Performances* (Boulder, Col: Rowman & Littlefield).

Gledhill, Christine (ed.) (1987), *Home is Where the Heart Is: Studies in Melodrama and the Woman's Film* (London: BFI).

Gledhill, Christine and Linda Williams (eds) (2000), *Reinventing Film Studies* (London: Arnold).

Harper, Sue (1994), *Picturing the Past: The Rise and Fall of the British Costume Film* (London: BFI).

Hill, John and Pamela Church Gibson (1998), *The Oxford Guide to Film Studies* (Oxford: OUP).

hooks, bell (1996), *Reel to Reel: Race, Sex and Class at the Movies* (New York: Routledge).

Neale, Steve (2000), *Genre in Hollywood* (London: Routledge).

Tasker, Yvonne (1993), *Spectacular Bodies: Gender, Genre and the Action Cinema* (London: Routledge).

Thompson, David and Ian Christie (eds) (1989), *Scorsese on Scorsese* (London: Faber and Faber).

Turner, Graeme (ed.) (2002), *The Film Cultures Reader* (London: Routledge).

Weddle, David (1996), *Sam Peckinpah: 'If They Move . . . Kill 'Em',* (London: Faber and Faber).

5. The Attraction of Stars and Genres

Using two detailed case studies in a similar way to Chapter 1, this chapter explores the importance of stars and genres in attracting audiences to specific films.

Once film studies had begun to focus on genre as a useful critical tool in the 1960s, it became a central feature of work on popular cinema. In 1975, Tom Ryall wrote an influential piece in *Screen Education* that contained the following definition of genre in film:

> The master image for genre criticism is a triangle composed of artist/film/audience. Genres may be defined as patterns/forms/styles/structures which transcend individual films, and which supervise both their construction by the filmmaker and their reading by an audience (quoted in Neale, 2000: 12).

Since 1975, there has been a great deal of work on genre theory in film studies, but the basic assumption set out by Ryall has been maintained. There is not space to explore that work in detail here, but we should note the following:

- Genres are not fixed or static – they change over time.
- The concept of **repertoire** is a useful way of thinking about the loose structure of elements that comprises a filmic genre.
- Although producers and audiences may both recognise enough elements to have some confidence about the kind of film they are considering, they may place emphasis on different elements and use different terms to describe them.
- Genres exist in all film industries, some are universal (broadly defined comedies, horror etc.), some are specific to certain film cultures (e.g. the *wu xia* films of Chinese cinema – see discussion of *Crouching Tiger, Hidden Dragon* etc. in Chapter 1).

- Filmmakers rarely set out to make a 'pure' genre film – most films draw on more than one genre repertoire.

Two of the leading names in the 'revision' of genre theory are Rick Altman and Steve Neale. Relevant texts for these authors are listed in the References at the end of this chapter.

Stars

The star system in Hollywood began to take hold in the 1910s. Early cinema tended to offer novelty and spectacle rather than star performers, but when films became longer and identification with strongly defined characters was the norm, it became clear that the most popular films were those featuring certain performers. The concept of star performers was not new, but previously it could only be achieved by personal appearances. Film allowed the emergence of a **star image** across the world (we will discuss this concept below). An early example of the attraction of stars was the establishment of a new studio in 1919. The studio's name, 'United Artists', referred to the four original partners: the performers Mary Pickford, Douglas Fairbanks and Charles Chaplin, and the director D. W. Griffith. These four names could all sell pictures to the paying public and over the next ten years the other studios attempted to build up a roster of star names to help promote their films. From the early 1930s through to a slow decline in the 1950s and 1960s, 'Studio Hollywood' saw the acquisition and development of stars as a crucial element in organising film production and distribution. During the studio era, stars were mostly contracted to specific studios and often appeared in a succession of genre films. Some studios operated a **unit system of production** in which the star worked with a small group of directors, writers, cinematographers etc. and other actors on a succession of films suited to a developing star image: e.g. the work of Errol Flynn and Olivia de Havilland in a series of 'swashbucklers' or action-adventure films at Warner Bros. in the 1930s (see Schatz, 1989: 208–9).

Every major film industry has had experience of a studio system and the development of contracted stars. Examples of films that deal with the lives of female stars in studio systems include *Centre Stage/The Actress* (dir. Stanley Kwan, Hong Kong, 1992), in which Maggie Cheung plays 1930s Shanghai star Ruan Ling-yu, and *Paper Flowers* (India, 1959), in which director and star Guru Dutt and Waheeda Rahman play a director and star in the Bombay studio system.

During the 1950s as the system broke up, actors were recruited by independent agents who became increasingly powerful in the new **package production system,** which sees each film produced and distributed as a separate entity (see Chapter 2). This remains the current system, with production companies obliged to pay very large fees to the top stars. These are the **A List** stars, capable of opening a film simply because of the presence of their name above the title. Membership of the A List is based on consistent performance at the box office. As a rule of thumb, the last three films released by a star should show an average box office of over $100 million to maintain that status.

Theoretical work on stars

The crucial theoretical work on stars was first published in the 1980s and included contributions from Richard Dyer (1979 and 1987) and John Ellis (1982), which was followed by Christine Gledhill (1991), Jackie Stacey (1994) and Christine Geraghty (2000) among others. As Geraghty points out (2002: 184), there have been three strands to this work on stardom:

- the place of the star image in a semiotic analysis of film;
- exploration of stars and their importance in terms of ideology and concepts of representing particular ideas and values;
- stars and reception studies, including references to psychoanalysis.
  (See the references to semiotics and psychoanalysis in Chapter 4.)

The suggestion that a star image is something that includes, but is more than, the star's appearance in specific films was an important part of the process of including work on stars in film studies. Dyer (1979) suggested two aspects to this. First, stars themselves are commodities who can be used in productions as valuable assets. This is manifest in both the perception by audiences that the presence of stars adds to the production values of the film (i.e. a film with stars feels more glamorous and exciting) and in the use of stars as promotional vehicles for films. Contemporary Hollywood uses stars to make appearances at premieres, to be interviewed on chat shows and in magazines etc. In addition, the private lives of contemporary Hollywood stars are now part of a general celebrity culture that focuses directly on them as distinct from specific films. Dyer's second area of work focused on the use of stars in particular kinds of roles that embodied typical qualities, such as those of the 'tough guy' and the 'good Joe', and alternative types such as the 'rebel' and the 'independent woman'. Dyer was drawing on earlier work and using it to suggest new approaches, but this did mean that he drew examples from earlier Hollywood periods. Geraghty and others have updated this in relation to contemporary Hollywood.

We can see the star image as a conglomeration of different aspects of the star's presence for audiences. This will combine the actual performance in specific roles, the recognition of those roles as relating to social types and issues in contemporary society, and, crucially what has been termed as the **secondary circulation** of the star's image in other media such as television and the tabloids. Each of these different elements can be confirmed, adding up to a single star image, or there may be a fruitful contradiction between different elements making the star image more intriguing. Sometimes a star's appearance in a film may involve casting against type. In Chapter 4, there is a discussion of *Brokeback Mountain* and a suggestion that for some audiences the star image of both Heath Ledger and Jake Gyllenhaal might have created a tension in relation to their roles in the film – but a slightly different tension in each case. In summer 2006, the star image of the A List star and director

Mel Gibson was queried in arguably a less productive way when he appeared dishevelled during TV news coverage of a drink-driving incident and allegedly made anti-Semitic remarks. Gibson's image perhaps draws on both the tough guy and good Joe types but adds a form of robust traditional Catholicism and, according to some commentators, an anti-Britishness.

John Ellis explored rather a different idea about stars that nevertheless referred to the idea of the star image and secondary circulation. In a discussion of the differences between cinema and television, Ellis suggested that audiences felt compelled to watch stars on a cinema screen in order to gain access to the complete star image that was introduced via the images in secondary circulation. He called this the 'photo effect'. Ellis argued that television was a more intimate medium in which the viewer can get close to the performance, and therefore the distance between the performer as actor and the character portrayed seems quite short. Cinema suggests a more powerful intrigue built into the larger gap between the star as a real life personality and the performance on screen. In Studio Hollywood this was articulated as the ordinary/extraordinary quality of stars. The great stars could be, at the same time, the boy or girl next door (we could identify with them) and magical, glamorous, unobtainable. This dual personality was the promise of big-screen entertainment. Ellis did his initial work before the video boom, which saw bigger audiences watching Hollywood films on a TV set rather than on a cinema screen. Even so, there is still mileage in the suggestion that the major stars of cinema exert a different kind of hold over audiences than those developed solely within television. Whether or not the increased access to stars for modern media audiences of all kinds compares to the controlled exposure of stars in the studio era is another question.

> Another question you might wish to explore is the movement of television stars into feature films for the cinema. This has been quite difficult for big TV stars such as the cast of *Friends* and crime TV stars like David Caruso. Why might this be so? How different is the star image on television?

This short introduction has established the importance of genres and stars in film studies. How can we use the concepts in thinking about the release of two recent Hollywood films?

Inside Man – An example of the release of a mainstream studio film with a strong personal stamp of the producer-director and stars.

When *Inside Man* was released in the USA in March 2006, there were a number of questions about how well the film might play in cinemas. The story concerns a bank heist in which the gang take hostages and lock themselves in so that they can recover something special from the vault. A detective is appointed to manage the police operation and he finds himself negotiating with both the gang leader and an agent representing the bank's owners. With a budget of around $40 million, this was not a blockbuster, but it was a more expensive film than is usually produced by producer-director Spike Lee, a well-known independent in the sense of maintaining his own production company, even if he has often dealt with the major studios. Lee's recent run of films had not been particularly successful in box-office terms. His 2004 film *She Hate Me* died at the box office, while 2002's *25th Hour* made a little money, but *Bamboozled* (2000), one of Lee's most personal and angry films, had also performed very poorly. Lee also works in television and on documentary films, and *The Original Kings of Comedy* (also 2002) was a major hit, grossing $38 million on a production budget of around $3 million. This spread of work keeps his company, 40 Acres and a Mule, viable.

THE DIRECTOR AS STAR

Contemporary American cinema does use the director's name as a marketing device. Sometimes this is merely a device whereby the director's name is linked to a previous box-office hit. We might not recognise the name, but we are made aware that they have been successful before. This is routine, but a number of directors have assumed a kind of star status. This began with the importation of the idea of film authorship from France in the 1960s, which added to the long-standing American tradition of the showman (including larger-than-life producer-directors such as Cecil B. DeMille in the studio era). The first group to gain widespread recognition as stars were the so-called 'Movie Brats' (Spielberg, Coppola, Lucas etc.). Spike Lee belongs to a later group that emerged as predominantly New York-based filmmakers in the 1980s and made their name in the newly defined American Independent cinema (see Pierson 1996). (Lee's contemporaries include directors such as Jim Jarmusch and John Sayles.) Lee is one of the most prominent independent directors in the USA. His central role in the new African-American cinema that emerged in the 1980s is undisputed, but he has also achieved a profile through appearing on mainstream television, often criticising African-American representations in Hollywood or commenting on representations of racist incidents. Lee has an image as an angry man committed to a certain position on African-American cultural life. Many potential audience members will have strong views themselves either pro or anti on Lee's cinema.

The Hollywood saying is that you are only as good as your last movie – so in Lee's case, he did not look like a good bet for a $40 million budget. On the other hand, Lee is an accomplished filmmaker, always controversial and capable of producing astonishing work. His previous big-budget picture was *Malcolm X* in 1992, on which he worked with Denzel Washington. Washington also worked with Lee on *Mo Better Blues* (1991) and *He Got Game* (1998), both films that had larger than usual budgets for the director and better than average box office. So the Lee–Washington pairing for *Inside Man* might have made the package much more alluring to Universal than a similar film without star presence.

Denzel Washington is an A List star. He does not belong in the group of megastars who will expect to appear in films that gross over $100 million. He sometimes appears in smaller films, but even so, *Screen International* (31 March 2006) reported that five of Washington's previous films had opened to more than

$20 million for the first weekend. Universal also knew that *Inside Man* co-starred Jodie Foster, like Washington a well-respected actor and a top draw when placed in a mainstream film.

Inside Man opened in North America and 19 other territories worldwide on 24 March, 2006. The three-day gross was $28.9 million in North America and $10.3 million in the international market, placing the film at the top of both charts. Jeremy Kay in *Screen International* (ibid.) quoted audience surveys (exit polls) of US screenings that suggested that 76% of patrons gave Washington as their main reason for seeing the film, while 44% went for Foster and 43% for the heist storyline. UK star Clive Owen was cited by 25% and Spike Lee by 22%.

It is probable that audiences for Lee's smaller independent films would be more likely to quote the director as the main attraction. The other figures no doubt reflect the overall status of the three actors as stars. Interestingly, each star possibly appeals to a different demographic, although Washington and Foster together is not that unlikely a pairing. Owen is a more recent star and may appeal to younger audiences. Foster's role in the film, as a cold, manipulative lawyer/political fixer, is perhaps an example of casting against type, which arguably makes her scenes with Washington more exciting. Washington himself has a complex star image. He manages to combine the attractions of a mainstream star with a clear identity as an African-American actor committed to what he would consider as roles that do not denigrate African-American culture and many that positively support it. Even so, this does not mean that he always plays versions of the good Joe. In films such as *Training Day* (2001) and *Out of Time* (2003), he plays police officers who are seriously flawed in terms of their honesty and professionalism. These two thrillers were also directed by African-Americans. Washington's performance in *Inside Man* as the detective in charge of the investigation is aided by knowledge of these other roles and the slight question mark over the good Joe reading of his star image.

The film features a complex plot involving hostages and a motive that is not fully revealed until late in the film. A first-time scriptwriter must have been a gamble for the studio, but the New York setting (with Lee exploiting his local knowledge) and the possible links to similar narratives in earlier films such as *The Anderson Tapes* in 1971 or *Dog Day Afternoon* in 1975 (both directed by Sidney Lumet) might have been attractive to older film fans. Since the tragedy of 9/11, films set in New York have been problematic for producers and distributors – when would audiences be ready for dramatic narratives focusing on public events in New York again? Spike Lee was one of the first filmmakers to feature the aftermath of 9/11 directly in *25th Hour*, but, in 2006, *Inside Man* seemed to be just the first of a series of films now prepared to explore the events in detail (e.g. *United 93*, 2006, directed by UK dramadoc expert Paul Greengrass). Universal also distributed *United 93*, so perhaps they considered coordinating the two release schedules?

The precise timings of a major film release are now a feature of both the North American and international markets. The months between the end of the Christmas holiday period and the start of the summer season are generally seen as a flat period, enlivened mainly by the promotional opportunities of the circus around the Academy Awards. Studios look at this as a period in which to slip out the more modest offerings from their slate or to carefully place films with a more defined audience profile. The most spectacular success in this respect was probably *Erin Brockovich* in 2000, which opened in North America on 19 March and took $28 million on its first weekend, before going on to make $125 million in total. Julia Roberts is the only female star consistently in the $100 million box-office group, but even so, the audience reaction to *Erin Brockovich* surprised the industry, given the nature of the story (i.e. it was not a romantic comedy, the main vehicle for Roberts' success). In 2005, Universal (which had also released *Erin Brockovich*) chose to go a few weeks later (UK 17 April, USA 24 April) with *The Interpreter*, another thriller by a well-established (indeed, veteran) director, Sidney Pollack, and featuring Nicole Kidman and Sean Penn. This claimed $22 million from its North American first weekend. What do *Inside Man*, *Erin Brockovich* and *The Interpreter* have in common? The suggestion is that they might be, in Jeremy Kay's phrase (ibid.), 'smart adult movies'. They are smart simply in the sense that they are driven by plot and acting/performance rather than action/effects. 'Adult' in this case means an audience older than the 15–24 age group targeted by the higher-budget blockbusters scheduled for a summer release. Quoting the same exit polls referenced above, Kay points out that 68% of *Inside Man*'s audience was over 30. We might note here that this observation fits the view that some smart films work by questioning or teasing the audience in terms of genre conventions. Like *Dog Day Afternoon* (featuring a bravura performance by Al Pacino), *Inside Man* tends to stop the action to allow us to enjoy the performances of Washington, Foster and Owen – almost as if it knows this will be what the older audience wants. Mainstream fans of more action-based crime films may find the film too slow.

This was how the second week of *Inside Man*'s release was described on <www.boxofficeguru.com>:

> Following its top spot debut last weekend, Spike Lee's bank hostage thriller *Inside Man* saw a standard 47% drop in the second weekend and took in $15.4M. After ten days, Universal has seized $52.5M giving the Denzel Washington–Jodie Foster film the largest ten-day cume of any film released before *Ice Age* this year. *Inside Man* has already become Lee's top-grossing film ever beating the $48.2M of 1992's *Malcolm X* which earned Washington an Oscar nod. Also, the bank heist flick is outdistancing *Man on Fire* and Foster's *Flightplan* which generated ten-day totals of $44.3M and $45.9M, respectively. Produced for $45M, *Inside Man* looks to reach around $90M domestically. The international cume to date stands at $22.5M after 11 days. (by Gitesh Pandya, accessed 4 April 2006)

Inside Man suggests that studios can get it right with a carefully planned release. We have identified the importance of stars, story and timing. The lack of competition from similarly adult films was a major factor in the first weekend success. The other new films available for audiences on that weekend were horror pic *Stay Alive* and comedy *Larry the Cable Guy*. The top films from previous weeks comprised mostly horror, action (*V for Vendetta*) and 'family' or 'romantic' comedies. Would Universal have seen so much success if they had released during November/December when Oscar contenders such as *Brokeback Mountain, Walk the Line* etc. were attracting adult audiences?

If age is one means of classifying audiences, gender and ethnicity are also possible classification criteria. *Inside Man's* first week was slightly skewed towards men (54%), but this is not so significant when action films and romances routinely see 60:40 or even 70:30 splits on gender lines. More pertinent is the skew towards an African-American/Latino audience, which made up 33% of *Inside Man's* total. As 'Box Office Guru' points out, African-American actors are often the top box-office draw for audiences, but in the case of Spike Lee and Denzel Washington working together, African-American audiences would expect a film that intelligently explored issues of black culture and racial difference. Spike rarely disappoints on this score, offering Washington's detective a partner in the form of the UK's rising star Chiwetel Ejiofor and a selection of important cameos, including Waris Ahluwalia as a Sikh objecting to being called an 'arab' because he wears a turban.

In a country as large as the USA, the African-American and increasingly the Latino audiences are significant (larger than the audiences for many national film

5.1 Jodie Foster and Denzel Washington, two established A-List stars together in *Inside Man.*

audiences elsewhere) and may behave differently – i.e. attend the cinema more or less frequently. There is evidence that although they are making attempts to understand these audiences, the studios are still not quite sure what to do with films that might target a specific African-American or Latino audience directly. Mainstream films with black actors appealing to all audiences do not present promotional problems, but when Denzel Washington starred in his own directorial debut, *Antwone Fisher* (2002), a story about the difficult childhood of a young African-American sailor, Fox Searchlight gave the film a **platform release**, eventually widening to just over 1,000 screens. *Inside Man* opened on over 2,800 screens.

Mona Lisa Smile – An example of the problems faced by a mainstream studio film with a big star that does not fulfil expectations, possibly because of a confusion over genre expectations.

Julia Roberts has been one of the most consistent draws in recent Hollywood history. By 2006, her 31 films had grossed over $2 billion and she had been involved in more $100 million movies than any other female star. *Mona Lisa Smile* (2003) was one of the few major releases for which her star presence could not propel the gross box office beyond the production budget figure. In this sense, the film failed at the US box office ($65 million production budget – a large chunk of which was probably Roberts' fee – and a North American gross of $63 million).

Mona Lisa Smile is not a bad film. It is competently directed by Mike Newell, a UK director with previous experience of similar period films focusing on independent women (e.g. Miranda Richardson in *Dance with a Stranger*, UK, 1985), beautifully designed and shot, and features a strong supporting cast of vibrant young stars such as Kirsten Dunst, Julia Stiles and Maggie Gyllenhaal – and Julia Roberts herself is fine. So what was the problem? Possibly the filmmakers failed to recognise what kind of film they were making and who the audience might be.

The classification 'women's picture' sounds very outdated now, but in the 1940s it described films that attracted a female audience because the stories in the films derived from the protagonist's position as a woman in a male-dominated society. Such a character would typically have to struggle between the competing demands of a lover, a family and her possible career. She could be punished for choosing one over another and the resolution of the story would probably mean that she had to give up something.

Julia Roberts plays a progressive art teacher from California (doubly marked as modern by her take on art and her Californian experience) who accepts a job at the ultra conservative Wellesley College, a private women-only university in New England, in the early 1950s. Her character finds herself caught between the demands of the institution and its pressure on her private life and her developing relationship with a class of highly intelligent young women, some susceptible to rebellion, others equally committed to conformity.

In essence, the film is similar to the classic 'women's picture' of the 1940s, in which all the main stars are women and the male leads are solid at best.

Such films, starring Bette Davis, Joan Crawford, Rosalind Russell etc., were eagerly received by mainly female audiences and helped to keep the stars high up in the box-office lists.

Erin Brockovich was in some ways an updated version of the 1940s women's picture – with an important twist. In most of the 1940s films the women, although powerfully played by such strong performers, were punished in some way for transgressing their social roles. In *Erin Brockovich*, Erin, played by Julia Roberts, walks away with a series of victories. But in *Mona Lisa Smile*, her character, Katherine Anne Watson, leaves the college at the end of an eventful year with only the knowledge that she may have influenced some young women who may remember her teaching in the future (which is, of course, important in real life, but does not work as a feel good ending for a Hollywood film).

The problem with *Mona Lisa Smile* is its appeal (or not) to younger audiences and whether this will also allow older audiences to enjoy the film. In North America, the audience profile is generally younger than in Europe and the 12–29 age group is arguably the single most important audience group for mainstream films. Why would this audience be interested in a film set in the 1950s, especially when it deals with issues about women's roles in education, business and domesticity, issues that, though still important, are viewed quite differently in a post-feminist society? The producers must have foreseen the possibility that the film would fail to satisfy enough younger or older cinemagoers, who in this case might have wanted something different. The burden of hitting the demographic here is heavy, because most of Julia Roberts' films tend to be seen by audiences as 'chick flicks' (to use the rather offensive industry jargon) – i.e. films primarily for women – to attend which reluctant male partners may need persuading. With only 25% of the audience as the main target, the appeal of the film has to be unambiguous, and the kinds of user comments on internet sites suggests that this was not the case. This comment was made in reply to a male viewer who had not enjoyed the film:

> 'I guess that since you're a guy you shouldn't have gone to this film in the first place. This one has 'chick flick' written all over it in big neon letters' (from <www.chokingonpopcorn.com>).

The problem may initially come from the script, written by two (male) writers whose previous films have mainly been remakes or adaptations of earlier TV shows (e.g. *Planet of the Apes*, 2001; *Mighty Joe Young*, 1998; *The Beverley Hillbillies*, 1993). The historical re-creation of the 1950s is authentic in terms of costume design, but the storyline itself does not ring true, failing to engage a younger audience and frustrating an older audience. Symptomatic of the overall approach is to include a soundtrack of classic 1950s popular songs, but then to re-record some of them with contemporary artists. It may be that some original recordings are not available because of problems over rights, but it seems a confused approach that again risks alienating both younger and older audiences. Of course, in some films that treat the use of popular music with a fresh approach, such as *Moulin Rouge* (2001), this can be a very successful ploy.

   Mona Lisa Smile is most of all confused about genre. Is it a 1940s 'women's picture', a modern 'chick flick', a social satire, a romantic drama? Most contemporary films do mix genre elements, but usually the audience is able to get a firm handle on how they want to approach the story. *Mona Lisa Smile* was unfortunate in that many reviewers and many individual audience members took it to be a film about an inspirational teacher and her students, and in this respect compared it (unfavourably) to the very successful 1989 film *Dead Poets Society*, directed by Peter Weir and starring Robin Williams.

The importance of star image and costume is outlined by Christine Geraghty in her analysis of Julie Christie in *Darling* (UK, 1965) (Geraghty, 1997: 159). Christie plays a character who sleeps her way to fame and fortune, only to be punished by loneliness and despair. Geraghty comments on the dominant reading of the film, suggesting that Christie's star performance transcends the narrative and invites young women in the audience to identify both with the array of fashionable clothes that she wears and her confidence in pursuing her desires. This, in turn, is linked to Christie's image as the young woman at the centre of London celebrity culture in the mid-1960s.

   As well as the genre angle, the film will succeed or fail on the basis of Julia Roberts as star. What is her star image? Partly it is physical. Although perhaps not conventionally beautiful, Roberts has distinctive features including a wide mouth and an engaging smile, sparkling eyes, fine facial bone structure and a slim but strong physique that audiences find attractive. *Erin Brockovich* exploited her physical appearance by contradicting her usual look with costumes suitable for her character, including high heels, short tight skirts and tight revealing tops (giving her a striking bust that mesmerised audiences), matched by 'big hair'. Her appearance became one of the major talking points of the film. By contrast, the 1950s fashions of *Mona Lisa Smile* did not help to make her performance memorable.

   The qualities associated with Roberts' star image include those of a strong, independent woman ('feisty' seems appropriate) with a sense of fun and a potentially rebellious streak. These qualities are evident in one of her biggest successes, *Runaway Bride* (1999). All female stars have to be able to develop a star image that will change as they get older. Roberts sometimes benefited from a girlish charm in her early career, but her intelligence is what is likely to work in more mature roles. Away from the screen, Roberts' secondary image has some association with charity work, whereas her celebrity status was to some extent created around her sudden decision to marry country singer Lyle Lovett after breaking an engagement to Keifer Sutherland. A sense of the complexity of her star image is provided by Christine Geraghty (2000: 196): 'her film performances have been patchy but her celebrity status is based precisely on this contrast between the successful life her beauty seems to deserve and the disasters to which her natural impulses lead her'.

I'm not exactly sure what makes julia special. maybe it's because of her portrayals of her characters, she's a fine actress. maybe it's that sadness that seems to cross her eyes once and again, it's very noticeable and there's nothing overtly tragic about it, it's just a flash of melancholy. something that her smile obliterates because when she smiles, the sun comes out.

a big part of why we all love Julia so much is her 'girl-next-door' appeal. She doesn't seem like that typical movie star – stuck up and materialistic. She does her own cooking. She takes care of her kids. She does her own laundry. You know? She's just like you and me! And it comes through in every character she plays.

i love Julia because her beauty is unique, not like the Hollywood standard or the other sexy actresses. i think there are actresses and there is Julia. she can be serious, funny, sexy, ugly, she can be everything. even if some people think that she's really ugly, maybe she has a big nose or a big mouth but she has been linked to a lot of hot guys.

5.2 Julia Roberts in 1950s costume for *Mona Lisa Smile*.

(Fan responses on <juliarobertsforums.com> to the question: 'Why do you like Julia over other actresses?')

There are plenty of audience responses to *Mona Lisa Smile* on various internet sites. They are not all negative and they include both younger audience members and some of the women who went to similar colleges. The ideas underpinning the story were certainly interesting enough to make the production worthwhile, but perhaps the studio made too many assumptions about how a Julia Roberts star vehicle would play? The dilemma is obvious. With Roberts starring, a much larger audience would be tempted to see the film on its initial release. Without her, and with a clearer idea of what kind of film was being made on a smaller budget, audiences might have been

RESEARCH SUGGESTION

Choose a major international film star and analyse his or her star image. Take the latest film in which he/she appears (ideally one that is about to be released) and research (1) how the star's image is used in the portrayal of the character in the film and (2) in the promotion of the film on television, in magazines, on the internet etc.

more satisfied, but would they have attended in sufficiently large numbers to make the project profitable? These are difficult questions for studio executives to answer. After the comparative failure of *Mona Lisa Smile* (which saw Roberts paid the highest fee yet to a female star), she appeared in smaller parts (i.e. with more ensemble playing) in *Oceans 12* and *Closer* (both 2004), followed by two voicing roles in animated features. It will be interesting to see how her star image is used in any new film that depends on her name to sell it.

References

Altman, Rick (1999), *Film/Genre* (London: BFI).

Dyer, Richard (1979/1998), *Stars* (London: BFI).

Dyer, Richard (1987), *Heavenly Bodies* (London: BFI).

Ellis, John (1982), *Visible Fictions* (London: Routledge).

Geraghty, Christine (1997), 'Women and Sixties British Cinema: The Development of the Darling Girl', in Robert Murphy (ed.), *The British Cinema Book* (London: BFI).

Geraghty, Christine (2000), 'Re-examining stardom: questions of texts, bodies and performance', in Christine Gledhill and Linda Williams (eds), *Re-inventing Film Studies* (London: Arnold).

Gledhill, Christine (ed) (1991), *Stardom: Industry of Desire* (London: Routledge).

Neale, Steve (2000), *Genre and Hollywood* (London: Routledge).

Neale, Steve (ed.) (2002), *Genre and Contemporary Hollywood* (London: BFI).

Pierson, John (1996), *Spike, Mike, Slackers & Dykes* (London: Faber & Faber).

Ryall, Tom (1975) *Screen Education* No.17.

Schatz, Thomas (1989), *The Genius of the System: Hollywood Filmmaking in the Studio Era* (London: Simon and Schuster).

Stacey, Jackie (1994), *Star Gazing: Hollywood Cinema and Female Spectatorship* (London: Routledge).

6. Theorising Audience Behaviour

Work on audiences is derived from the social sciences – sociology, anthropology, ethnography, psychology etc. It is more comfortably situated in media studies and cultural studies than film studies for this reason. This chapter explores how ideas from these disciplines, some of them controversial in their methodologies and conclusions, have been incorporated into (or excluded from) film studies.

> I have long supposed that the quickest way to make friends and pleasant casual acquaintances was to go walking with a dachshund. I know now that it is even better to be writing a book about the movies. (Margaret Thorp, *America at the Movies*, 1939)

These are the opening words of a book about the sociology of American audiences written at the height of the Studio System in Hollywood. Thorp recognised that movies were so important in people's lives that they were happy to talk about them and what they enjoyed about cinema going at length, with anyone. 1939 saw the release of *Stagecoach*, *The Wizard of Oz* and *Gone with the Wind*, and 85 million Americans went to the movies each week. What is surprising, perhaps, is that most of the major issues examined in Thorp's book are still relevant nearly 70 years later:

- stars and celebrity;
- fashion and representations of social behaviour;
- relationships with literature, music and dance;
- censorship;
- propaganda;
- studying film in higher education – 'taking films seriously'.

The parallels between 2006 and 1939 are strong. If we are surprised about this, it is partly perhaps explained by the relatively few attempts to deal with cinema going in such broad terms in the years between. Chapter 4 looks at the different approaches adopted to studying films and how spectators read them. Here we shift the focus to the audience itself.

Audiences, were until the 1980s, largely ignored by formal film studies – i.e. how real audiences behave during and after their experience of a film screening. Instead, audience theory developed in media studies mostly in relation to broadcasting (and then almost entirely in relation to television) and subsequently to films watched at home on a television set. There are good reasons why this focus developed, but it has skewed theoretical work on audiences. We need to consider the impact of the television-focused work on the different approaches required to study film audiences.

Sorting out the history of audience theories

Although 1960s and 1970s film theory might have largely ignored audience theories, there is plenty of evidence that audiences and their reaction to films were the subject of all kinds of speculation from the earliest days of cinema onwards. A very good overview of 'the tradition of research on actual film audiences, as it has developed in response to the history of the medium' is found in Jostein Gripsrud's entry to the *Oxford Guide to Film Studies* (1998). This provides a useful complement to Gripsrud's own brief history of audience theories across all communications media (Gripsrud, 2002) and also Jensen (2002, Chs. 9 and 10).

> The British Board of Film Censors was set up in 1912 (see <www.sbbfc.co.uk/student_guide_history.asp>)

> Cinemas were indeed unhealthy, especially in poorer districts, where they became known as 'fleapits', 'bug-hatches' or 'the germ exchange'. Patrons were doused in a perfumed disinfectant spray, which then mixed with the fug of cigarette and pipe smoke.

Cinema began in the late-Victorian period and there was evident concern by the 'male elders' in positions of authority in the UK and the USA that it would become a major source of attraction for the working classes, and for women and children of all classes – all easily susceptible to its excitement and influence. The crucial period was around 1910 when cinema began to be established in permanent buildings and the screening programme had begun to move towards forms of sensationalist fictions – melodramas, crime stories and anarchic comedies. This was the period when public concerns led to various attempts to measure audiences and to document what was happening in cinemas. Censorship in different guises began to be established in many Western countries and, as Gripsrud suggests:

> Such efforts characteristically sought to verify the intuitive feelings of educators, religious leaders and many social reformers that movies were for the most part

detrimental to the psychic, moral, and even physical health of those who regularly went to see them. (Gripsrud, 1998: 203)

The initial response to cinema as entertainment was similar to what we now often call a **moral panic**, seeming over-reaction by older people to any new entertainment form that is popular with young people. The reaction often comes from people who have no direct experience of what they are criticising. This is not to suggest that there is not some legitimate cause for concern, but that it is often exaggerated.

These early attempts to survey audience behaviour were essentially pragmatic and empiricist. **Empiricism** refers to attempts to test a hypothesis by searching for evidence in actual experience – as distinct from hypothesising what might happen. The researchers hoped to find examples of the degradation they feared. At the same time, especially in the 1920s, various authorities began to suggest that the new media of the period (which

Moral panic, as a concept related to media forms or representations of behaviour widely circulated in the media, is generally seen to have been introduced by the sociologist Stanley Cohen in his book *Folk Devils and Moral Panics* in 1972. Cohen was analysing the media coverage of the competing youth sub-cultures of 'Mods' and 'Rockers' during the 1960s. The term was used subsequently in relation to the **video nasties** of the early 1980s and more recently of various kinds of internet and mobile phone use by young people.

now placed radio alongside the press and the cinema) could be a positive force in educating the citizenry as well as a potential threat to moral order. A good example of this in relation to film was the beginnings of support for the documentary work of John Grierson and his collaborators in the UK at the end of the 1920s (alongside the nationalisation of the BBC after the General Strike in 1926). Questions about the cinema as a dangerous entertainment form continued into the 1930s, and film historians point to three research projects, each different in scope, but each noteworthy.

Three early research projects

The earliest of the three was not recognised in the Anglo-American world until the 1980s, and *A Sociology of the Cinema: The Audience* by Emilie Altenloh did not appear in English until 2001, with a translation in *Screen* by Kathleen Cross. Working in the crucial transitional period when cinema was becoming established as mass entertainment, Altenloh provided a detailed survey of the cinemagoing experience of a wide range of people in the provincial city of Mannheim in south-west Germany (population in 1914 roughly 200,000, served by 12 cinemas, all recently built). She was able to get the cooperation of cinema managers and school authorities and also worked with several professional and trade associations, sending out surveys and also meeting individuals for face-to-face interviews, ending up with 2,400 personal responses. As the *Screen* editorial for the issue carrying the translation of her work remarks:

Besides standing as a contribution to the historical study of film reception and to cultural and sociological studies of the consumption and use of popular media forms, *Zur Soziologie des Kino* offers a methodological template for the sort of ethnographic study of media audiences which is being reinvented today: for in attempting to understand the appeal of cinema, Altenloh's investigation aligns itself in spirit with the ethnographer's quest – in this case, to document cinema audiences' experience from the inside. (*Screen*, Vol. 42, No. 3, 2001: pp 247–8)

Ethnography is the study of specific communities of people undertaken through extensive fieldwork in which a researcher attempts to gain an insight into all aspects of the community's social behaviour, often through participation in their activities. Ethnography is derived from the Greek words **ethnos** (the nation) and **graphein** (writing) and as an academic study is linked to travel writing and colonial administration.

Altenloh's findings were remarkably similar to some of the later work undertaken in the UK and North America. Instead of discovering a single audience susceptible to the power of sensationalist fictions, she found a varied set of audiences with divisions along class and gender lines, and a range of ways of approaching films. One particularly interesting observation related to a group of apprentices from the town of Heidelberg (some 20 km from Mannheim). Altenloh reports that they 'show a greater degree of work-related interest. For example, they will watch pictures in the cinema with the eyes of an electrical engineer, a construction worker or a gardener' (Altenloh, 2001: 269). Although Altenloh had her own agenda, governed by the institutional demands of German academic work in the period, she was not as single-minded in her approach as those in the UK who were looking for evidence of moral decay. She did indeed find some examples of youths whose

whole imagination is geared in this way [i.e. to crime adventures], and it is these obsessions that must be understood as the basis of juvenile crime. For a group as weak, as morally wayward and as irresponsible as this, moreover, it is the lowest grade film material that holds the greatest attraction. (Altenloh, 2001: 265)

On the other hand, she also finds plenty of very different kinds of responses to cinema.

In the USA, the late 1920s and early 1930s was a period of prohibition of alcohol and persistent pressure to curtail the effects of a sensationalist cinema on young people in particular. The USA was one of the few countries not to have adopted some form of cinema censorship or classification by 1910–12. This finally came in 1930 with the **Production Code** (often referred to as the Hays Code after the then President of the Motion Pictures Producers and Distributors Association), which was fully applied for the first time in 1934. The Production Code was formulated by the major Hollywood studios to pre-empt criticism by

One of the most famous prohibitions of the Production Code referred to men and women in bed together. This was only allowed if the man kept one foot on the floor.

various pressure groups. Filmmakers were required to submit scripts in advance and the Production Code listed various themes and depictions that were not allowed.

Around this time, the largest and possibly most influential empirical research project on cinema going was set up with funds from a philanthropic foundation, the Payne Fund. A series of different research projects was carried out between 1929 and 1932, which eventually produced 12 separate volumes of research reports in the period up to 1937. The Payne Fund Studies encompassed a whole range of research methodologies, from content analyses, large-scale surveys and laboratory experiments to **participant observation** and autobiographies of individual movie going habits. Their importance for subsequent work on media audiences is that as well as trying to measure audiences and describe them, they attempted to explore the effects of movie going. It is also important to recognise that the studies were organised in the context of the most developed scientific methods available and the latest psychological theories. The USA in the 1930s was at the forefront of scientific management and behaviourist psychology – an ideological position that embraced the possibility of measuring and predicting behaviour. Gripsrud suggests that already in some of these studies it is possible to see the early methodological problems associated with much of the later **effects studies** (see below), but he also suggests that because of the range of studies of different kinds, 'at least some of the Payne Fund Studies were more nuanced and theoretically reflective than much post-war research' (Gripsrud, 1998: 206).

In Britain in the 1930s and 1940s, there were similar attempts both to measure audiences and to discern the possible effects of cinema going, but neither on the scale nor with the claimed scientific contextualisation of the American studies. The most interesting British research used much simpler forms of empirical research, such as participant observation of cinema audiences, direct responses and letters to magazines, diaries etc. As with the Payne Fund, there was an umbrella organisation for several different activities. This was **Mass-Observation** established in 1937. A very British kind of organisation, Mass-Observation recruited a large number of (mainly middle-class) volunteers, who undertook to keep diaries and send in reports on their observation of everyday life in the UK (i.e. on all aspects of everyday life, of which cinema was just a part). There were also paid investigators. One central project was focused on a study of 'Worktown' (in reality, Bolton in Lancashire). Observers sat in pubs and went to the cinema and even accompanied workers on holiday to Blackpool (resulting in the publication *The Pub and the People* in 1943).

The work of Mass-Observation carried on until the 1950s and was revived again in the 1980s. There is a clear link between Mass-Observation and the Grierson inspired Documentary Movement of the early 1930s. In some ways it was the case of middle-class observers in working-class communities (also to be found, with consequent reflection on the political questions such participation raises, in the work of writers such as George Orwell (e.g. *The Road to Wigan Pier*, 1937)). When interest in Mass-Observation was revived at a later date, it became clear that the material from the 1930s and 1940s revealed the same range of audience responses and variety of approaches present in Altenloh's earlier work and in the ethnographic studies that began to become a feature of cultural studies in the UK from the late 1970s onwards.

Some of the cinemagoing material from Mass-Observation was collected in *Mass-Observation at the Movies*, edited by Jeffery Richards and Dorothy Sheridan and published in 1987. This collection of material is drawn directly from the archives of Mass-Observation housed at the University of Sussex, nearly all of it previously unpublished. The focus on Bolton was somewhat fortuitous, as this was also the home town of the popular film historian and later film buyer for ITV, Leslie Halliwell, whose book *Seats in All Parts* (1985) paints a vivid complementary picture of cinemagoing in the town. In the 1990s, John Sedgewick (1999) carried out a statistical analysis of box-office takings in Bolton and London West End cinemas during the 1930s, which generally confirmed the impressions gained from the Mass-Observation period. These included the observation that the cinema in Britain was both an agent in the process of developing a national popular culture, where certain stars and genres were popular in both the upmarket West End and 'Worktown', and that it also allowed the possibility of surviving regional preferences (e.g. for tough Hollywood actors and local comedians and against Continental-style costume pictures). This dual role of developing the national/regional balance passed from cinema to television, especially after the arrival of ITV from 1955. The value of this research lies in the breadth of its approach to a wide range of films and its capacity to identify a very wide range of personal responses. This forms the basis of a riposte to some of the very generalised assertions about British cinema and audience concerns that might arise from concentration on textual analysis of a selected number of classic films.

Little of this material on cinemagoing was published during the Second World War, even though the research continued. It is worth remembering that during the war, cinema was increasingly viewed as an important agency for propaganda in all the combatant countries. In Britain, the scarce resources available to filmmakers were utilised to make morale-boosting films of all kinds. There was a clear recognition that cinemagoing did have effects and that successful propagandist films could boost the war effort and help to explain '*Why We Fight*' (the title of a series of films made for the American War Department by the Hollywood director Frank Capra between 1942 and 1945). Sometimes it was not clear what that effect might be (e.g. in the case of the production of the popular British film *The Life and Times of Colonel Blimp*, 1943, which the British Prime Minister Winston Churchill attempted to stop). Nevertheless, since the declaration of support for cinema by the Russian Soviet leader Lenin as the most important art and as an agency of **agitpropaganda,** this effect of cinema was almost unchallenged.

Film audiences and mass media

After the Second World War, the attention of researchers gradually shifted towards television and away from cinema as audiences declined in the USA and the UK. This was not total – as cinema became more focused on the youth audience, it became one of the sites for the possible moral denigration of youth, alongside comics, popular music, dancehalls etc.

For the next 30 years, the major work on audiences began to be seen as part of the emerging discipline of media studies. If you have taken any kind of media studies course at an introductory level, you will probably have come across some basic ideas about audience theory. For instance, students are often introduced to the seemingly opposite models of the **passive** and **active audience**. Although these are potentially useful as a starting point, they can also be confusing. Partly this is because they are often taken to be contemporary models. In fact, they both refer to work first undertaken in much earlier periods. However, although the models may be dated, they are still current in certain kinds of public discourse, allowing fierce debates to develop featuring scholars versus newspaper commentators (most notably in the 1996–7 furore surrounding the release of David Cronenberg's film *Crash*). To try to put this in some perspective, Jostein Gripsrud (2002: 42–44) refers to three distinct periods in terms of attitudes towards the media:

One of the most celebrated instances of the link between cinema and 'juvenile delinquency' (as it was called in the 1950s) came with the release of the film *Rock Around the Clock* (USA, 1956) which featured Bill Haley and the Comets. The film was banned in some towns in the UK, while in others, cinema staff struggled to prevent jiving (dancing) in the aisles and vandalism of the seats. The *Manchester Guardian* reported that the Odeon had to stop a screening for 18 minutes because the audience of 900 were in uproar. (Everett, 1986: 24)

- 'Almighty media' (1920–40), when the passive audience models held sway.
- 'Powerless media' (1940–70) when the **uses and gratifications model** proclaimed the active audience.
- 'Mighty media' (1970–present), when more sophisticated theoretical ideas recognised the long-term effects of media in societies where individuals and groups in the audience struggled to make their own readings in the face of dominant media messages.

Almighty media

The period of 'Almighty media' corresponds with the discussions above about the Payne Fund Studies. The suggestion here is that the researchers began from the premise that the media (i.e. in this case, the cinema film) 'did things to audiences' who sat passively in the theatre. This view could be found at opposite ends of the traditional political spectrum. The **Frankfurt School** of German scholars observed in horror the ways in which the Nazi propaganda machine held the majority of the German population in thrall in the 1930s, through the use of radio and cinema newsreels. When the Frankfurt scholars (Theodor Adorno, Max Horkheimer,

British cinema in the 1950s and 1960s produced two distinct kinds of youth pictures. The sensationalist aspects of youth culture were explored in films such as *Cosh Boy* (1952), but more common were liberal social problem films that tried to 'understand' youth, with titles such as *Mix Me a Person* (1962) and *Violent Playground* (1958). See Hill (1986) for an analysis of these and similar films.

Herbert Marcuse etc.) fled to the USA to escape Hitler's power, they began to recognise a similar problem in the United States. But here the problem was the great power of corporate America to dominate media production and to stifle what the scholars thought of as innovation or originality. In a sense, the Frankfurt School saw the US audience passively accepting the American Dream of boundless consumption (and also accepting American Cold War propaganda about the communist threat from the Soviet Union).

The Frankfurt School position tended to validate **high culture** over popular culture and there have been echoes of this approach within British culture at different times. For instance, the furore over the 'teddy boys', the first youth sub-group in the UK to define themselves via a style of dress (Edwardian = teddy) in the 1950s (see the margin entry above on *Rock Around the Clock*), referred to various aspects of 1950s cinema. High culture critics warned against the Americanisation of British youth culture and the influence of horror films and teen films featuring violence.

6.1 The youth gang depicted in *Cosh Boy*, one of the more sensationalist entries in a UK cycle of juvenile delinquency films made in the 1950s.

The debate about high culture and popular culture had an impact within formal education in the UK in the 1950s and 1960s – which again has echoes in contemporary debates. In his book *The Uses of Literacy* (1957), Richard Hoggart explored the ways in which contemporary mass-produced popular culture was beginning to displace the more traditional working-class culture he had

> Behaviourist psychology has often been studied in opposition to cognitive psychology. See Chapter 4 for discussion of the cognitive approach to reading films.

experienced in Leeds. The book proved influential and Hoggart went on to be one of the founders of British cultural studies. Other important names from this period include Stuart Hall and Paddy Whannel, who wrote *The Popular Arts* in 1964, influencing the development of film and media education in the UK at a time when teachers were beginning to bring films into the classroom. Stuart Hall then joined Richard Hoggart at the Birmingham Centre for Contemporary Cultural Studies (**CCCS**) (see below).

A different view of audiences, but one that still sees them as passive, has been derived from the work of behavioural scientists such as B. F. Skinner (1904–90). The **behaviourists** believed that, following close observation of the behaviour of particular groups or individuals in laboratory conditions, programmes of learning could be developed through repetition of rewards and punishments. In other words, the social behaviour of passive subjects could be shaped in specific ways, just as laboratory animals could be trained to respond to particular stimuli.

In an education context, behaviourism suggested *positive* ways in which children's learning could be improved. When these ideas were applied to the mass media, they tended to be used to support the identification of *negative* media effects. Behaviourist studies suggested that, for example, the repeated exposure of audiences to scenes of sex and violence would inevitably have an effect on subsequent behaviour – and that this would be a generally negative effect of increasingly violent behaviour and sexual promiscuity.

These ideas gained currency, especially in the USA, but also in the UK, partly because they seemed to be provable in scientific experiments (and also because they seemed like 'common sense'). In a practical sense, it was possible to make assumptions and then fund a project to find evidence. The techniques of the behaviourist scientists, developed in performing experiments on laboratory animals, could, it was argued, be applied to humans. A group of people could be given tests to determine their attitudes towards violent behaviour. They would then be exposed to violent imagery and re-tested. The results would show the effects of the exposure. This has been termed as the **effects model** of audience behaviour. It is important to note here that within film and media studies, the assumptions of the effects model were discredited a long time ago, but that within the popular discourse of pub conversations, phone-in programmes and newspaper columns, it has thrived and continues to do so.

The 'common sense' appeal of the effects model is one of its main weaknesses as a theoretical model. 'Common sense' is often the basis for **hegemonic** control over societies (see below). If we do not question claims that appear natural or self-evident, we will not learn much. Common sense suggested that the world was flat.

The behaviourists were working in similar territory to the Frankfurt School, but with quite different political objectives. They were not criticising media corporations – rather it was the nature of the learning process implied by the mass media that was the problem. The behaviourists were generally seen as right wing and promoting policies that would ensure that the behaviour of the mass of ordinary people could be controlled. But the work of the Frankfurt School and the behaviourists shared the same premise – a belief that the passive audience needed to be protected from harmful media messages. At this point, it is useful to consider the role of the BBFC as the UK film industry regulator. The BBFC is often caught in the firing line during controversies associated with media effects questions.

The BBFC and the audience

The British Board of Film Classification (which changed its title, replacing 'Censors' with 'Classification' following the acquisition of statutory powers under the 1984 Video Recordings Act) has in the last few years become highly effective in explaining its decisions on classification and publishing information on its very useful website,

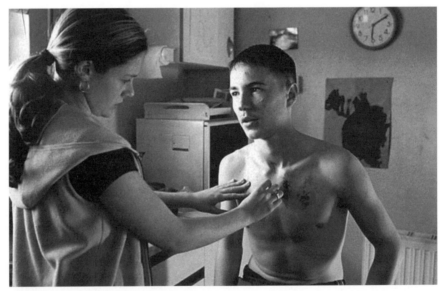

6.2 Annemarie Fulton and Martin Compston as brother and sister in *Sweet Sixteen*, a film about teenagers which was given an 18 Certificate by BBFC because of the constant use of 'offensive language'. The audiences who might identify with the central characters were unable to see the film on its cinema release, although certain schools screenings were later negotiated.

which now has a parallel students' site at <www.sbbfc.co.uk>. On this site is a Student Guide to classification as well as various case studies on specific films and downloadable reports that give an insight into how the Board responds to public opinion. (For more on the background to the BBFC, see Chapter 3.)

The new open face of the BBFC followed publication of written guidelines to classification in 1998 and the decision to hold extensive public consultations in 1999. The report (available on the website as *Sense and Sensibilities: Public Opinion and the BBFC Guidelines*) on these consultations showed that, in the main, the public agreed with the Board's conclusions and decisions. In other words, there was an endorsement of the view that audiences are quite sensible and able to make up their minds unless provoked by press campaigns. This view is echoed by academic research, funded by BBFC and other agencies, into 'Young People, Media and Personal Relationships' (2003), a **qualitative study** by David Buckingham and Sara Bragg. Buckingham and Bragg argue that children are capable of being critical viewers, that they do consider moral questions in respect of their use of the media and so on – overall a refutation of any simple notions that children are led by films and television (a more important medium in this debate). These findings have given the BBFC more confidence in its work and, especially, confidence that the decisions they make are largely consistent with general public opinion. A further example of this occured in research commissioned by BBFC and carried out by Guy Cumberbatch and Sally Gauntlett, entitled *Knowing it When You See it: The Difference between '18' and 'R18' Video Works:*

A viewing panel representing a wide cross-section of opinion from liberal to conservative was established. Participants watched a selection of sexually explicit film material under natural conditions in their own homes. Each recruit was given at least one full '18' film, one full 'R18' film and a compilation of six R18 excerpts. The viewing order of these was randomised and participants were not provided with any means of knowing the BBFC's classification. Telephone interviews focused on whether participants thought that the titles should be rated 18 or R18. The distinction between these two categories (and the consequences of this) had been fully explained at recruitment, at film delivery and was repeated at the start of each interview. Additionally, two focus groups (one female and one male) considered the arguments for and against the R18 classification of the kind of films watched in the compilation. (From the Summary of the Report)

The results were 'exceptionally clear-cut' with the participants confirming the BBFC decisions and in interviews demonstrating confidence in the distinction between 18 and R18 ('material which appears to be simulated is generally passed '18', while images of real sex are confined to the 'R18' category' (BBFC Guidelines, 2000: page 17).

This general confidence does not mean that there is no controversy about how audiences might be affected by films in the cinema or on video (which as it is less easily policed and can be replayed at will, is thought to be potentially more harmful to under-18s). There are still calls for more control over what audiences might see and also calls for more freedom. The BBFC Guidelines refer to the following main areas of concern – i.e. areas that examiners must consider in making classification decisions (as well as identifying any representations that are unlawful under other legislation, such as that concerning animal welfare etc.):

- **Theme** – what is appropriate for each age-related certificate (it is unlikely that any themes would be disallowed for over-18s, or even over-15s).
- **Language** – there is evidence that offensive language is an issue for significant elements of the general audience, especially in relation to films for younger audiences.
- **Nudity** – 'Natural nudity, providing there is no sexual context, is acceptable at all classification levels except 'Uc''.
- **Sex.**
- **Violence.**
- **Imitable techniques** – includes 'behaviour which young children are likely to copy . . . combat techniques, hanging, suicide and self-harm'.
- **Horror** – only in terms of 'the young and vulnerable being protected from too intense an experience'.
- **Drugs** – 'Any detailed portrayal of drug use likely to promote or glamorise the activity may be cut.'
  (All quotes taken from BBFC Guidelines, 2005.)

Powerless media and the active audience

During the 1940s, audience work shifted towards consideration of a more active audience. 'Active' in this sense meant that instead of media texts doing things to audiences, theorists considered the ways in which audiences might do things with the media texts that they used. For instance, audiences might watch a film to escape from everyday concerns, to learn something about a world different to their own, to help them rehearse their own thoughts about difficult social situations etc. This became known as the uses and gratifications model. To some extent, this is a straight reversal of the moral position taken in effects studies. Why should audiences not allow films to take them away from reality? If they feel better after seeing a film is that not that a positive thing? So goes the argument, and it is clear that certain uses of the film experience have definite social benefits. Audiences have learned how to flirt, how to kiss, how to behave in all sorts of social situations by watching stars on the cinema screen. They can also learn how to rob banks and break up a marriage, but this approach works on the basis that audiences can decide for themselves which kinds of behaviour they might seek to emulate.

Although active audience theories offered a corrective to the earlier theories, they were in turn critiqued. It was noted that advertisers and industrial corporations seeking to promote consumerism were keen to support such theories. Advertising could be justified because it was useful to consumers. DVDs are consumer products that can be bought for collections. Watching films becomes part of a consumer culture and thus sanctioned in a materialist society that asks us to keep on buying. Audiences seeking out films for particular purposes suggests a discerning and discriminating public, but the functioning of the market suggests that audiences can be bought to a certain extent and that they may be indulging themselves as much as selecting for use – fulfilling certain desires at the expense of others. This model also underestimates the will of large corporations to persuade audiences.

Mighty media: audience theories since the 1970s

Both the active and passive models of audience behaviour have been found wanting and since the 1970s more sophisticated models have developed. One of these is associated with work undertaken at the CCCS. Stuart Hall argued for a model of audience activity that allowed for different kinds of audience response from groups from different social backgrounds. Hall, and later David Morley and Charlotte Brunsdon were concerned with television viewing, mostly of news and current affairs, but the model also began to influence thinking about cinema audiences. Hall suggested three kinds of audience reading response:

- the preferred or **dominant**
- the **negotiated**
- the **oppositional**

The first of these suggested the kind of response that the text appeared to expect and that conformed to the prevailing views of the majority culture. This was argued by many theorists in the 1970s to be an example of the **hegemonic** control that dominant ideas in a culture exert. **Hegemony** describes a situation in which a population is under the control of a certain set of ideas. Importantly, this control is maintained not by force but by persuasion. In media and cultural terms, the majority audience is persuaded to support those in power. In film studies, you may come across references to the hegemonic power of Hollywood in dominating the international film industry.

However, Hall argued that not everyone would accept the idea of a preferred reading. Some audiences would negotiate a reading in which they accepted some, but rejected other, aspects of what they were being offered. Their **negotiated** readings would be significantly different. There might also be audiences who rejected everything about the preferred reading and who instead created their own reading in **opposition**. Morley and Brunsdon analysed an early evening television programme featuring news stories about the economy in order to discover what kind of ideological work was being carried out. They were intrigued by the sense of 'we' that such programmes assumed for the audience when discussing the economy and social issues. Who was this 'we' – was the audience an homogenous group? Morley then organised qualitative research among specific groups of viewers: managers, trade unionists, apprentices, students, student teachers etc. These groups watched selected programmes and discussed them. As Hall had originally requested, Morley was carrying out empirical research and, not surprisingly, he found enough examples of the three types of reading to suggest that Hall's initial ideas had validity.

Hall's ideas pushed audience studies into projects that were more concerned with both the identity issues among audience groups and the social context of viewing. Morley's research was a form of **ethnographic research** (see Chapter 7). Much of what followed was concerned with television rather than film. Where film was the focus, it was often a historical survey such as those conducted by Annette Kuhn and Jackie Stacey, exploring the experiences of audiences of women in the 1930s–1950s. More recently Matt Hills (2005) looked into the world of fans of Japanese horror in the USA (see the *Ringu* case study in Chapter 1). Hills conducted his research in the virtual world of a fan forum on the internet, where he found distinctive patterns of response to the Japanese film *Ringu* and its American remake *The Ring*. Hills' earlier book, *Fan Cultures* (2002), sets out some of the problems for scholars researching film audiences.

Researchers are drawn towards audiences for cult films (especially fans of cult horror films), if only because these are identifiable groups with their own means of discussing and presenting their views about films. It is possibly more difficult to research a range of fan responses and general audience behaviour in respect of more mainstream fans, as the audience itself is more diffuse. The problem, however, is similar to that of other forms of participant observation. Fans and academics do not necessarily get on and they speak slightly different languages, even though they study the same films. Hills is a 'scholar fan', trained as a professional scholar, but also a fan and he berates other academics who don't understand the fan position (Hills, 2002: 5). One of his targets is Martin Barker, who in 1998, with Kate Brooks, produced *Knowing Audiences: Judge Dredd – Its Friends, Fans and Foes*. However, Barker was at least interested in asking audiences what they thought of the film they had seen and in going to multiplexes to find out how the film was being promoted.

Audience studies is one of the most contentious areas in film and media studies and it has its fair share of in-fighting between academics about which are the most useful forms of research and which audience models are worthwhile adopting (Hills, for instance, is not dismissive of the Frankfurt School). It is not surprising then to discover that when there is a major controversy over a research report using the effects model or a campaign against a film thought too violent, it can sometimes lead to a dispute between academic positions as well as a spat between scholars and lobby groups. This was certainly the case with the *Crash* controversy in 1996 and with other instances when particular films were singled out for coverage in what is a protracted debate about 'media violence'. Martin Barker and

Julian Petley edited an important collection of essays entitled *Ill Effects* in 1997, with a second revised edition in 2001. This was followed by a book on the *Crash* controversy by Barker with Jane Arthurs and Ramaswami Harindranath, also in 2001. These essays comprehensively dismiss the arguments promoted to suggest that watching violent films leads to violent behaviour. Perhaps most influential has been the work of David Gauntlett whose essay appears in the 2001 edition of *Ill Effects*. Another version of material from that essay comprising the 'Ten Things Wrong with the Media "Effects" Model' can also be found on his website <theory.org.uk/david/effects.htm>. You can look up Gauntlett's arguments and decide for yourself if the case against the model is proven. We simply note two of the points he makes here. One is the artificiality of many research projects. Instead of talking or observing people who have visited a cinema or watched a DVD at home, selected subjects are shown videos in laboratory or classroom conditions. Second, the research project is effectively back to front. Instead of starting with a film that the researchers consider violent and 'testing' its effect on viewers, Gauntlett suggests that they should research what might have motivated offenders to become violent and assess their film viewing as part of more wide-ranging investigations. He quotes a survey that did this and that found no significant relationship between violent behaviour and film viewing.

However, this refutation of the effects model is problematic in the sense that it might lead to the conclusion that films have no effect. Film and media studies obviously believes that films do have effects – it was to study those effects that many academics embraced the new disciplines. But it is not the immediate effects of watching a single film that are important, but the development of an understanding of film culture over time. One aspect of this may be an issue of sensitisation or desensitisation to particular types of representation. It has been suggested, again in relation to issues of sex and violence, that audiences can become desensitised to shocking images over time through constant exposure. This is a common claim: 'Violent video games "desensitise" players' (*Daily Mail*, 17 August 2006). A long-term study of what is screened in terms of sex and violence may well reveal that depictions of violence are less frequent now than in, for example, the 1970s. Demonstrating a clear correlation of any kind between violent crimes and media representations is likely to prove extremely difficult.

One conclusion might be that watching films has effects, but that these effects vary from one person to another. The effects may be different in kind and in strength. There is no way of predicting what impact a single film title might have on audiences. Our only recourse is to rely on an independent film classification board that seeks to give advice on potentially offensive films and to monitor the level of satisfaction shown by the general public with the classification system. At the moment, the system seems to work. As an example of the ways in which the social context of film viewing can change, there are several case studies of classification decisions on the student website of the BBFC. One of these covers the history of submissions for *Straw Dogs* (UK/USA, 1971). Controversial and cut on its cinema release, *Straw Dogs* was denied a video certificate after the 1984 Video Recordings Act came into force. The major issue about the film concerned two acts of sexual violence that raised questions about the reaction of the main female character to a rape. Several re-submissions were made, but it was not until 2002 that an uncut video version of the film was given an 18 certificate. The case study includes the following findings:

> The issue of context was also important to the members of the public to whom the video was shown as part of a research exercise into the acceptability of images of sexual violence. A focus group of 26 people viewed *Straw Dogs*, with 20 people accepting '18' uncut as the most appropriate category, five suggesting only minor cuts, and only one favouring rejection. No respondent asked for major cuts of the kind required by the Board in 1999.
>
> Discussion in the subsequent focus group about the film was generally very positive, with most members finding it a powerful, compelling and well made work. The controversial scenes were not considered to be a gratuitous exploitation of sexual violence. It was felt that the quality of the filmmaking and the narrative context allowed the director to explore through them some difficult and complex issues. (<www.sbbfc.co.uk/case_study_strawdogs.asp>)

RESEARCH SUGGESTION
Visit the student website of the BBFC at <www.sbbfc.co.uk/student_guide_casestudies.asp> and select one of the recent case studies explaining why a specific classification system was awarded. It would be best to choose a film that you have seen recently. Do you agree with the reasoning behind the classification decision? Try applying some of the audience models discussed in this chapter to the film. Can you see any ways in which you could discuss what an 'active' audience might do with the film?

Is it clear that preferred, negotiated and oppositional readings are possible for the film?

What should we conclude from this? Over a period of 30 years, a film has moved from being unacceptable to being judged as a 'well made work' that at least some viewers found worthwhile in terms of exploring difficult and complex issues. The film has not changed, so are we desensitised now or have our attitudes and understanding of sexual behaviour and violence developed? Or, perhaps, if the BBFC had conducted a focus group in 1971 it would not have made the cuts for cinema release (which, it has subsequently been argued, confused audiences and had the opposite effect to that intended, making the film more, not less, offensive).

If there is some cause for optimism in the current practice of the BBFC, there is no general agreement on how to theorise about audience behaviour. Perhaps this is a good thing in a film studies context. As Toby Miller (2001: 304) argues, film students are often given potted histories of film studies that suggest a neat story of moving from authorship, to texts and then to audiences as a focus for attention. This, he argues, misses out the struggles between competing discourses of popular criticism, political campaigning, social science research etc. That is something I have tried hard not to do and I hope it is clear that there are still plenty of different ways of thinking about how to theorise audiences and their variety of behaviour.

References

Altenloh, Emilie (1914/2001), 'A Sociology of the Cinema: The Audience', transl. Katheen Cross, *Screen* Vol. 42 No, 3, Autumn.

Barker, Martin and Julian Petley (eds) (1997, 2nd ed 2001), *Ill Effects: The Media/Violence Debate* (London: Routledge).

Barker, Martin and Kate Brooks (1998), *Knowing Audiences: Judge Dredd – Its Friends, Fans and Foes* (Luton: John Libbey).

Barker, Martin with Jane Arthurs and Ramaswami Harindranath (2001), *The Crash Controversy: Censorship Campaigns and Film Reception* (London: Wallflower Press).

Brunsdon, Charlotte and David Morley (1978), *Everyday Television: 'Nationwide'* (London: BFI)

Everett, Peter (1986), *You'll Never Be Sixteen Again* (London: BBC).

Gripsrud, Jostein (1998), 'Film Audiences', in John Hill and Pamela Church Gibson (eds), *The Oxford Guide* to Film Studies (Oxford: OUP).

Gripsrud, Jostein (2002), *Understanding Media Culture* (London: Arnold).

Hill, John (1986), *Sex, Class and Realism: British Cinema 1956-63* (London: BFI).

Hills, Matt (2002), *Fan Cultures* (London: Routledge).

Hills, Matt (2005), 'Ringing the Changes: Cult Distinctions and Cultural Differences in US Fans' Reading of Japanese Horror Cinema', in Jay McRoy (ed.), *Japanese Horror Cinema* (Edinburgh: Edinburgh University Press).

Jensen, Klaus Bruhn (ed.) (2002), *A Handbook of Media and Communication Research: Qualitative and Quantitative Methodologies* (London: Routledge).

Kuhn, Annette (2002), *An Everyday Magic, Cinema and Cultural Memory* (London and New York: I.B. Tauris).

Miller, Toby (2001), 'Cinema studies doesn't matter; or, I know what you did last semester', in Matthew Tinkcom and Amy Villarejo (eds), *Keyframes: Popular Cinema and Cultural Studies* (London: Routledge).

Morley, David (1980), *The 'Nationwide' Audience* (London: BFI).

Sedgewick, John (1999), 'The Comparative Popularity of Stars in Mid-1930s Britain', *Journal of Popular British Cinema* No. 2: Audiences and Reception in Britain.

Stacey, Jackie (1993) *Star Gazing: Hollywood Cinema and Female Spectatorship* (London: Routledge).

Thorp, Margaret (1939/1946), *America at the Movies* (London: Faber and Faber).

7. Researching Audiences and the Film Market

This is a practical and descriptive chapter offering resources that could be used in student research projects. It also provides information to support work in other chapters, including the case studies in Chapters 3 and 4.

Film studies and media studies have a great deal to say about research. It is needed for several different purposes. **Production research** involves both work on background for the content of the film and on resources, permissions etc. for physical production activities. This is an important element in pre-production on any film, but is not our focus here. We are concerned with **market research**, tracking the performance of films in the marketplace, and **audience research,** creating a profile of audiences and their preferences and behaviour. It is important to recognise some of the fundamental differences in the types of research activity required for each purpose.

A distinction is made between **primary** and **secondary** research. Anything that involves collecting raw data (e.g. the box-office receipts of a cinema) or eliciting a direct response from audience members (e.g. interviewing individuals who have just seen a film) is *primary research*. Once the results of primary research are processed and presented as a report, they become available as *secondary sources*. A new researcher attempting a larger-scale exercise or perhaps comparing a current situation with a year or ten years earlier can go to various secondary sources for material.

A second distinction is made between **quantitative** and **qualitative research**. These terms generally refer to the methodologies employed within academic research programmes, but we can also use them to classify some industrial activities. In our example above, collecting box-office information is a number-crunching exercise, *quantifying* or measuring the size of the audience. An interview question about whether someone enjoyed a film, thought it controversial or worth recommending to someone else etc. is an example of *qualitative research.* This is not such a clear-cut distinction as primary/secondary, as qualitative statements can also be quantified: e.g. 70% of audiences said that the film was 'good' or 'very good'.

In this chapter, we will also be sliding between audience research and market research. In an industrial context, everything discussed here is effectively market research which could be defined as 'the process of systematic gathering, recording and analysing of data about customers, competitors and the market' (Wikipedia definition). Within the different sectors of the film industry, managers will have different marketing aims. In some cases, they will want to know about overall trends in the industry and in particular customer preferences. A cinema chain will look carefully at attendance patterns for different audience groups, spending behaviour regarding concessions, merchandising etc; a film production company will look at what kinds of films are popular in the contemporary market, which stars attract audiences etc; and a distribution company will seek out information that will help to sell a specific film.

Marketing organisations that specialise in film and media will generally offer two kinds of research data (or *market intelligence*) in relation to audiences: an overall audience profile for a territory, identifying trends in composition and behaviour (i.e. preferences), and an individual profile for specific films. Audience research is effectively an element of market research in relation to a market where consumption takes place in conditions unique to the filmed entertainment industry.

Finally, we need to distinguish between **industry research** and **academic research.** Industry research is primarily concerned with producing data and analyses that will enable film businesses to maintain their market position and become profitable. Academic research is designed to produce data and analyses that will increase our understanding of how films produce their meaning and are understood by audiences, and how the industry functions. Between these two relatively distinct positions, we can also recognise a third type of research, mainly concerned with *audience behaviour.* Some types of audience behaviour are related directly to the cinema visit and are therefore conducted for exhibitors, as noted above, often in conjunction with advertisers. Arbitron is an American marketing company specialising in reports on media opportunities for advertisers. Its 2002 survey of the American cinema audience is available from <www.arbitron.com/study_o/cinema_study.asp>. Once you get past the relentless message of advertising opportunities, this detailed survey gives an interesting picture of how time is spent going to the cinema and within the building itself. It also stresses the attempts that cinemas make to sell you something else besides the film. The ideal cinemagoer (for the cinema, selling audiences to an advertiser) emerges as a family that includes shopping and dining out as part of the cinema experience. (One surprising aspect of cinema advertising in the USA is that it is a relatively recent innovation. This comes as a shock considering that the UK has experience of 70 years or more of cinema ads.) The findings also emphasise that cinema is a communal activity for all age groups in the USA. Over 80% of interviewees in each age group agreed with the statement (about going to the cinema): 'It's something I like to do with my friends'. Like several other research projects referenced in this chapter, Arbitron explain their data-collection methods in detail.

Other forms of research into audience behaviour not associated with advertising are conducted on behalf of lobby groups or regulators. Lobby groups will often have a specific hypothesis to 'prove' about audience behaviour, with researchers funded to find evidence. Regulators are possibly more objective (e.g. the BBFC carried out research to help them reform classification of films utilising feedback from public consultation). Much of the research into audience behaviour is controversial because of the methodologies used. The BBFC and some of the methodologies used by researchers for lobby groups are discussed in Chapter 6.

Industry research

The cinema industry in North America and the UK has had a very long history of collection of box-office receipts. It might be argued that this is an ideal entertainment medium for the collection of data. The box office must keep receipts for accounting and tax purposes. For mainstream films, tickets for the same film are being sold in cinemas all over the country at more or less the same time. As the system became increasingly automated and computerised in the 1990s, it was possible to give an almost immediate verdict on a film's popularity. With the internet being used to publish the 'top line' of results for new film releases, it is now possible for anyone to find out whether a film might be counted a success by Sunday afternoon in North America, following a Friday release (the industry itself will have a pretty good idea by Saturday morning).

Box-office figures are so important that their collection has become almost an industry in itself. The major company collecting data worldwide is Nielsen EDI, part of the Dutch information company VNU. Included in VNU's holdings are other companies that track music, DVD and book sales, television ratings, internet 'hits' etc., as well as industry publications such as *The Hollywood Reporter*. VNU companies also carry out market research into every aspect of consumer behaviour, and according to its website, VNU's 'strategic focus for Marketing Information' is:

- be the global authority on consumer behavior;
- provide more detailed information on consumers and markets (global markets are increasingly complex);
- offer expert analysis and fact-based advice;
- strengthen client relationships through delivery of value added insights.

All of this is accompanied by 'Media Measurement and Information' (see <www.vnu.com>). VNU's global reach in regards to box office includes the UK, but as yet in cinema terms not important territories such as India and China. In order to get as full a picture as possible of global film audiences, it is necessary to consult a variety of sources.

Much of the industry research into audiences is too expensive to be easily accessible for film and media students. In the UK, research into film audiences is undertaken by BMRB under the heading of **CAVIAR** and distributed via Pearl and Dean and Carlton, the companies selling cinema advertising. CAVIAR offers film industry executives two main services: (1) an annual report on the UK film audience, identifying changes in audience composition and behaviour; (2) a quarterly 'film monitor':

> Over 120 films are profiled every year and the film monitor now boasts a library containing more than 1,000 film profiles, going as far back as the early 1980s. The demographics included for each film are:
>
> • sex
> • social Class
> • age
> • household composition
> • regions
> (<business.pearlanddean.com/research/caviar.html.)

These reports are detailed and the Annual Report plus film monitor costs around £12,000. Fortunately, some of the 'headline' results of this research are published for free access by the UK Film Council. The Statistics Yearbook published by UK Film Council is a very valuable resource and should be downloaded by every serious student of British cinema. It combines CAVIAR data with other material and is one of the activities of the Research and Support Unit (RSU) at the Film Council. The RSU has these aims as part of its remit:

• To gather and maintain up-to-date market intelligence on film in the UK and internationally, and respond to enquiries about the data.
• To undertake research projects to support and inform UKFC strategic development. (<www.ukfilmcouncil.org.uk/information/statistics/rsuwork/> accessed 15 June 2006)

As well as the *Statistical Yearbook*, the RSU produces occasional bulletins (also downloadable) and other reports, one of which is explored below.

In North America, similar headline data to that reported by UK Film Council is available from the **MPAA**. Useful data is also obtainable from **EIRIN/MPAAJ** in Japan and **CBFC** in India, but the single most useful source of information that is accessible to everyone is the **European Audiovisual Observatory,** which operates the **LUMIERE** database of film admissions and the **FOCUS** series of annual reports on all the world's film markets (see <www.obs.coe.int/medium/film.html>).

Analysing the data

The main variable in general cinema audience data in the UK is 'frequency of cinema visits'. These figures are collected via a sample of 'face-to-face interviews' with 3,000+ people in the UK aged 4 and over, selected according to **ACORN** criteria developed by the marketing organisation CACI and widely used in the UK and globally for 25 years. ACORN places individuals in lifestyle groupings such as 'Wealthy Achievers' or 'Hard pressed', each of which is then broken down into more precise demographic classifications. The sample is selected to be representative of the UK population across all the ACORN groupings according to their distribution across the country.

The standard questions attempt to find cinemagoers who visit:

- at least once per year
- once a month or more.

From this data, it is possible to plot trends in cinemagoing from year to year, and because the sample is carefully structured, to measure changes in the demographic profile of the audience – considering frequency in relation to gender, age and social class in particular. Historically, the cinema audience has shown significant changes in composition over time. In 2004, there were more females than males in the population (51%:49%), but 73% of males visited the cinema at least once per year compared to 72% of females. A glance at the overall age profile of the UK population will show that there are significant 'bulges' when there are more people in a particular age group (see Fig. 7.1). As these bulges pass through different age groups, the effect on cinema audiences can be dramatic because the frequency of attendance is markedly different. Some concern is being expressed as the 15–24 age group is going to shrink over the next few years as the mid-1980s bulge moves up into their late 20s. The UK population has bulges at roughly 20-year intervals – the result of increases in the birth rate during the late 1940s, mid-1960s and mid-1980s. The current bulge seems to be less pronounced in babies born around 2004. Significant immigration of people aged 20-35 following the expansion of the European Union may alter the overall demographic profile.

This base data is then explored in relation to the kinds of films that are more likely to be watched by women (confirming what some might see as a stereotype, the female audience prefers to watch romantic comedies, romance and family dramas, whereas male audiences favour action, horror, comedy (but not romantic comedy)). It is possible to estimate a skew in the audience for the most watched films – i.e. those films watched by a larger proportion of males or females in the sample.

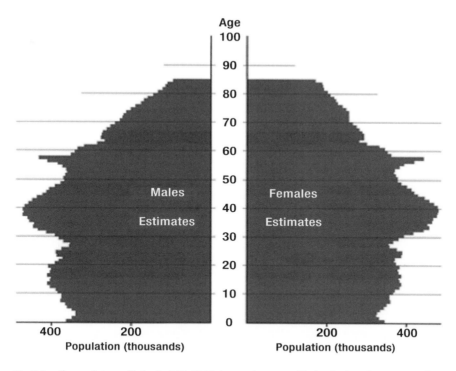

Fig 7.1   The population profile for the UK in 2004 showing the impact of births, deaths and migrations in the age range 0–85.

The UK Film Council publishes tables showing an indication of this skewing process in relation to age, region, social class and ethnicity. These skews can be quite dramatic, with big disparities in frequency of attendance between London and other regions.

The demographic data can also be related to a preference for Top 20 films and to UK films. The latter is particularly important for the UK Film Council, and it must be worried that younger audiences are less likely to watch British films than older audiences. This is partly explained by the small numbers of British films made for young people, but it may also be a function of popular culture that in the last 20 years has become more globalised/American influenced (television also sees younger audiences preferring American drama to mainstream UK drama series).

More intriguing may be the finding that middle-class (ABC1) cinemagoers are more attracted to Top 20 films (as well as Top UK films) than C2DE audiences. This is a very long-standing difference that can be traced back to the 1930s when **Mass-Observation** found an aversion to the middle-class Southern voices of most British films among the communities of 'Worktown' (Bolton) and a preference for Hollywood (and northern stars such as Gracie Fields and George Formby) (see Chapter 6).

Preview screenings

One well-known strategy for film producers and distributors is the preview screening. The practice of showing a completed screening to an invited audience has been adopted for two quite different purposes. In the UK, such screenings are usually held in order to generate a buzz, leading to word of mouth on a new film. Distributors will offer free seats at a preview screening to groups likely to fit the intended audience profile of the film. Approaches might be made to student unions or through offers in newspapers or radio stations. In these cases, the previews are held shortly before a release and are effectively part of the promotional strategy for the distributor. With the growth of online media such as 'upcoming film releases' websites, bulletin boards and blogs, you will often notice reports from someone who has attended a preview screening.

American practice is to call trailers 'previews' and preview screenings 'test screenings'.

The second purpose of a preview is to give the producer/distributor direct feedback on a film that may not yet be a final edit. In this case, the audience may be asked to complete a feedback questionnaire designed to gauge reaction to particular elements of the narrative. Sometimes this might lead to a decision to change an ending, remove certain scenes or to increase the focus in the marketing campaign on particular aspects of the film. This practice appears to be common in Hollywood, but is relatively rare in the UK for British films.

> Hey folks, Harry here . . . this is an extremely early test screening for a Martin Scorsese picture. Nearly 5 months out – he's finally putting his film in front of an audience, gauging and taking note of exactly what works and doesn't work with his film. (<nitti.aintitcool.com>, 7 June 2006)

These kinds of preview screenings are usually for mainstream films. Previews may take place in public cinemas outside normal opening hours (mornings, late night), in special preview cinemas used mainly for industry events (in the UK, several smaller cinemas in the West End are available purely for business use) or sometimes in particular venues related to the theme of the film, the interests of sponsors etc. The location of the screening and the atmosphere created could have a significant effect on what audiences feel about the films they see. More specialised films are likely to be shown at film festivals as a means of previewing, sometimes as gala screenings for cast, crew and friend or as Q & As (question-and-answer sessions with a director, writer or star present to discuss the film afterwards with audience members). These screenings can also help to generate word of mouth. However, in many ways, the best way of gauging audience reaction is to visit a cinema with a paying audience.

Darren Aranofsky's film *The Fountain* premiered at the Venice Film Festival in 2006. It was booed at the press screening, but then given a 10 minute standing ovation at a public screening the next day. (Geoffrey Macnab, *Guardian* 7/9/06)]

Cultural cinema and public funds

Some of the most interesting research into cinema use is undertaken by market research agencies or consultants on behalf of publicly funded specialised cinemas or arts agencies. Commercial cinema pays for data on audiences and may well be interested in new audiences and how to reach them. The bottom line, however, is profitability. The publicly funded sector is interested in the social benefits of cinemas and film culture. Research is undertaken to find out what people actually want, how they use facilities and what kinds of barriers there might be to greater access to a more diverse film culture. The public sector has a wider range of objectives, but it still needs evidence about how money is spent and if the benefits generated are worthwhile. Here are two examples of audience research with a clear social benefit focus.

Leeds Film Festival

Most of the UK's large cities have a modern art cinema complex, but Leeds has long suffered by comparison with Manchester, Sheffield and Liverpool. It compensates by having two well-established film festivals and a municipal commitment to film culture. The Leeds International Film Festival has been innovative in many ways, not least in finding new venues and embracing video games and new media. In 2001, it sought to find out more about African-Caribbean and Asian 16–18 year-olds, a distinct audience group that it believed was possibly under-represented in the festival audience. **Qualitative research** was undertaken by a local marketing organisation and funded by a New Audiences scheme managed by the then regional arts organisation.

The 1991 Census suggested a target population of around 2,300 black and Asian 16–19 year-olds in Leeds. Three focus groups were formed comprising 15 Asian females, 13 Asian males and a mixed-gender group of ten African-Caribbeans. All the participants were non-attenders of the film festival. The researchers taped the discussions and transcribed them. The overall findings of the research reveal some of the problems faced by a specialised cinema organisation attempting to attract a diverse range of audiences. The young people were to a certain extent satisfied by what was being shown by mainstream cinema and were unaware of the festival and what it offered. In particular, they were not attracted by the festival brochure – in many ways both the major source of information about what is showing and the main marketing tool for creating a festival brand. The design and layout of the brochure was not appealing and this did not help to promote content that was already to a certain extent off-putting because it did not reflect familiar mainstream concerns (especially with the inclusion of 'ancient films' and the relative absence of stars and celebrities the target group recognised). The problem here is that festival brochures must focus on a core audience with very different tastes. The solution has to be a range of promotional materials and brands that are appropriate for different audiences. This is more expensive, but there are also opportunities for different sponsors to be involved.

Qualitative research with face-to-face contact allows researchers to tease out a variety of responses, and the final report was able to suggest a range of possible strategies for future audience work, many of which were suggested by the target groups themselves, who were interested in ideas beyond the mainstream, but possibly not in the same way that older audience members might be. There were also findings in relation to perceived differences in cinemagoing within the Asian community (such as attending events in family groups of either older or younger relatives). The target group was also conscious of not wanting to be singled out by promotional materials, but rather made to feel more welcome by a general sense of being part of a multicultural scene.

This kind of research was clearly useful for the specific festival in question, but was also valuable for similar festivals and specialised cinemas in other parts of the country. Such research work is circulated within networks and complements work undertaken centrally by the RSU at the UK Film Council and other national agencies.

The impact of local cinema

In November 2005, the UK Film Council published a report on 'The Impact of Local Cinema'. This collated research funded by several agencies focusing on five local cinemas in different parts of the UK:

- Lonsdale (2 screens, 150 seats), Annan, Dumfries and Galloway, Scotland (pop. 8,000).
- Curzon (1 screen, 380 seats), Clevedon, Somerset (pop. 22,000).
- Rio (1 screen, 402 seats), Dalston, London
- Metro (1 screen, 126 seats), Derby.
- Savoy (3 screens, 273 seats), Penzance, Cornwall (pop. 17,000)

This Local Cinema research can be downloaded from the UK Film Council website at <www.ukfilmcouncil.org.uk/information/statistics/localcinemaproject/>. There is also information for researchers on this project and advice on similar work at <www.ukfilmcouncil.org.uk/information/statistics/lcprsrchinf/> (both accessed 16 August, 2006).

The objectives of the research were much wider in scope than simply audience studies. Beginning from the premise that the multiplex building programme in the UK had been largely confined to urban areas of high population, the aim was to study how cinema functioned in a social, economic and environmental sense in areas without a multiplex. Aspects of the final report are interesting for audience study, as they do point to important issues that are not immediately obvious. In a small town with limited amenities, the social function of the cinema is very important, encouraging people to use the town centre and to become part of a community (as distinct from sitting at home and watching satellite television).

The five local cinemas surveyed include two city-based cinemas offering a specialised programme, raising different questions about serving a local community. The Metro in Derby and Rio in Dalston cater mainly for 'a particular sub-group of the local population – typically described by the cinemas as predominantly middle class, middle-aged, well-educated and interested in independent film'. However, without attempting to compete with multiplexes, both cinemas also offer screening programmes and events to other local audiences.

In the small towns, it is often the case that older teenagers and young adults will be prepared to travel (up to 20 miles) to larger towns for a wider choice of entertainment. This means that the local cinema focuses mainly on audiences of families and children and older adults.

The Lonsdale, Annan, similarly caters well for families, particularly those with young children. Among its most successful films in 2003 were *Peter Pan*, *The Haunted Mansion* and *Looney Tunes: Back in Action*, and 60% of the annual screenings were of films were certificate PG or U. However, the cinema also does well with older people, and this is a reflection of both the cinema's programming (which includes weekly matinees with free tea and biscuits for older audiences) and the profile of the local population – Annan has a higher than average proportion of pensioners among its residents.

7.2 The Lonsdale Cinema, Annan, a small local cinema in South West Scotland.

The Curzon, Clevedon, views its audience as a mixture of family groups, and adults (predominantly women) aged 35 or older. Its programme therefore caters for both groups. A third of the screenings are of PG or U certificate films (70% are films of 12A and below). However, in the top ten most popular films shown at the cinema during 2003 were *Calendar Girls*, *Chicago*, *Love Actually* and *The Hours*, films which appealed to the older, female members of the audience.

In addition, the cinemas also offered a series of events, such as these in Annan:

- Saturday-morning birthday parties for young children, involving private screening and special trip to the projection box.
- Regular end-of-term screenings for several local primary and secondary schools.
- Regular private screenings for local youth groups, such as the Girls' Brigade, Scouts and Beavers.
- Weekly tea and biscuit matinees for older people.
- Weekly world cinema screenings.
- Occasionally hired by local groups for special fund-raising events.

Small mainstream cinemas in market towns (Annan) and seaside resorts (Clevedon) offer an alternative to more expensive and, for young families and older cinemagoers, more 'challenging' urban multiplex experiences: 'Parents are probably more willing for them to come here on their own than travel to Carlisle. And so they can have their bit of independence by coming here without mum and dad.' (Regular Lonsdale visitor). The smaller specialised urban cinemas attract an audience with similar, if more robustly expressed, views:

> You do not get the kids here so often: that puts me off going to a mainstream cinema, with kids screaming. You often can't hear anything, and I can't watch the film properly . . . that's why I come here. Because you know that people generally are going to be avid film fans (regular Metro visitor).
>
> I think that is what independent cinema is all about . . . it's not for the young people to hang out. It's to appreciate the movie (regular Rio visitor).

These comments represent a real dilemma to many cinema managers. How do you cater for different audiences, attracting one group without alienating others? In a commercial cinema, it is possible to focus on the one or two groups that will fill the cinema and provide the necessary revenue. In a publicly funded or supported cinema (many small cinemas will receive some form of public funding in order to provide the social benefits discussed here) favouring one group over another is less justifiable. Similar comments about attitudes towards others in the audience are echoed in a different kind of survey presented in *The Place of the Audience* (Jancovich et al., 2003). This book is an academic study of 'the cultural geographies of consumption', primarily in the city of Nottingham. It is a form of **longitudinal**

study in which the authors trace the changing use of cinemas and the social context of film consumption over the whole period of cinema history. It is one of a number of historical surveys that have used a variety of research methods, including forms of oral history and reminiscence – discussing memories of cinemagoing with older people – and questionnaires. The Nottingham researchers asked questions about the specialised cinema provision in the city, which developed from a film society in 1950 into the current Broadway Media Centre complex:

> Some respondents referred to the place as 'arty farty', while others described it as 'snooty', 'trendy' and 'elitist' . . . for both those who identified and disidentified with the Broadway, the cinema was discussed in terms of an opposition between entertainment and cultural knowledge, in which both groups associate the Broadway with the values of cultural knowledge rather than entertainment. (Jancovich *et al.*, 2003: 222)

The Place of the Audience is a useful survey and an excellent source of material that is taken up in Chapter 8 on film culture. It prompts several ideas that might be adopted by groups of students undertaking research into local film history and film culture. This is another area in which 'non-academic' researchers have plenty to offer. Most major towns and cities have a local historian interested in the cinemas that once operated locally and there is often a local publication available. The Cinema Theatre Association has members who have worked in cinema exhibition or have had an interest in cinema architecture and it offers useful resources for local research (see <www.cinema-theatre.org.uk/>). Other useful reference sources for local cinema history include the Regional Film Archives (listed on <www.bufvc.ac.uk/faf/members.htm>) and the Insight Gallery of the National Media Museum in Bradford (<www.nationalmediamuseum.org.uk>).

There is a wealth of material for research into audiences and cinemas – both as secondary sources and as examples of methodologies. Film studies still needs more, so now is a good time to start.

The Place of the Audience includes the questionnaire given out in Nottingham.

RESEARCH SUGGESTION
Carry out a small-scale research project into the cinemagoing habits of your local population. Review the discussion of research into the impact of local cinemas in this chapter and draw up a list of questions that will inform an analysis of local cinemagoing. Focus on the audiences for at least two cinemas used by local people, ideally a larger multiplex cinema and a smaller community-based cinema. Negotiate with cinema managers to get access to audiences. You should also interview the managers. Analyse your results in terms of the expectations of the cinema managers and the comments by audience members.

References

Jancovich, Mark and Lucy Faire, with Sarah Stubbings (2003), *The Place of the Audience: Cultural Geographies of Film Consumption* (London: BFI).

<www.bmrb.co.uk>

<business.pearlanddean.com/research/caviar.html>

<www.carltonscreen.com>

<www.cbfcindia.tn.nic.in/statistics.htm>

<www.eirin.jp/english/index.html>

<lumiere.obs.coe.int/web/search/>

<www.mpaa.org>

<www.obs.coe.int>

8. The Culture of Film Viewing

How important is social context in terms of film viewing? This chapter considers how the actual watching of films has changed over time and finishes with a consideration of viewing culture in a digital environment.

The French watch films in a theatre as if they were in a cathedral – with awe and reverence. In India, going to a movie is more like going on a picnic – the audience chats, sings, wanders out for a smoke.(Meenakshi Shedde, 'Bollywood Cinema: Making Elephants Fly', *Cineaste*, Vol. XXXI, No. 3, Summer 2006)

During the evolution of the film audience in the 100 years or so of cinema, the viewing experience has almost gone full circle for significant groups of cinemagoers. In the 1890s and early 1900s, many people would have experienced cinema as a fairground attraction – literally so in some cases, with filmshows staged in tents on a fairground or in meeting halls and other buildings used for public events. Gradually, permanent venues developed. In the USA, these were known as nickelodeons and were often little more than high street store spaces converted into small cinemas seating 50–300 people on wooden chairs or benches.

> Unknown in December 1904 (according to *Variety*), nickelodeons were established so quickly that by 1910, estimates ranged from 5,000 to 10,000 across the USA (Gomery, 1992: 18).

You may have experienced something similar as part of a contemporary film festival, with short films being shown in clubs and bars, projected from DVDs. Nowadays, the licensing of public screenings is more carefully regulated, but otherwise the similarities are there. In some parts of the world, cinema has nearly always been like this. In Nigeria, for instance, one of the world's most popular film cultures (sometimes referred to as 'Nollywood' and now claimed to be the No. 3

8.1 Keighley Picture House, one of the early 'purpose-built' cinemas sited in a manufacturing town in West Yorkshire, opened in 1913 and was still open in 2007.

industry behind Hollywood and India) exists almost solely on video films watched at home. Occasionally, people go to improvised cinemas:

> The power of the ['occult movie'] genre is evident during a visit to one of Nigeria's improvised backstreet cinemas. The cinema is essentially a grimy concrete shelter with a billygoat tied up by the door. Inside, a dozen or so men and women are watching a Nollywood video on a small TV.
>
> The crowd sway and click their fingers during musical interludes, and giggle and shove each other during comic passages. But they watch enthralled when a woman in the grip of an occult mania is exorcised by a man in a giant blue turban and flowing robe. (Jeevan Vasagar, *Guardian* 23 March 2006)

For much of the 20th century, cinema was the principal location for film culture. Purpose-built cinemas began to appear in the UK from around 1910–12 and several early cinemas are still showing films today. They tended to seat 300–500 people and their audience was relatively downmarket. In the 1920s, cinema began to appeal more directly to middle-class patrons and the idea of an evening at the cinema as a glamorous night out began to develop. The period from the mid-1920s to the late 1930s has been seen by some commentators as a Golden Age of **super cinemas**. The biggest and most magical of the cinemas of this era in the UK were the Astorias, Gaumonts and Granadas. The Finsbury Park Astoria was conceived in what in the USA was known as the atmospheric style. The ceiling of the auditorium was painted like a night-time sky with twinkling stars, and from the arch over the screen, turrets and minarets spread out as in a Moorish fantasy. The Moorish idea was followed through downstairs in the auditorium with a water fountain that might have graced a square in the Alhambra at Granada. In Streatham in south London, the Astoria had an Egyptian theme and other cinemas explored Spanish and Italian fantasies.

The Finsbury Park Astoria became a famous venue for rock concerts in the 1970s as the The Rainbow and is now owned by the the Universal Church of the Kingdom of God, which has restored it to its former 1930s glory.

The super cinemas of the 1930s seated 3,000–4,000 people for single screenings. The Kilburn Gaumont State is reputed to have had room for 4,000 waiting in its 'crush halls' for the next performance, and a restaurant/cafe capable of seating 400. Many cinemas built in this period had restaurants or cafés (with full service for high tea), as well as ballrooms for dancing. In many ways, going to the

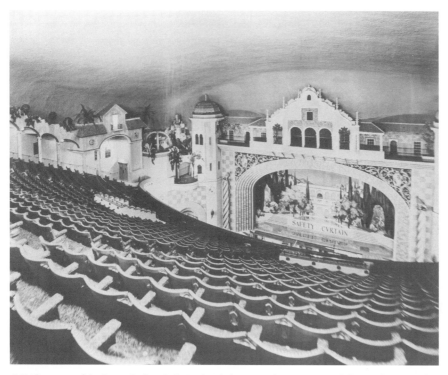

8.2 The interior of the Astoria Finsbury Park (London) built in 1930 for Paramount and showing the extent of the 'Moorish fantasy' decor in this super cinema.

cinema in a city-centre cinema in the late 1920s and 1930s was much like going to the theatre or the opera today.

In the late 1930s and again in the 1950s, the consolidation of the cinema exhibition business in the UK led to an increased emphasis on cinema brands for the three main circuits of Odeon, Gaumont and ABC (the Odeon and Gaumont chains were both owned by Rank and eventually merged). Cinemas built by these chains (as distinct from those they took over from smaller chains) were more functional and standardised (although the Odeon cinemas were certainly distinctive and are perhaps now best remembered in the form of the company's flagship, the Odeon, Leicester Square, still the most prestigious cinema in the UK, opened in 1937). This standardisation led to a more uniform viewing and entertainment experience across the country, as there was an Odeon and/or ABC in every main town and suburb, as well as city centre. The 1950s saw cinemagoing become an organised leisure activity that became part of youth culture in particular as

Circuit cinemas encouraged a sense of community by setting up children's clubs that featured Saturday-morning screenings. *ABC Film Review* was a magazine featuring films released on the ABC circuit and sold in its cinemas. Both these long-standing ideas have been adopted by contemporary cinema managers – although children's clubs are now frequented more by middle-class children in art cinemas rather than working-class children in the ABC.

that sector of the overall audience profile became more important. One feature of this was that as popular music became more youth orientated, it was often the larger circuit cinemas that had the capacity and the stage facilities to host tours of pop music acts. As commercial television drew away the older audience from the mid-1950s onwards, some of the cinemas that had closed re-opened as bingo halls, attempting to entice that older audience back for a different kind of entertainment.

Up until the late 1960s, despite the closure of large numbers of older and smaller halls, cinemas remained part of the community. Cinemas still existed in most town centres and in the suburbs of most large cities. Anyone could go to the cinema and still experience a reasonably inexpensive entertainment offer. Nevertheless, that experience was changing. Gradually, the cinema programme shrank and instead of the two features plus cartoon, newsreel etc. that made up a full programme for a night out, audiences got used to the idea of a single feature. They may have accepted this because the other elements in the programme had become less relevant as television advanced – but allied to the lack of investment in the fabric of cinema buildings, this gave an overall impression that cinema was declining.

RESEARCH SUGGESTION
You can discover something about how the film culture of the area in which you live has changed by studying some of the newspaper records in your local reference library. If you look at the local newspaper cinema listings (usually on microfiche) for the 1920s and the mid 1950s you should find that in your locality there were several cinemas showing a wide variety of films. How does this compare to what is available now?

In the 1980s, that decline seemed inevitable once the possibility of video rental was fully realised. As with bingo, some cinemas embraced the new medium by setting up video stores within the cinema building, perhaps utilising the space where the café or bar used to be in the 1950s. Some exhibitors even attempted to set up video cinemas – either as new operations, in non-traditional venues (in pubs) or in existing cinema premises. But cinema exhibitors were caught in a downward spiral. Because of cinema closures, in most local communities there was only one cinema (possibly crudely twinned or tripled), changing films once per week. But at the video shop it was possible to rent a film from a comparatively large selection. The more cinemas that closed because they could not sustain a large audience, the more appealing the video rental shop appeared.

Video in the 1980s

It is perhaps worth exploring in more detail the impact of the video revolution in the 1980s. The whole history of cinemagoing/film watching is important in understanding audience issues, but the 1980s experience is still relatively recent (and therefore memories are easily to hand if you wish to research it) and it has several potential lessons to teach us about film viewing culture.

As a new technology, video was seized on by the pornography industry (just as DVD, the internet, mobile phone technology etc. in the succeeding years). In the USA this meant the rapid rise of a hard-porn sector. In the UK, both soft porn and extreme violence became available in a host of largely unlicensed/unregulated new outlets, often as a video equivalent of top-shelf magazines – with the two on offer together in local newsagents. The result was that films that might not have made it into local cinemas were now available in local shops. Audiences were introduced to a wider range of viewing material. This included material that had been shown in cinemas, but which some would-be viewers might not have wanted to watch in a public cinema. Now they could watch it in the privacy of their own home. They could also play the video more than once and select scenes for repeat viewings.

Video rental took off in the UK faster than in most other territories because of the long tradition of renting rather than buying television sets and then VCRs. This allowed more UK homes to get access to a VCR quickly. The fact that UK VCR manufacturers/renters favoured VHS over Sony's rival Betamax format also helped VHS rentals to come out on top.

In 1979, when I was 12 years old, we got our first video recorder. The local video store was a few hastily cleared shelves in Hurley's record shop, run by two middle-aged men, Archie and Cliff, who knew what the public wanted: a complete set of Clint Eastwood movies and an impressive array of modern horror films. (Jones, 2002: 1)

These opening lines of Darryl Jones' book *Horror: A Thematic History in Fiction and Film,* perfectly capture the sense of wonder and liberation that many 12-year-olds must have felt when videocassettes began to appear in corner shops.

Two older horror fans' experiences of video (and magazines, late-night film screenings and festivals) can be found in Newman (1988) and Kermode (1997).

One inevitable outcome of this was a **moral panic** about the corruption of audiences, especially minors. The brief period of video freedom ended in the UK in 1984 with a new statutory power to regulate the presentation of videotape material, using revised certification categories decided by the BBFC. (Jones tells us that he watched many horror films at home with his mother that were subsequently banned.) Within a few years, the moral panic had shifted to satellite television and then to DVD. Several of the **video nasties** (i.e. horror films with 'unacceptable' themes or depictions of violent acts) refused a certificate after 1984 have now been re-submitted and classified without fuss (although some titles have still been refused a certificate). The important changes were the development of new approaches to certification and regulation and the potential broadening of film viewing habits. A third development was the shift in status and appeal that the possible divergence of cinema and video audiences produced.

As had happened earlier in cinema history, the 1980s saw a change in the social class composition of the cinema audience. Whereas in the 1950s, cinema in the UK had been a predominantly working-class form of entertainment, by the 1980s the dwindling audience was becoming more middle class. As cinema ceased to be mass entertainment, its core working-class audience began to migrate towards video, arguably for two reasons. First, video was cheaper – one rental fee could be shared by several viewers – and second, the wider range of popular genres, including comedy, action, martial arts etc. as well as horror and erotic thrillers was more appealing than the limited selection of titles available at the cinema. In the early 1980s, it was small, independent video distributors who led the industry, rather than the Hollywood studios, which were slow to exploit the new video market. As a consequence, new 'straight to video' stars developed, such as the martial arts star, Cynthia Rothrock. Later, when Hollywood did learn to love video, it became apparent that certain films could do very well on video release, even though they might have failed at the cinema box office. There could be several reasons for this, but one must surely be that video attracted a different audience, which did not necessarily go to the cinema.

The initial video boom had further effects. For instance, it threatened the survival of 16mm film, the format that had allowed films to be seen in non-theatrical venues since the 1930s. These included local film societies, institutional cinemas in schools, prisons etc. and in cinemas on ships and for in-flight screenings on long-distance air services. Although 16mm gave a better image than video, it could not compete on cost grounds and video gradually replaced film in many of these sectors. The main concern here was what would happen to the hundreds of titles in film libraries – could they all be converted to video? Those who did not want to change were threatened by the lack of viability for the format caused by the switchover in other sectors. (Those with the biggest investment in 16mm, the film societies, struggled on until DVD projection emerged as their saviour in the early 2000s.)

If the first impact of video was via rental, possibly the more fundamental shift came with retail video. Hollywood was suspicious of video at first and the studios were reluctant to let anyone own a copy of a film that conceivably they might re-release. When Hollywood films were first distributed for rental, the price of the same videocassette to a private customer was over £80. Eventually, this price came down to a more realistic £12–15 and video retail began in earnest. Very quickly, retail sales, driven by massive numbers for certain key titles, overtook rental income. How do we explain this and what changes did it suggest in viewing culture?

The possibility of owning a video copy and viewing it as many times as required over a long period – and possibly lending the tape to others – did change viewing habits. Its first noticeable impact was on films for children – films to be watched in a family context and films in front of which small children could be safely 'parked' (a practice that prompted another form of moral panic among those without small children). One fear of the studios and local exhibitors might have been that this practice would seriously damage the audience numbers for such films at the cinema. However, as numerous subsequent research reports have suggested, consumers who regularly buy videos (now DVDs) are very often frequent cinemagoers. A family may see a film in the cinema and then buy a video copy as soon as it is released for repeated home viewings. Favourite films have become like books, so that they can be passed down to younger children (although videotape is certainly more fragile than a book, and DVDs, although physically more robust, can be scratched and become unplayable).

The ownership of films on video has had various consequences. We can identify the collectability factor as individuals buy copies to keep. There may be several different motivations here. Collections may be important because they focus on favourite stars or directors, specific genres, foreign-language collections etc. They may be collected as an inspiration for production/creativity, to confer prestige on the owner, for use in education or simply as favourite films to be watched repeatedly. See Dinsmore (1998) for a detailed research account of two interviews with film collectors.

There have always been mechanisms for seeing certain films again and therefore a canon of culturally valued films as well as simply a list of popular films has been with us since the 1930s. Hollywood would remake certain films and re-release others. Film societies and specialist cinemas would show films celebrated in film history and, up until the 1980s, there were significant numbers of repertory cinemas that regularly showed popular and cult films long after their wide release. (The Prince Charles Cinema in London's West End is perhaps the last example of this kind of programming.) Television took over this function in the 1980s, at first on the main terrestrial channels and more recently on digital-only channels. But

> **RESEARCH SUGGESTION**
> Oral history is an excellent means of discovering how the cinema experience has changed over time. Find three people to interview, if possible aged around 40, around 60 and around 80. Ask them about their memories of going to the cinema when they were 17-18. Which cinemas did they go to, what did a night out at the pictures involve, what did they most enjoy about the whole experience?

none of these platforms/outlets could compete with retail video/DVD and the joy of owning the film. Of course, an important element of consumerism has also been added, especially since the advent of DVD, with more and more special editions of films offering different edits and additional material of all kinds, so that many well-known films exist in several different versions.

The multiplex

The idea of putting two or more cinema auditoria into the same building is not as recent as you might think. The Picturehouse Cinema in London's Oxford Street was 'twinned' in 1936 to produce two cinemas and one box office in the form of Studio 1 and Studio 2. But this practice was not widespread in the UK until the 1970s, with the twinning and tripling of most circuit cinemas. In North America, the multi-cinema concept was developed in relation to the shopping malls being built in the 1960s. Although these were new builds, they were sometimes of rather poor quality and did not match up to the cinema palaces of the 1930s. Even so, they were economically successful and gradually they got bigger with more and more screens. In 1985, AMC (American Multi-Cinema Inc.) brought the concept of the multiplex to the UK with The Point, a 10 screen cinema in Milton Keynes. The change in the

A multiplex generally means more than five screens and a **megaplex** 20 or more. A **miniplex** might be three to five and if the films shown are specialised, it might be an **artplex**.

UK was dramatic because it brought about not only an improvement in general standards of projection and sound, but also a social revolution – a new kind of cinema experience for an audience used to an ugly conversion of an old building. New multiplexes appeared on out-of-town sites in retail and leisure parks with acres of car parking and good lighting.

By the time AMC and then Showcase, Warner and UCI (all three with direct Hollywood studio connections) began to establish chains of multiplexes in the UK, the concept had developed further in North America. The Canadian company Cineplex is often credited with stimulating a move to better-quality architecture and a real attempt to make the modern cinema experience an event comparable to the best cinemagoing experience of the age of super cinemas. The 18-screen Cineplex theatre in Toronto opened in 1979, after which Cineplex expanded across Canada and into major American cities. Douglas Gomery (1992) analysed the development of the company and the concept of a new-style picture palace. He notes that Cineplex was devoted to detail. When patrons complained of dirty floors the company employed more cleaners and in a particularly telling comment, Gomery refers to the opening of a Los Angeles Cineplex where, as well as the usual concessions, 'Perrier water and Cadbury's Fruit and Nut bar' were on sale (see below for further discussion of concessions). In Canada, Cineplex also commissioned original artworks for the lobby and waiting areas, supporting local Canadian artists.

It would be an interesting exercise to survey the multiplex chains across the UK and to try to assess how much care has been taken to make audiences feel comfortable and safe on the one hand and excited at the prospect of an event on the other. For every attempt at some form of creativity, there seem to be several 'sheds' with sticky floors across the UK.

The importance of concessions

The stark economic facts of exhibition mean that the multiplex cinema exists to draw in audiences who will buy concessions, especially popcorn and soft drinks. The mark-up on these products is very high and so, although tickets for screenings might create more revenue for the exhibitor, the concessions sales actually create more profit. 'Concessions account for a quarter of all revenue in UK cinemas but half the profits' (*Screen Digest Report*, April 2005). Cinema exhibition in the UK in 2006 was dominated by four large chains, only one of which is a dedicated 'entertainment company' (National Amusements, owners of Showcase and effective controllers of Viacom/Paramount). The other three are owned by venture capital organisations whose main

The spate of mergers and acquisitions of cinema chains in 2005 produced a new chain announced in summer 2006. Empire Cinemas was formed out of the group of UGC and UCI cinemas that Cineworld and Odeon were forced to sell to comply with competition laws. They were bought by an Irish company that may bring something new to the UK exhibition sector.

concern is for cash turnover (at the time of writing, a management buyout of Vue has been announced and this may change overall policy). What kind of experience do you have when you visit a Vue, Cineworld or Odeon multiplex? Does the cinema itself excite your senses – or do you rely on the film to do that? How does it feel to visit the cinema 'off season' in October or February when big-budget event films are thin on the ground?

Popcorn and Carrot Cake

Paul Brett, Head of the British Film Institute's Cinema Services in 1999, used the terms 'popcorn' and 'carrot cake' to distinguish multiplex mainstream cinema and art house or specialised cinema in a Strategy Consultation Document. This distinction captures something about audiences that continues to trouble exhibitors and cultural agencies like the UK Film Council. Popcorn conjures up images of audiences associated with youth, American culture, issues of taste (both in the gustatory and aesthetic sense) etc. that are opposed to carrot cake, referring to older more European-orientated and possibly more middle-class cinemagoers. For audiences in outer suburbia and rural areas where they may be little choice about where to watch a film, the distinction may be academic, but in towns and cities where sometimes the same film will play in both a multiplex and a specialised cinema, some audiences will always prefer one type of venue over another (see Chapter 7 for local research on this issue).

> Recent research by the All Industry Marketing Committee for the UK cinema industry proposes two new audience segmentation schemes. The 'lifestage' categorisation draws attention to the elements of the cinemagoing experience that each group seeks – popcorn, comedy and thrills for the teenage audience contrasting with a bar drink and a quality film for 40+ year old adults. (Baker, Inglis and Voss (2002)

In terms of numbers, specialised cinemas are thin on the ground in the UK – fewer than 200 screens compared with over 3,000 mainstream screens. The crucial point here is that the audience and the income for the two types of cinema is different and therefore the exhibitors have to adopt a different mindset in order to attract customers. This is an institutional difference that also carries over into the categorisation of the films themselves as mainstream or specialised. Certain films are almost free of categorisation – e.g. *Toy Story, Lord of the Rings* – and they will be successful wherever they are shown. Others have much more clearly defined audiences. A mainstream teen comedy is unlikely to play in a specialised cinema, because the target audience probably would not think of going there. Similarly, an Iranian art film will not play in a multiplex. But there are a host of films that fall somewhere between the two institutional categories and it is this territory that the multiplex and the specialised cinema fight over.

Most of the successful independent cinemas that show specialised cinema will cater to audiences with a restaurant/bar, possibly a shop selling film magazines, DVDs etc., provision of film notes and education events. They will screen films in seasons, hold festivals and special events, all listed in a detailed brochure each month. The multiplex operation will want an ethos of entertainment and fun to prevail without too much earnest discussion – and they know they will make more profit from concessions than from the films. The large foyer area of the multiplex is designed to create a buzz of excitement and is generally noisy with the sound of video games and video trailers. By contrast, the art cinema may have a small foyer, but larger spaces for bars and restaurants.

Smart Cinema

A distinctive group of films and the audiences who watch them in a similarly distinct type of cinema is neatly described by the term 'Smart cinema', taken from an article by Jeffrey Sconce (2002) in *Screen*. Sconce traces the development of a new sensibility in the 1990s that comes together at the turn of the century in films such as *Ghost World* (US/Germany/UK, 2000). *Ghost World* is an adaptation of Daniel Clowes' graphic novel about two young women who rebel against the conformity of suburban American life (the 'ghost world'). Similar youth-orientated American independent films such as *Rushmore*, *Election* and *Donnie Darko* could also be included under this banner, producing:

> An interesting shift in the strategies of contemporary 'art cinema', here defined as movies marketed in explicit counterdistinction to mainstream Hollywood fare as 'smarter', 'artier' and more 'independent' (however questionable and manufactured such distinctions might actually be). (Sconce, 2002: 350)

This definition attempts to describe both the filmmakers' attitude towards narrative and characterisation and the approach taken in marketing the films to what Sconce refers to as the bohemian audience that frequents the artplexes of North America and Europe. The films are clever and smart and so is the audience. The marketeers must make sure that the two connect through an ironic marketing campaign – thus the tag line for *Ghost World* is 'Accentuate the negative'. This is a clever slogan – perhaps too clever. The meaning is fairly clear and in one sense it describes the mood or tone of the film, which is 'down'. It is also a clear riposte to the values of mainstream Hollywood cinema that nearly always promotes success and the positive aspects of life. Finally, the phrase itself is a play on a song title ('Accentuate the positive') originally performed in a Hollywood musical from 1944 by Bing Crosby. The opening lines are:

> You've got to accentuate the positive
> Eliminate the negative
> Latch on to the affirmative
> Don't mess with Mister In-Between

The song embodies everything about the 'up' values of Hollywood entertainment. It is also possibly the kind of reference that would be enjoyed by one of the characters in the film who collects old vinyl records and other memorabilia.

Smart cinema plays with the more traditional notion of art cinema. Typically, art film narratives have either been avant garde in terms of telling a story or political ideology, or else they have been conventional in appearance, with an emphasis on exploring character rather than offering the narrative pleasures of popular genres. A smart film like *Ghost World* is fairly conventional in appearance and relatively conservative in terms of politics – the difference comes in the attitude that produces the tone of disaffection (or, in more extreme cases, nihilism – belief in nothing). Overall, this is an attitude that questions both the liberal political values of the left and the moral certitude of the right.

The attitude in these films has been traced to the concept of 'Generation X' or the 'Slacker Generation'. These are the people born in the late 1960s or 1970s who were teenagers or young adults in the 1980s and who, by 2000, were 30-somethings. Generation X values have been celebrated in literature as well as in films and popular music. Sconce makes various references:

- the Douglas Coupland novel *Generation X: Tales for an Accelerated Culture* (1991);
- the music of bands like Velvet Underground;
- fascination with black clothing and other forms of 'anti-fashion' fashion.

We could add the graphic novels that inspired a film like *Ghost World*. The antagonism of the heroes of these texts is directed towards the generation who came before – the **babyboomers** who were born in the late 1940s and the early 1950s (and possibly including those born up to the early 1960s) – and those who came later, the 'yuppies' and 'consumer babies' of the 1980s and 1990s. (The earlier group includes both the director and scriptwriter of *Ghost World*, born in 1948 and 1961 respectively.)

Smart cinema is concerned with a view of the world that on the one hand abhors the conformity of consumer culture and on the other celebrates the possibilities for difference that exist because affluence allows choice. This is illustrated in *Ghost World* in contrasting scenes. The first shows the lead character, Enid (played by Thora Birch), failing to hold down a job selling concessions in a multiplex because she cannot resist insulting the customers who want to buy the 'chemical gloop' that passes for popcorn and Cola. Elsewhere in the film, she enjoys what she sees as 'cool' popular culture products such as Hindi films and English punk records (although Enid would not use a word like 'cool').

A South Asian view of the cinema audience

The quote at the beginning of this chapter highlights the different approaches to the experience of sitting in a cinema audience in India and the West. Indian cinema, the only national cinema to rival North America in the number of films and the size of the audience, offers a useful contrast. There are all kinds of cinemas across India, from modern multiplexes (and shopping malls) in major cities to village compounds and travelling cinemas in rural areas. Indian film and cultural studies scholars have also begun to think about exhibition, reception and the cinema experience. S. V. Srinivas is a fellow at the Centre for the Study of Culture and Society in Bangalore. He has written widely on various topics relating to cinemagoing in the state of Andhra Pradesh, South India, including the distribution of Hong Kong action films on the 'B cinema' circuits and the fan associations for major stars, many of whom have political ambitions. In a discussion of film culture, politics and industry, Srinivas develops an argument about the relationship between the film industry and the audience and how cinema managers have attempted to persuade audience members to behave in such a way to improve the viewing experience. Overall, he argues, Telegu cinema (the regional language cinema of the state) has not managed to gain the full economic benefits that the passion of the audience and the massive importance of cinema in local culture could bring. The producers are reluctant to make a 'quality product', but the exhibitors are at least trying to offer a better quality of presentation. Here he describes one strategy to control audiences:

> In Madanapalle, Srikrishna, the town's first air-conditioned cinema hall, segregates the sexes both at the booking counters and inside the auditorium. The management of the theatre does not permit the audience to whistle after the first week of a film's release. This, I argue, is an industrial aspiration of the kind that film history is familiar with and much has been said about this mode of cleaning up the cinema halls in the histories of American cinema.
>
> But it is not only air-conditioned cinema halls aiming to attract the middle class customer that aspire to standardise the conditions of viewing. Jyothi theatre, also situated in Madanapalle, is a typical example of a B circuit cinema hall for it still has wooden benches in the lower stalls and is notorious for screening soft-porn films. When it screens a soft-porn film it ensures that the booking counter is closed when the film commences. No one is allowed to whistle or make lewd comments. No one can leave the auditorium till the screening is over. Precautions against police raids, certainly. But perfect customer compliance is achieved and stable conditions of viewing have been created. (from Seminar No. 525, 2003, accessed via <www.india-seminar.com/2003/525.htm>)

As Srinivas points out, similar scenes were evident in British and American cinemas in earlier decades, as were other aspects that he explores in this and other papers (all of which can be accessed via <apache.cscsarchive.org/ Hongkong_Action/html/fans_01.htm>). For instance, audiences in India have in the past been segregated according to social caste and class, with middle-class patrons in more expensive seats. When the multiplex arrived in the UK, it helped change seating patterns, with a single price gradually replacing the idea of 'cheap seats' at the front and more expensive seats at the back (or upstairs in the circle/balcony). But multiplex operators have also tried to re-introduce the idea of more expensive seats in 'executive cinemas' with extra features – more comfortable seats, a bar and seat service etc. Both live theatre and football stadiums routinely segregate spectators according to seat price and facilities. Film studies needs to consider how this concept of status influences the viewing experience.

> Where do you sit in the cinema? For many people, there seems to be a psychological imperative to sit at the back, but some people prefer the sides, giving an angled view. Many film buffs argue that the best seat is in the middle of one of the first four or five rows, allowing the big screen to fill their field of vision (and keeping most of the rest of the audience out of view). The film buff choice contradicts the idea of cheap seats at the front.

Srinivas makes reference to an article by Linda Williams (1994) on *Psycho*, pointing out that in the USA (and the UK), it was the showmanship of Alfred Hitchcock (and the nature of the film itself) that changed the cinema viewing experience profoundly in 1960. Before *Psycho*, audiences would often enter a cinema auditorium part way through a screening and then remain for the rest of a long programme, perhaps staying to see the opening of the film they missed as part of the 'continuous performance' that was then a feature of cinema programming. Hitchcock ran a campaign that announced that no one would be admitted after the film began. Inside the auditorium, the audience was taken on a rollercoaster ride of thrills that Williams argues was a major influence on the blockbuster action narratives that followed *Jaws*. Srinivas sees this as the filmmaker training the audience to watch films in a particular way. Similar arguments have been put forward to explain the use of the soundtrack for blockbusters in the multiplex, which often use the power of sound systems like DTS to literally hail audiences: 'Hey you, sit down, the show is about to start'. The music and sound effects pin audiences back in their seats.

The Indian experience reminds us of the range of potential audience behaviour and some of it may still resonate with UK audiences. Many people enjoy going to the cinema in groups, and it is not unusual in multiplexes to see a constant coming and going of group members in and out of auditoria to buy concessions etc. The use of mobile phones inside the auditorium is something that many people might now find 'normal', but which drives others to distraction (and which the exhibitor attempts to control with on-screen announcements). What do you think is acceptable behaviour? Does it affect your enjoyment of the film? Once again, this is probably an issue in the distinction between mainstream and specialised cinemas. What might be acceptable to the rest of the audience in one type of cinema (despite the exhibitor's request not to talk during the film, keep phones switched off etc.)

Cineworld have used a short animated feature in which a young woman (modelled on Lara Croft) sternly deals with audience members who talk, use phones etc. In reality, few multiplex auditoria have ushers, who in traditional cinemas had a visible presence representing the cinema management.

may not be in another. It may be that 'acceptable behaviour' is related to age, social class and experience of other art forms. The mobile phone problem is arguably more acute in live theatre, where on several occasions audience members who have allowed a phone to ring have been harangued by angry actors on stage.

These questions about audience behaviour may have important institutional effects in separating certain kinds of audiences into certain kinds of cinemas, but they are also important in potentially influencing how we read and understand films. Film scholars need to experience films with audiences to understand the range of responses. Here is an extract from a paper on the films of Robert Aldrich, often perceived as a leftist director of macho action films in Hollywood from the 1950s through to the 1970s:

> I went to see Aldrich's Great Depression proletarian epic, *Emperor of the North Pole* (USA, 1973) at a big, unclassy theatre on Hollywood boulevard with an audience of mainly young, mainly black and chicano, people. The theatre was packed, several hundred people. At the end of the film's triumphant final sequence, the entire audience spontaneously stood and cheered: a standing ovation, something I had never seen in a movie theatre before, and only once since, when I went to a similar theatre to see Aldrich's *The Longest Yard* (USA, 1974). (Rick Thompson 'Robert Aldrich: An Independent Career', *Screening the Past* No. 10. <www.latrobe.edu.au/screeningthepast/firstrelease/fr0600/rtfr10a.htm>)

More than just the film

In their book *The Place of the Audience* (2003), Mark Jancovich and his colleagues explain that they wish to discuss 'film consumption'. They use this term to distinguish the whole range of ways in which people engage with film culture from the familiar academic concept of the single spectator having a relationship with the film on the cinema screen. They intend consumption to include all the cinema-related experiences described in this chapter plus the consumption of films and engagement with film culture via television, video and new media. We have shown here that contemporary multiplex exhibition practice has reduced the actual screening of the film to a single event. But this has not stopped the foyer of the cinema becoming a meeting place or prevented the film from becoming part of an evening out. Audiences have also found different ways of consuming films in cinemas. Here are just two examples.

Repeat viewings and celebration

The Odeon cinema chain introduced the slogan 'Fanatical about cinema' a few years ago. It is not clear exactly what this means (is it them or their audiences?), but there are certainly fans who are fanatical about cinema. In the days before VCRs and DVD players, anyone who wanted to watch a film again had to go back to the cinema. In the 1960s, many people were prepared to do just that, especially for the big **roadshow** films such as *The Sound of Music* (USA, 1965). A roadshow screening was a special screening, often on the superior 70mm format, for major films that could command a higher ticket price and that were booked for several weeks into the same cinema rather than being on

In 2006, the large IMAX screen was increasingly used to show digitally converted mainstream blockbusters. When 3D was added to this experience with a 20-minute sequence in *Superman Returns*, admissions rose further with London's BFI IMAX cinema recording record box-office figures. (*Screen International* 4 August 2006)

general release (see Chapter 3). Figures collated by Sheldon Hall (2005) show that in many cities in the UK, the attendance figures for *The Sound of Music* were higher than the population of the city itself – this might not be a surprise in resorts like

Blackpool and Brighton, but in Manchester and Leeds? The only explanation is that many people went more than once. Indeed, there were many newspaper reports at the time claiming a local resident as the film's 'No. 1 fan' after 50 or 100 visits. In recent years, *The Sound of Music* has again become the centre of fan attention – this time as a participation sport, involving dressing up and performing the songs along with the film at special screenings.

The Sound of Music has followed earlier films such as *The Rocky Horror Picture Show* in terms of participation. This might be linked to other types of exhibition, such as the late-night screenings of classic horror and cult films, which although not as widespread now, still linger on in some cinemas and the more recent practice of open air Summer screenings in non-cinema venues sponsored by beer companies (like the major music festivals). Two other rather different types of cinema events that attract audiences looking for something more than a standard screening experience are the revival of 'silent cinema' classics in large concert halls, complete with full orchestra, and the recent developments in IMAX exhibition. In each case, the audience wants to be part of a special event.

8.3 The audience for a 3-D screening, a form of 'special event' first staged in the 1950s and available in selected IMAX cinemas around the world in 2007.

Festivals and conventions

Film festivals became much more important elements within film culture once cinemas began to close and cinema became less of a mass medium that audiences attended on a regular basis. Festivals make films special and they provide extra attractions ('added value' in marketing terms) for both audiences and distributors/exhibitors.

There are several kinds of festivals that attract different audiences and serve different purposes. The most famous film festivals have two primary (but related) functions: to confer prestige via the award of prizes and to provide a film market where international buyers and sellers meet. The film calendar is constructed around four such festivals. Berlin hosts an international festival in February where often a low-budget, controversial film wins a 'Gold Bear', with individual 'Silver Bears' for directors, actors etc. In May there is Cannes, a high-profile event attracting many celebrities as well as an important film market, where a large number of prizes (the Palme d'Or etc.) are awarded for films and creative people in many categories. Venice hosts the late-summer festival in August/September, while Toronto lays on the major North American festival a week or so later. These four festivals each have a different flavour. With the exception of Toronto, which is perhaps more geared to a public audience (the main prize is called the People's Award), the three European festivals' main function is to promote specialised cinema titles. All the festivals need sponsorship and press coverage, so Cannes in particular tends to flirt with Hollywood, inviting stars and screening blockbusters that otherwise look out of place. The lack of 'real' as distinct from 'industry' audiences at Cannes can create potentially misleading profiles for some films and help launch others.

Toronto is important, because it enables international films to be shown to North American audiences and can help some films to open successfully. Its timing is also significant as it leads nicely into the Academy Award season, with leading contenders generally opening in North America in the last three months of the year. Every country has several festivals and, as far as the more general audience is concerned, they allow either the chance to see territory premieres of new films or to get immersed in specific film genres. In the UK, festivals are likely to be supported by both national and regional cultural agencies as well as commercial sponsors. The sponsorship money allows the festival director to bring in directors, screenwriters, stars etc., for personal appearances and Q & As with audiences, and also to airfreight in copies of films not normally in distribution.

We have mentioned elsewhere in this book (see Chapter 7) that festivals are not as attractive to mainstream film audiences. However, many local/regional festivals (i.e. as distinct from Cannes etc.) are eagerly awaited by the more devoted film fans, because they offer all those exclusive attractions that in a sense define fan culture. Fans get to see films first, they get to meet (or at least see) directors and stars in the flesh, they can buy merchandise and memorabilia (the festival T-shirt?) and meet other fans. And festivals are not necessarily about art films. Some are, but others celebrate horror, animation, crime films, porn films, science fiction and fantasy etc.

The ultimate in fandom is the fan convention, often associated with television series and characters. The *Star Trek* conventions have come to define the concept in popular discourse and were celebrated in a kind of homage in *Galaxy Quest* (USA, 1999). The convention idea (often held in a hotel or exhibition centre, not a cinema) brings together fans, producers and stars, and the possibility of all kinds of markets for fan material, screenings etc. This is film culture moving out into a broader leisure culture. It can be related to other leisure activities, such as film quizzes (sometimes held in cinemas, or in bars attached to cinemas), home cinemas with friends invited round, fancy-dress parties that feature screen characters etc. Film culture exists outside cinemas in a host of different manifestations.

Audiences and the internet

Access to the internet and mobile telephony has changed people's lives in quite profound ways. There are still many parts of the world where the general population is too poor and the infrastructure is not available (and there are parts of the developed world where broadband access is still not possible), but the spread of services is wide enough to have altered both the way in which the industry works and ways in which audiences get to see films and discuss them. The changes are very recent: perhaps only since 2001 have they become really significant, although we can trace several developments back ten years or more. Changes are ongoing and responses are swift. To give just one example, as soon as blogging was generally understood and services freely available, the Hollywood studios began to adjust to the new environment and to court bloggers in an attempt to benefit rather than damage film promotion.

How should we approach these developments? It might help to think about specific uses of the new technologies (which could also cover DVD and developments in personal computers):

- in helping studios to promote/build a profile for a new release;
- in providing information for audiences about films, both current and library titles;
- in making new digital prints available (for cinema screenings and as DVDs);
- in making it easier to find film screenings and to purchase/rent DVDs;
- in providing fora to exchange views on film releases;
- in building fan communities.

It goes much further than this, and we could consider the wholesale changes to the process of film distribution and exhibition that the digital projection revolution promises (but is yet to fulfil on a large scale). On the negative side, we would need also to discuss the piracy issue that threatens to undermine the whole economic relationship between distributors/exhibitors and audiences. We do not have the space for all of this, so let us stick for the moment with the legitimate relationship between the distributor/exhibitor and the audience.

Promoting a film in the digital environment

Distributors have always sought new ways to engage audiences with forthcoming product. Appearances by stars, stories in magazines and newspapers, merchandising tie-ins with sponsors – all these have been used in different ways since the 1930s. But arguably the most cost-effective way of reaching the target audience for a film has been the traditional cinema trailer. The argument has been quite simple. Most people do not go to the cinema very frequently – fewer than three times per year for most of us. Those who do go on a fairly regular basis are therefore of great interest to distributors. Show a trailer in a cinema and the audience is already one step towards commitment. Advertisers calculate the efficiency of an ad campaign on the cost per thousand of the target audience who see the ad. Everybody who sees the trailer is a potential viewer of the film. Of course, it may not be their favourite genre and the trailer may be poorly made, but the audience for the trailer is still more likely to return to the cinema than the average person on the street outside. The same trailer (probably much shorter) may also be used for a television advertisement, which will cost significantly more. It will be seen by many more people, most of whom do not attend the cinema regularly. In this sense, it can be wasted promotional spend.

Traditional promotion is designed on a push basis – promotional material is *pushed* towards prospective audiences on their cereal boxes, as part of their favourite TV chat show, or in their newspaper. The internet has introduced the possibility of *pull* technologies for finding information. Instead of being bombarded with *Spider-Man* images in the supermarket, a film fan can now search for information about a favourite star or director's latest film. Fans can pull together information about new releases. Studios are alive to this and can to some extent control or guide the fans by releasing information at specific moments. The very big franchises for *Star Wars*, *Lord of the Rings* etc. are able to tease fans long in advance of a film's release, prompting discussion and stirring up interest.

It could be argued that the pull possibilities of the internet have been overplayed and that really fans are being pushed towards exactly what the studios want them to find. Overall use of the internet has also changed significantly over the last ten years. At one point, it looked like the early freedom and anarchy of the net would be replaced by corporate control of players such as Microsoft and AOL, who would control access, sucking consumers into their portal websites, where all kinds of services would be pushed to unsuspecting users. At that point, Time Warner merged (as junior partner) with AOL to create a new form of media corporation. Five years later, after the 'dot.com' boom was over, Time Warner quietly dropped AOL from the brand name. Now, it would seem, sites like MySpace and YouTube are proving so popular for sharing music and videos that they may be 'absorbed' by larger corporations (at the time of writing, MySpace had recently been acquired by News Corporation). Inevitably, as the internet grows, the large corporations will try to preserve their revenues by exploiting each change in use. What is important here is not the actual ownership of a website, but the sense of ownership or autonomy felt by the consumer/viewer. Someone who seeks out and selects a trailer or a website for a new film could feel quite differently towards the film than if they had felt compelled to watch the film following months of paid promotion. Some media companies have recognised this in their attempts to exploit **viral marketing**. This sees an organisation releasing a short advertising film that is posted on a website or emailed to selected customers. If the film is entertaining enough, it may well be emailed by the recipient to a circle of friends – eventually spreading like a virus (and costing the originating company nothing in distribution). Even more effective is an interactive campaign, which gets users to create something around the marketing concept. A Google search for 'viral marketing film' produced this result as the first hit in June 2006:

Twentieth Century-Fox Pushes UK Garfield Release with User Generated Content (Posted on Wednesday June 21, 2006)

According to Digital Bulletin, Twentieth Century Fox is launching a viral site that will use user-generated content to promote the U.K. release of *Garfield: A Tale of Two Kitties*.

Located at worldwidewhiskers.com, the site enables users to create a special 'cat profile', which allows the user to pick attributes like color, food favorites, and pastimes. Users can then scour the globe to find other 'cat buddies' that share similar interests. (<www.indiescene.net/archives/movie_marketing/viral_marketing/>)

Studios' use of the internet to promote films tends to employ different strategies for different markets (and it is not only the large studios – the first major internet promotion campaign was for *The Blair Witch Project*, an independent film made on a tiny budget with little to spend on marketing but inventive ways of spreading word-of-mouth promotion). Whereas some of the viral marketing, and seemingly everything on YouTube, is of fairly poor visual quality, with a small on-screen window and a home-made feel (a major part of its attraction for younger audiences?), at the other end of the scale, High Definition trailers from Apple's website are of a quality that exceeds DVDs. These require broadband access, powerful computers and large displays, but the impact for more upmarket viewers ('early adopters' of technology in the marketing speak) is considerable. It is hard not to be impressed by such images (although, again, if the trailer is poorly thought out, the impact is lost).

Blogging offers a rather different approach to promotion. As far as the studios are concerned, blogs can be simple text, audio (podcasting) or video. All of these offer ways in which a virtual community of film fans (and critics) can quickly link up and exchange ideas. *Screen International* (13 May 2005) recognised the importance of this in a cover story headed 'Up Close and Personal. Can the Two Worlds of Blogging and Film Distribution find a happy equilibrium between Inside Gossip and Controlled Spin?' As Denis Seguin writes, 'you can hear, see and read the future of film marketing right now on-line and it is personal, highly subjective, in-your-face, unvarnished and uncontrollable'.

What concerns the studios most, as it concerns many traditional media organisations, is the spectre of a new generation of young people termed 'young millennials' by an interactive marketing executive at Paramount Pictures. She quite possibly means you, dear reader, if you fit that demographic. The young millennials grew up in a world in which they saw the internet as the norm, along with multi-channel television and most other forms of new media. The demographic terrifies media buyers (the people who buy advertising space) and even more traditional media outlets like commercial television, because these young people are generally well-educated, relatively affluent and totally disinterested in traditional media. To reach them, the studios have to trust to new media and its uncertainties. Fortunately, the demographic does like movies and is indeed the single most important market for mainstream films.

The studios can certainly see the advantages in the free advertising they can generate by feeding the bloggers from an early stage in the production process, but they are also aware how quickly 'zubb' ('negative buzz' – does anyone apart from marketing people actually use these terms?) can circulate and kill a new film. Equally, though free advertising on the viral principle can spread exponentionally (via the concept of the **RSS** feed, which tells users of blogs that a new message has been posted), it must be transparent and not faked. If studios are devious in engineering a viral campaign, they will be found out and it will backfire, warns Seguin. However, if the studios can 'get into bed with the webheads' they may succeed. What might happen is that the studios learn how to use the new media environment creatively. For example, they could release ideas about how a franchise might develop and gauge reaction before deciding to go ahead. In this way, the 'blogosphere' becomes an agent similar to the traditional preview audience, but at an earlier stage and with potentially considerably more power.

RESEARCH SUGGESTION

Select two film titles that are currently 'in production' and due for release in a few months. (Go to the Internet Movie Database and see what is listed for well-known directors and stars). If possible, choose a potential blockbuster and a smaller more specialised title and search for information about the release. How much information is out there? How much is being circulated by fans and how much is clearly coming from the distributor?

Audience choice and diversity

The issue of what audiences have the chance to see is important. There are some 500 films and more released in the UK each year, but many of these do not reach multiplex screens or independent cinemas in all parts of the country. Cultural agencies (primarily the UK Film Council) are charged with developing a diversity of audiences and a diversity of films for them to see. The **Digital Screen Network** initiative and the support for specialised film releases are part of this overall strategy. At the same time, the multiplex operators, in the way of many modern media organisations, will always claim that their operation maximises consumer choice. Whether either the private or public sector is actually succeeding in increasing audiences for a wider range of films is a moot point, but it could be argued that because of the new technologies available, it is much easier to

- find out where and when films are playing at the cinema;
- discover when films are going to be released and plan leisure time accordingly;
- buy or rent a very wide range of DVDs.

The internet has made available plenty of information about screenings and also provided the means to acquire or at least get access to DVDs. Someone dedicated to seeing films outside the mainstream can now usually find them. This includes DVDs of films never released in the UK. Provided you have a multi-region DVD player (a relatively cheap purchase), it is possible to enjoy English subtitled versions of many East Asian and South Asian films from websites in the UK and in Hong Kong and South Korea. Often other films not released on DVD in the UK will be available from North America. Although this is not be something that the mainstream audience will consider, there are now significant numbers of fans of martial arts, horror etc. who have effectively escaped from the constraints of UK distribution/exhibition. Audiences generally should feel more in control over what they go to see. The point here is that although only a small percentage of the audience actually seeks out overseas DVDs, the fact that they can and do has at least some influence on UK distributors, encouraging them to consider a wider range of material.

> In the US there were 45,000 film titles available on DVD in 2005. (US Entertainment Industry 2005 Market Figures, available from <www.mpaa.org>).

> A different kind of control is offered by the various American lobby group websites that will warn you about violence, explicit sex, questioning of Christian values etc.

Cinema as 'public sphere'?

The concept of the **public sphere** is usually associated with the work of Jürgen Habermas. It refers to the space into which we enter in order to make comments and exchange ideas about society. It is therefore related to ideas about **identity** and status and also confidence in that space being available and protective of the free exchange of ideas etc. Questions about the development of different media and their impact on the public sphere are an important aspect of media studies. For most of the latter half of the 20th century, the public sphere in terms of media institutions was dominated by the 'quality press' (the former broadsheet press in the UK) and radio and television broadcasting (most of which, outside the USA, has been regulated in the public interest, producing examples of 'public service broadcasting').

The cinema has tended to be seen much more as part of the private space – even though we all like talking about movies, it has tended to be with friends rather than the world at large. Now the internet is usurping the role of traditional media – newspapers such as the *Guardian* are now possibly better known for their web presence (certainly in North America) than for their print products. The internet has also made it possible for our talk about movies to be made available to anyone who wants to read it – and to reply to others.

There are many, many websites devoted to films and film culture, but let us focus on perhaps the most prominent site. The Internet Movie Database (imdb.com) began life as a project for film fans that eventually made it onto the web via the University of Cardiff. Now it is part of the Amazon.com empire. The database itself is a useful resource for tracing the careers of actors, directors etc. and getting information on individual films. But there are two other major attractions, especially for the film studies student – the user comments and the bulletin boards (some of which are general, others related to specific films, but both of which require registration). Generally, user comments are considered pieces at some length. For a mainstream film with wide appeal, 2–300 comments is not unusual. *Inside Man* had over 350 by June 2006 and, as is often the case, the same page of commentary will include those who thought the film brilliant and those who found it completely worthless. What are we to make of this?

The range of opinion immediately destroys any sense that audiences passively follow a preordained narrative path through a movie. Spectators see different things and attach different importance to what they see. It is also possible to discern that different users have completely different expectations about what they are going to see and what they want to see. The commentaries are also interesting in relation to the voting system. Some 15,000 people voted on *Inside Man*, using a 1 to 10 scale, and the overall result was (in June 2006) a score of 7.5, a relatively high score, brought down by a relatively small number of voters who gave votes of 1–5. The largest group of voters gave 8, a sign of a major film. Spike Lee is a controversial director and although the film itself is not seen by many of the users as controversial, there are certainly those who love or loathe the director and will vote accordingly. One interesting aspect of the voting is that overall far more men than women voted (6:1), but that the women who did vote gave the highest score: 8.3 for females under 18. It is likely that the actual cinema audience was skewed towards men (see Chapter 5's discussion of exit polls), but also are men more likely than women to vote on IMDb? The higher score given by women does suggest, however, that perhaps they have been put off seeing a film that, once they are inside the cinema, they seem to have enjoyed – or at least valued highly. On the other hand, a check on user ratings for other films suggests that women, and young women under 18 in particular, nearly always give the highest scores.

Voting is less onerous than writing a commentary, but even so, IMDb users/voters are only a tiny proportion of the people who see a feature film. The people who have the energy to write or even vote are those who feel strongly about a film, for or against. The more controversial, newsworthy or perhaps affecting the film, the more votes will be cast. *Brokeback Mountain* has collected over 50,000 votes, half of them registering a '10' and 9% a '1' for an overall 7.9. Voters will tend to come from the USA more than any other country, although this skew may be disappearing (*Brokeback Mountain* had more votes from non-US sources). Where there are so many voters, it is tempting to invoke 'the wisdom of crowds' in determining whether any meaning should be attached to these figures (the phrase refers to a model of crowd behaviour discussed in a book with that title by James Surowiecki, 2005). Ask yourself, would you take more notice of a film critic or the votes of 25,000 who thought a film merited a '10'? It certainly throws up a challenge for the professional critics.

One other important aspect of user comments is that they continue after the film's initial release, with additional comments by those who view the DVD, re-releases etc. The comments can offer film students a very useful guide to how opinions can change over time or perhaps to the ways in which DVD responses differ from cinema responses.

The second interactive aspect of IMDb is the range of bulletin boards. As with user comments and votes, you must register before you can post on the boards, but this formality does not prevent some robust exchanges, with several posts routinely 'deleted by the administrator'. Bulletin boards do offer a different kind of response. Whereas most user comments are quite considered and in many cases written in a formal style using the conventions of professional journalism, board messages are more personal and conversational, and they are part of an interaction. If you can wade through some of the tedious arguments, you can find genuine debates and sometimes information not available to formal commentators. Board members may live in the area where the film was made, have been extras on the shoot etc. They may know the detailed history of a controversial true story used in the film. Because of the international spread of viewers, members can translate film titles, explain dialects etc. They may ask for and receive advice on where to see a film, how to acquire a DVD etc. Bulletin boards certainly contribute to that growing sense of a filmic universe in which it seems possible to find out whatever we want about most films and that, despite the vagaries of distribution, we might finally be able to see a particular film that has always eluded us.

The viewing experience in the digital world

In 2006, when this book was written, film culture yet again seemed poised on the brink of major changes. It could be argued that it has always been on the brink of change, so we need to tread carefully in thinking about any predictions. We might begin with just a couple of observations:

- Films remain popular all over the world, even if the way in which audiences watch them and where they watch them changes.
- Hollywood remains the dominant force in cinema worldwide, but other film industries are making a comeback and box-office income is rising fastest outside North America.

There is a tension embodied in these two observations that may have a major impact on audiences in the future. The tension is there in the power of the Hollywood studios and their capacity to remain in power and successfully exploit technological developments. There are question marks about both the theatrical and domestic futures of cinema.

Those of us who love cinema screenings and for whom a TV screen is no substitute can be reasonably sure that cinemas will remain important, at least as a promotional medium. Films will open in cinemas to gain a profile for subsequent viewing on domestic formats. Cinema building – multiplex development – is continuing in the world's new markets. Cinemas are facilities that have become accepted as a marker of affluence and confidence in recovering economies – in August 2006, *Screen International* featured multiplex development in Vietnam. In the biggest potential market, China, exhibitors have an advantage over Hollywood companies, in that new cinemas can be equipped with digital projection from the outset. In North America and Europe, the big problem will be to re-equip existing cinemas for digital projection and to organise digital distribution. Who will pay for the conversion? So far, it has taken longer to get the process moving than some experts suggested. China will become a world leader in digital cinema and with the emergence of South Korea as a major international film industry and a resurgent Japanese industry, three East Asian economies, all with strengths in electronics manufacture, are in a position to threaten Hollywood's control of electronic image-making. Add to that the combination of a vibrant information technology culture and the world's largest film industry in India, and the near future presents Hollywood with a serious challenge. Hollywood is alive to the challenge, and partnerships with East Asian and South Asian partners are under way. The likelihood is that we will see more American co-productions with Asian partners and possibly more East Asian and South Asian films in cinemas in the West. Cinemas will remain important venues, but most of us will still watch more films on a video screen, either on a TV set or a computer screen.

Home cinema

The American–Chinese axis is important for films in the domestic sphere as well. DVDs have boosted Hollywood's profits, but also increased the levels of piracy. DVDs are cheap to produce, but easier to pirate than previous film media. Piracy is a problem throughout the world, but it is particularly rife in China, where the cinema audience fell from a peak of over 4 billion in 1959 (Thompson and Bordwell, 1994: 478) to around 140 million in 2004 (FOCUS 2006, European Audiovisual Observatory). Many of the lost billions will now be watching recent films on pirated DVDs at home. MPAA figures claim that piracy cost the film industry worldwide $18.2 billion in 2005 (<www.mpaa.org/piracy_economies.asp>), with $2.7 billion of lost business in China (where official box office takings were only $250 million).

Hollywood has considered and implemented several strategies, including education/exhortation (evident in the UK with on-screen announcements by FACT – the Federation Against Copyright Theft (see <www.fact-uk.org.uk>)) – and various encryption methods. Prosecution of pirates and seizures of illegal discs merely reduce losses on a temporary basis, and with films set to join music files as easily tradeable in digital formats online, the film industry faces an uncertain future. Illegal files are already traded via peer-to-peer services such as BitTorrent, but access to new studio films for purchase was limited before 2006.

Film audiences will make decisions and either enjoy or suffer the consequences. The music companies eventually embraced digital downloads and made deals with Apple's iTunes and other distributors. They did this only when it was obvious that sales of CDs were falling. There are some signs that Hollywood will be quicker to embrace the digital download. In 2006, Universal and UK company Lovefilms began a scheme that makes available films for rental or purchase on digital download. (Similar deals between Universal and local operators established schemes in other European countries in 2006.) Purchase allows the download of new films the day before DVD release. Purchasers receive three copies of the film – downloadable versions for desktop and portable film player and a DVD mailed on the same day. Universal conducted research that suggested 12–18 year-olds were most interested in watching films on laptops and handheld devices (<www.cnn.com/2006/TECH/ 03/23/movie.download/>). Ironically, Universal's scheme operates only on Windows XP systems, excluding most Apple users. iTunes itself began offering television programmes for download in 2005, and in summer 2006, there was a widespread assumption that iTunes film downloads would be available in the near future.

The concept of the long tail has been around for some time, but its relevance to 'e-tailing' or selling on the internet has been explored by Chris Anderson, editor of *Wired* magazine, in *The Long Tail: How Endless Choice Is Creating Unlimited Demand* (Random House, 2006).

If film downloads become as commercially successful as music downloads, a number of changes to distribution and access to films could result. The retail music industry has seen the gradual decline of the local record shop and even the beginnings of decline for the larger retail chains, which have come to increasingly rely on DVDs rather than CDs. The winners overall appear to have been Apple and online retailers like Amazon, who can stock any title for delivery by post without the need for expensive high street retail space. One theory is that the consumer gets much more choice in this new market, mainly because of the **long tail** effect. This refers to a graph representing the sales of popular items and those selling only one or two copies. Whereas high street shops mainly stock the Top 20 records or books, with few others available, Amazon stocks everything and eventually all titles will sell one or two copies. This is the long-tail of sales. However, a *Guardian* report ('A musical tail of hits and misses', Adam Webb, 17 August 2006) suggested that there was little evidence of this on iTunes. Indeed, if anything, iTunes seemed to be selling a higher proportion of chart songs (90% rather than the high street norm of 80%)

DVD viewing culture

Barbara Klinger (2006: 365–374) has produced one of the first analyses of how DVD viewing culture might be theorised. She suggests a number of central features that characterise this new domestic social practice (some of these will be familiar from other sections of this book, but is useful to bring them together here):

1. The techno-aesthetic refers to the double advantage of DVD in both bringing into distribution a wide range of films from all over the world and from previous decades and in providing the technical quality of sound and image that reproduces the quality of the cinematic experience.
2. 'Remote' viewing enables very different ways of watching films, improving the access to specific scenes and enabling control of playback. She also notes that refusal to use the remote, submitting instead to a 'theatrical presentation' is also a mark of a new cultural position on spectatorship.
3. Special editions offer extras such as interviews, 'making ofs', alternative endings etc. Klinger suggests that these are now expected by audiences, especially for high-profile films, and she wonders if the extras are beginning to change the conception of what a film might be and whether this might in turn lead to a questioning of formal film criticism and academic practice.
4. Alternative canons – different lists of the top films – become more possible as the DVD market expands, with some films being recognised as working better on DVD as well as the success of titles not released theatrically. Again, this challenges the sense of film culture developed by critics and some scholars.

5. Film collecting, especially in terms of special editions, moves film culture closer to other forms of leisure such as book collecting, antiques and philately, with their different social status. It also makes possible different forms of study, when, for instance, it is possible to log the ways in which re-issues of classic films use different approaches to promotion and contextualisation of the same film for a different period. The marketing of boxed sets covering a genre or an artist's (director or star) work offers different ways for audiences to explore film culture.

6. Repetition of viewing has always been possible, but DVD makes it much easier and much more likely. It pushes film consumption/use much closer to the position of popular music in domestic life. Your favourite movie moments are always there ready to enjoy and share with friends, much as you might once have played them a CD.

In 2006, DeAgostini, the part-work publishing company that offers collections on a subscription basis and through newsagents' distribution in the UK, began several series of DVD collections featuring the films of John Wayne, Clint Eastwood, Robert De Niro and 'Hong Kong Legends'.

RESEARCH SUGGESTION
Consider a group of films of different genres/time periods etc. presented on DVD. What kind of 'bonus material' is included in each case? What kinds of bonus material and/or new technologies available on DVD increase your viewing pleasure? Try to formulate about how the experience of watching films at the cinema and on DVD compares.

Klinger's work is a useful starting point and she is aware that there is much to be done. The new viewing culture has already started to make us query the audience work of the last 30 years, rooted in cinema studies. The future of film studies should be interesting.

References

Anderson, Chris (2006), *The Long Tail: How Endless Choice Is Creating Unlimited Demand* (London: Random House).

Atwell, David (1980), *Cathedrals of the Movies: A History of British Cinemas and their Audiences* (London: Architectural Press).

Dinsmore, Una (1998), 'Chaos, Order and Plastic Boxes: The Significance of Videotapes for the People Who Collect Them', in Christine Geraghty and David Lusted (eds), *The Television Studies Book* (London: Arnold).

Gomery, Douglas (1992), *Shared Pleasures: A History of Movie Presentation in the United States* (London: BFI).

Hall, Sheldon (2005), 'The Hills Are Alive in East Anglia: *The Sound of Music* Comes to Norwich', *Picture House*, No. 30.

Jones, Darryl (2002), *Horror: A Thematic History in Fiction and Film* (London: Arnold).

Kermode, Mark (1997), 'I Was a Teenage Horror Fan: or 'How I Learned to Stop Worrying and Love Linda Blair', in Martin Barker and Julian Petley (eds), *Ill Effects* (London: Routledge).

Klinger, Barbara (2006), 'What Is Cinema Today? Home Viewing, New Technologies and DVD', in Linda Ruth Williams and Michael Hammond (eds), *Contemporary American Cinema* (Maidenhead: Open University Press/McGraw-Hill Education).

Newman, Kim (1988), *Nightmare Movies: A Critical Guide to Contemporary Horror Films* (New York: Harmony Books).

Sconce, Jeffrey (2002), 'Smart Cinema', *Screen*, Vol. 43 No. 4, Winter.

Surowiecki, James (2005), *The Wisdom of Crowds* (London: Abacus).

Thompson, Kristin, and David Bordwell (1994), *Film History: An Introduction* (London: McGraw-Hill).

Endpiece

This book has attempted to introduce film audiences and the film industry. I am conscious that, in some cases, I could have gone much further in exploring aspects of film theory, but to do so would have required work at a much higher level of complexity. Instead, I have tried to provide a starting point for further exploration. I am also conscious of raising questions that I have not been able to answer. I accept this situation if what I have achieved is a sense of how industry and audience relate and also what kinds of work film studies might attempt to do.

I do worry that film studies, especially at an introductory level, is in danger of being too narrow in approach and I think it should reach out to embrace ideas from media studies and cultural studies. Film students should have their eyes open for links to all kinds of other academic activities and to the discourses of the industry and other commentators. Throughout the book, there are many references to *Screen International*, a wonderful resource for students and teachers alike. Trade publications like this and the industry websites that provide the basic data on audiences and film box office offer a useful complement, and sometimes a corrective, to academic textbooks.

I hope that some readers will use the book as a starting point to undertake their own research, both into the industrial background of film and into real audiences at their local cinemas. I have enjoyed writing the book and exploring a wide range of background reading. I have also learned a great deal. I am more interested in audience studies than when I started – I hope you are too.

Glossary

1970s theory Refers to the intense period of the 1970s when new theoretical ideas (mainly from France) entered film and media studies in the UK and USA. Also sometimes referred to as *Screen* **theory**.

A List A Hollywood reference to the drawing power of the biggest stars and directors.

academic research Research undertaken in order to increase knowledge and understanding about film production, distribution and exhibition, and about film culture generally.

ACORN A market research classification system devised by CACI that takes broad lifestyle categories and breaks them down into more precise classifications. In the UK the break-down is often related to postcode districts.

active audiences Audience models that assume that audiences 'do something' with what they see and hear, or that they have a reason for watching and listening.

agit-prop Cinema (and other media) used for propaganda purposes. Famously introduced by Lenin during the early years of the Russian Revolution, as a means of getting political messages across quickly, and in a direct style, to a large audience.

anime A Japanese form of animation, that draws large audiences and, like the associated form of *manga*, is now influencing filmmaking in the West.

apparatus theory A reference in 1970s theory to the idea of cinema as a meaning-making machine in which the spectator is held in a particular position to ensure a specific meaning is read.

art film A term used to loosely describe a film outside the mainstream. Art films generally focus more on style and/or characterisation than on entertainment narratives.

arthouse/art cinema Cinemas that play art films. Also the idea of a social institution understood by filmmakers and audiences.

artplex A small multiplex cinema devoted to more specialised films.

aspect ratio The shape of the cinema screen defined by the ratio width:height, e.g. 1.85:1.

audience research Research into cinema audiences which looks at overall attendance patterns and the audience profile of individual films.

audience segmentation The process whereby distributors and exhibitors target segments of the audience separately, i.e. youth, families with children etc.

auteur The concept of the film director as author. Deriving from the polemical writing of the French critics in the 1950s, some of who became directors during the New Wave period between 1958 and 1962.

avant garde This refers to work in any art form that is in some way 'ahead' of what is being produced by the mainstream at that time. What was once avant garde is usually absorbed into the mainstream at a later date.

babyboomers A term used to describe people born during a period of significant rises in birth rates. As these people grow older, they can have an impact on popular culture because of the size of their age group. In the UK, the term was first applied to those born between 1947 and 1950, but in the USA it refers to a larger group born between 1946 and 1960.

BBFC British Board of Film Classification. The UK regulator for the film and video industry.

behaviourism A school of psychology in which the behaviour of animals and humans in laboratory conditions informs ideas about how behaviour can be conditioned by various factors. Behaviourist ideas are behind many of the effects models that have been suggested to explain how media audiences might behave.

binary oppositions A technique used in a structuralist analysis which recognises that texts are produced in cultures in which conflict is expressed by opposite qualities which, in turn, form the basis for narratives. Common oppositions would include good and evil, male and female, conformity and rebellion.

CAVIAR Cinema and Audio Visual Industry Audience Research. A UK audience research programme conducted regularly by the market research organisation BMRB for the Cinema Advertising Association (CAA).

CBFC Central Board of Film Certification. The Indian film and video industry regulator. (Publishes statistics on film releases.)

CCCS The Centre for Contemporary Cultural Studies was a hugely influential department of the University of Birmingham in the UK. During the 1970s and 1980s, it played a major role in the development of British Cultural Studies, which in turn prompted more attention to audience studies.

character functions The idea that certain familiar characters can be recognised by the role they play in a narrative, e.g. the hero or villain. A systematic analysis of a whole range of such functions is associated with the work of Vladimir Propp.

cinephile A person who loves the cinema. Used like **cineaste** to distinguish someone whose interest and enjoyment of cinema goes beyond enjoying individual films as sources of entertainment

cognitive approach In psychology, a theoretical position which starts from the premise that human beings tackle most situations through a process of acquiring knowledge and understanding based on experience. In film theory, the cognitive approach to 'reading' a film is associated with the work of David Bordwell.

counter-booking The strategy adopted by distributors and exhibitors in selecting specific films which will appeal to audiences not attracted to a major blockbuster or another major entertainment event, e.g. counter-booking a romantic comedy against the opening of a big action picture or during a football championship.

crossover The term used to describe a film (or a music recording) that sells in another market as well as the one toward which it would usually be promoted.

cult In film culture, 'cult' is often used to describe a specific group of films (and their stars and audiences) which is clearly not mainstream, but does have a loyal and significant group of fans. There are no strict definitions, but a large number of cult films refer to genres such as horror and science fiction.

demographic Jargon – when used as a noun – which describes a particular segment of the audience, defined by age, gender etc.

Digital Screen Network An initiative by the UK Film Council that is intended to create a network of cinemas capable of projecting digital film prints. All participating cinemas receive some public funding towards installation of digital projectors and must programme a quota of 'specialised film' screenings.

dominant reading The reading of a film that corresponds to the dominant ideology, and therefore appears the most likely. Also described as the 'preferred reading'.

EIRIN Administration Commission of Motion Picture Code of Ethics in Japan. Japanese film and video industry regulator.

effects model The idea that films have demonstrable (and usually negative) effects on audiences that could be predicted/prevented. Circulates widely in popular discourse, but is largely discredited in academic film and media studies.

empiricism A philosophical position that emphasises the importance of experience. In film studies this refers to research into 'real' audiences.

ethnography The study of specific communities of people undertaken via detailed fieldwork by researchers who may become participant observers.

European Audiovisual Observatory 'The Information Portal for the Audio visual Sector'. Invaluable source of data about the media in Europe.

expressionism An artistic style or aesthetic in which the internal emotions of characters or the general emotional state of the society as a whole is expressed visually and aurally in the filmic image through *mise en scène*, camerawork etc. Shocking when introduced in the 1910s, it is now a familiar element in horror, melodrama and other genres.

fetish The idea, in Freudian psychology, that sexual desire can become channeled through attention to a specific object or part of the body rather than a relationship with a whole person.

film market An international event, often part of a film festival, where sales agents attempt to sell both completed films and films in production to distributors in different territories.

four quadrants Used in film marketing to refer to the very desirable prospect of a film that can be sold to all types of audiences (e.g. to the youth market, 25–34 AB adults, older audiences of 55+, families with children etc.)

franchise (1) A licence to broadcast a terrestrial television service in the UK, (2) used to describe an established series of high budget films with the same central characters and setting, often developed from a single very successful film with a strong central character (e.g. James Bond, Harry Potter)

Frankfurt School A group of academics who worked across several disciplines from the 1930s onwards and who had a great influence on the foundation of cultural studies. Some of their work focused on popular culture and they were criticised for taking what was seen as an elitist position.

gaze theory Associated with the adoption of both feminist and psychoanalaytical ideas in film studies, gaze theory suggested initially that the representation of women on screen was constructed to appeal to the viewpoint of the male audience. Later adapted to include consideration of the 'female gaze', such ideas are associated with the work of Laura Mulvey.

grading The process of adjusting the colour palette for the final projection copies of a film.

grand theory Sometimes referred to as a 'grand narrative', various ideologies have been seen as attempting to explain 'everything'. This is the typical charge made against Marxism by postmodernists.

greenlighting The process by which a film studio or major financier gives the go-ahead for a film to move into production.

hard money Money put up by risk-taking investors, as distinct from **soft money**.

hegemony, hegemonic The dominance by one group with a specific set of ideas in any society, achieved by persuasion rather than simply by coercion.

high culture Traditional arts such as opera, ballet, fine art painting and sculpture have been accorded great cultural value. Cinema is described from this position as a 'popular' art form.

identification: In textual analysis, the concept relating to the spectator's involvement with one or more of the characters in a story. In psychoanalytical analysis, the child's adoption on the behaviour of one parent as part of self-development.

identity politics In relation to film audiences, the potential clash between ideas of personal identity, developed in the social world outside the cinema, and representations on screen. Also relates to questions about the identity of filmmakers (and critics) and the representations in their films.

industry research audience research/market research undertaken for commercial motives.

intertextuality A term used in relation to films that depend on references to other films in order to release all their meanings. Argued as a feature of postmodern films – but also of earlier films in the studio period.

intertitles Onscreen text that gives information to the audience, often about time and place, or about the start of a new episode or chapter.

letterboxing The effect of preserving the correct **aspect ratio** of a film when shown on a television screen, resulting in black bars above and below the image.

long tail The suggestion that modern retail markets developed online are more likely to extend the range of commodities sold (e.g. DVDs) with not only bestsellers, but a 'long tail' of titles selling only a handful of copies. This is possible because of the low fixed costs of online retailing.

longitudinal study A form of research attempting to trace a set of practices/behaviour over a long period – several years at least.

low resolution image A reference to the visible 'lines' of pixels on the screen of the standard TV set. Film offers a high resolution image, now matched by high resolution digital projection.

LUMIERE Database of film admissions in Europe.

mainstream Generally used to represent the prevailing conventional cinema produced by the major studios in Hollywood and other major film producing countries.

manga Japanese literature similar to Western 'graphic novels' or comic books, but targeted at a much wider range of readers and with much higher public status.

market research Research into the market for films (in any format) and audience behaviour.

Mass-Observation A large scale social survey conducted by teams of professional and amateur observers in the UK from the late 1930s into the 1950s.

mediate/mediation The process whereby the content of a message is in some way changed by the medium used to communicate it, e.g. in cinema by use of framing and editing etc.

megaplex A multi-screen cinema complex with 20 or more screens.

melodrama A film genre with a long history and a derivation in live theatre. Often used loosely as a pejorative term for any form of exaggerated performance and with changing meanings throughout the history of the film industry. In film studies, it now usually refers to films focusing on personal relationships with expression of characters' inner feelings revealed through aspects of *mise en scène*.

miniplex A purpose-built cinema with three to five screens.

mise en scène A theatre term referring to the use of decor, costume, colour, lighting etc. in putting together a scene.

moral panic Refers to any new medium or new kind of media product, usually associated with youth culture, that is perceived to threaten social norms. The potential dangers to society are usually highly exaggerated.

MPAA The Motion Picture Association of America (and its international counterpart, the MPA) is the trade association of the American film industry. In practice, it represents the views of the six major studios. The MPAA acts as the film and video industry regulator in the USA. It began life as the MPPDA (Motion Pictures Producers and Distributors Association) in 1922.

MPPAJ The Motion Picture Producers Association of Japan (see also **EIRIN**).

multiplex A multi-screen cinema with more than five screens.

negotiated reading The idea that some audiences do not accept everything in the **dominant** or preferred reading of a film and construct their own understanding which may include extra or different interpretations.

New Wave A general term for any new film movement (usually defined in terms of a national cinema). First used extensively to define films by first-time filmmakers in France between 1958 and 1962, and often seen as a reaction against the prevailing modes of mainstream cinema.

oppositional reading A reading of a film by individuals or groups opposed to the dominant ideas and values in society. This audience not only resists the dominant reading but also constructs another in opposition.

P & A Prints & Advertising is the industry term for the major elements of the distribution budget.

package production The current mode of film production in which films are made as single productions that originate as a package of director, writer, stars and property.

pan and scan Technique for presenting a widescreen film on a standard 4:3 TV screen, by showing only the part of the image that contains the main action.

participant observation A form of field research in which observers take part in the activities being observed.

passive audiences Audience models that treat the audience as passive in terms of what media texts do to them. Confusingly, it is passive audiences who are potentially dangerous because they might go out and be violent after watching a violent film, i.e. they are more likely to be subject to the **effects** of violent films.

pester power Refers to the impact of promoting products to children, who then 'pester' parents to buy them. A function of advertising on children's television and 'tie-in' promotions for films on cereal boxes etc.

platform release A film release strategy that opens a film on a limited number of screens in key cities and expands to a wider release once a 'profile' for the film has been achieved.

postmodernist A widely used term with several meanings. In film studies it refers to (1) a philosophical position opposed to the certainties of 'grand theories' such as Marxism, (2) a description of social, economic and cultural conditions in contemporary society, (3) a description of films themselves, stressing their mixing of styles and genre elements and general 'playfulness'.

post-theory A general term for the shifts in film theory during the 1990s which critiqued 1970s theory and encouraged a re-thinking of general approaches.

primary research Refers to the first handling of what will become research data – i.e. data collected by a researcher from interviews, observation, study of raw box-office data etc.

Production Code The detailed code governing what was allowable in Hollywood films from the mid-1930s to the late-1950s. Scripts had to be submitted in advance to the Production Code Office. Sometimes known as the Hays Code after the President of the MPPDA, Will Hays.

production research Activities carried out by film production teams that are directly concerned with the content of the film and the practical questions about shooting. It is not part of **audience research**.

property In film production, this refers to any source material that can be copyrighted and subsequently exploited in a production, e.g. the rights to adapt a best-selling novel.

public sphere The concept of a virtual debating arena in which people can exchange ideas. Cinema (and discussion about cinema) could provide a space for this.

qualitative research Research designed to find out what audiences think about films or why they do certain things in relation to films. It asks how and why questions.

quantitative research Research which sets out to measure audiences and their responses to films in quantifiable ways. It asks what, where and when questions.

reception theory General term referring to the shifts in film studies away from studying the idealised spectator and the single film text, towards studies of real audiences in cinemas in all their variety.

rentals The money returned to the distributor of a film by the exhibitor after deduction of the exhibitor's take.

repertoire In genre theory, this is the concept of an ever-changing repertoire of genre elements from which a filmmaker can draw when putting together a new genre film. Each new film will be a new mixture of elements in different arrangements.

rights The legal rights to distribute and exhibit a film title. The copyright holder will sell the rights for a fixed period to exhibitors in different territories.

roadshow A form of film release adopted in the 1950s and 1960s in which a big-budget film is shown in selected cinemas for an extended run with higher ticket prices for a more exclusive, 'event-orientated' presentation.

RSS 'Really Simple Syndication' or 'Rich Site Summary' is a form of automatic feed of web-based information to registered users. Potentially a means of spreading promotional material. (See **viral marketing**.)

safe area The area of a filmic image that can be guaranteed as visible on a standard 4:3 TV set – filmmakers are often required to ensure that important action is always contained within this frame (as indicated in a camera viewfinder).

Screen **theory** See **1970s theory**. *Screen* is now a UK academic journal for 'screen studies'. In the 1970s it was engaged in a more overtly political project to develop the theoretical base of film and media studies.

secondary circulation The circulation of a star image in other media besides cinema, e.g. when a star appears on a TV chat show or in a magazine interview.

secondary research Research data that has already been collected, collated and presented for reference in journals, books, archives etc.

self-regulation In the UK and the US, cinema has been largely self-regulating, but video releases in the UK are subject to **statutory regulation**, since it is required by legislation.

semiotics/semiology The study of sign systems which became influential in film studies during the 1970s.

slate The films that a studio intends to make within a specific production period.

soft money Usually refers to the funding available to filmmakers from various schemes using public funds. These may include tax concessions, grants of various kinds or investment by public sector organisations such as the UK Film Council or the BBC.

specialised cinema Term used by the UK Film Council to distinguish films that do not receive a 'wide' commercial release.

spectatorship A general term for the approach to audience adopted in the 1970s – that of the idealised spectator and their relationship with the single film text.

star image Refers to the meanings associated with a particular film star that have accreted over the period of the star's career, including through performances in films and the **secondary circulation** of the star's image in publicity and promotional material.

structural film A form of avant garde film concerned with exploring the material properties of film as a medium.

structuralism A major movement in philosophical thought in the latter part of the 20th century. In film studies, structuralism challenged the assumption that meaning was rooted in the film itself, arguing instead for the recurrence of structural elements across texts and the importance of the context of production and consumption. Attention in textual analysis turned from 'What does this mean?' to 'How does this produce meaning?'.

super cinema Very large (around 3,000 seats) and extravagantly decorated cinemas built in the 1920s and 1930s. The basis for cinema as 'dream palace'.

synergy/synergistic The concept of two separate agencies (e.g. two media such as cinema and television) working together and generating new energy from 'feeding off' each other.

tentpole A major film used by a studio as the main focus for an annual **slate** of films – literally building a distribution strategy supported by the biggest and strongest 'tentpoles'.

territory A geographical area in which a distributor will control the rights to show a particular film on one or more media platforms for a set period.

theatrical (rights) This refers to the distribution of a film to cinemas (as distinct from DVD, pay TV, free-to-air TV etc.).

turnaround The period when a property or proposal for a film has been 'developed' but has not been 'greenlighted' and is effectively put into a 'waiting' state, from which it might be rescued by another producer.

typing The use in film narratives of character types, related to social types, to give audiences knowledge and to stimulate expectations of character behaviour.

UK Film Council The agency charged by UK government with supporting and developing UK film in both industrial and cultural terms.

unit production system A mode of production at some Hollywood studios during the 1930s and 1940s. A star worked with a producer's team of director, writer and crew on a series of similar films.

uses and gratifications model This is associated with the concept of **active audiences** who use media texts for their own purposes.

VCD A digital format that compresses a film onto (usually two) CDs. Generally unknown in the UK, the VCD is popular in South Asia and East Asia, offering a convenient format costing less than DVD.

vertical integration The acquisition by one company of other companies, operating in different stages of the production process. For example, when a production company acquires a distribution company.

video nasties A small number of violent horror film titles released on video in the early 1980s that provoked a **moral panic**, leading to the statutory regulation of video films.

viral marketing A form of marketing in which fans are recruited to spread promotional material such as film trailers via email, websites, blogs etc. like a virus.

window The gap between the release dates of a film in different markets: e.g. between the DVD release and Pay TV release.

Resources

Textbooks

Gill Branston and Roy Stafford (2006) *The Media Student's Book* (4th edition) (London: Routledge) is an introductory textbook which can be used to complement this guide, providing introductions to other key concepts and putting audience studies in film studies into a wider context.

Graeme Turner (2006) *Film as Social Practice* (4th edition) (London: Routledge) is a more specific textbook on film culture and John Hill and Pamela Church Gibson (eds) (1998) *The Oxford Guide to Film Studies* (Oxford: OUP) is a more advanced guide to academic film studies.

This book has attempted to represent the trend towards a more inclusive approach to film studies, with more attention to real audiences and to the social and economic context of film production and reception. The following are useful collections that share this aim:

Christine Gledhill and Linda Williams (2000) *Reinventing Film Studies* (London: Arnold)

Graeme Turner (ed.) (2002) *The Film Cultures Reader* (London: Routledge)

Online resources

Most of the industry research material used in this book has been obtained from the websites of various organisations. Most of the sites listed here make material freely available. The exception is *Screen International,* whose website at <www.screendaily.com> is only available to subscribers to the weekly magazine.

The UK Film Council site at <www.ukfilmcouncil.org.uk> offers a great deal of extremely useful material for free download. In particular, the Research and Statistics Unit (RSU) offers a Statistical Yearbook and regular bulletins relating to the UK film industry.

The equivalent US website is <www.mpaa.org> which will email free documents to visitors who register.

The European Audiovisual Observatory offers free downloads and the Lumiere database for film admissions at <www.obs.coe.int/medium/film.html>

FOCUS reports on all the world's film industries are available from <www.obs.coe.int/oea_publ/market/focus.html>

Box office figures for the UK are available from the UK Film Council (see above) and for the US (and worldwide) from various sources, including:

<www.boxofficeguru.com>
<www.boxofficemojo.com>
<www.the-numbers.com>

The British Film Institute website at <www.bfi.org.uk> carries a wealth of material including the essential guide to setting up an independent cinema: Robin Baker, J. Ron Inglis, Julia Voss (2002) *At a cinema near you: strategies for sustainable local cinema development*

The associated BFI website at <www.screenonline.org.uk> also carries a great deal of useful information about distribution and exhibition.

Index

Selected Key Terms and Names

A List 105–8, 111
academic research 134–6
ACORN 138
active audiences 123,
    128–9, 132
agit-prop 122
art film/arthouse/art
    cinema 12, 15–22, 28,
    31, 35, 60, 62–3, 66–7,
    70–3, 79–80, 88, 98, 141,
    145, 149, 154–7, 163
aspect ratio 51–4
audience research 42,
    134–45
audience segmentation 45,
    155
auteur 36, 73, 79, 89
avant garde 51, 73, 79, 81,
    157

babyboomers 157
Barker, Martin 87–8,
    130–1
BBC 16–17, 23, 46–50, 65,
    67, 119

BBFC 13, 59–60. 118,
    126–8, 131–2, 136
behaviourist/behaviourism
    121, 125–6
binary oppositions 81
Bollywood 15, 22, 26–9, 71,
    147

CAVIAR 42–5, 137
CCCS 125, 129
Channel 4 50–1
character functions 81
cinephile 19, 21, 75
cognitive approach 84, 87,
    92, 125
counter-booking 39
crossover 19–23, 71
cult 23–6, 53, 130, 153, 161

demographic 13, 37–8,
    42–6, 75, 109, 113,
    137–9, 166
Digital Screen Network 64,
    72, 167
dominant reading 86–7,
    114, 129–30
Dyer, Richard 85–6, 106

effects model 86, 125–6,
    130–1
Ellis, John 106–7
empirical/empiricism 84,
    119–21, 130
ethnography/ethnographic
    research 120, 122, 130
European Audiovisual
    Observatory 137
expressionism 79

fetish 82
film market (1) trade event
    37, 162 (2) marketing
    territory 3, 57, 134, 138
four quadrants 10
franchise (1) TV licence
    50, (2) blockbuster film
    7, 10–11, 164, 166
Frankfurt School 123–4,
    126, 130
Freud, Sigmund 82–3

gaze theory 82–3
Geraghty, Christine 106, 114
greenlighting 33, 38
Grierson, John 119, 121

Hall, Stuart 125, 129
hard money 38
hegemony, hegemonic 126, 129
hybridity 29

identification 25, 82, 85, 97, 105, 107, 114, 126
identity politics 85–6, 95–6, 109, 130, 168
industry research 135–40
intertextuality 83
ITV 46–8, 50, 122

Jung, Carl 82

Lee, Ang 19, 21, 88–90, 98–9
Lee, Spike 108–12, 168
letterboxing 52–3
long tail 172
longitudinal study 144
LUMIERE (Database) 16, 40, 138

mainstream cinema/films 8, 12–29, 34, 39, 43, 51, 60, 63–4, 66, 70–5, 83, 88, 102, 107–13, 136, 140–4, 155–6, 159, 161–2, 166–8
manga 12, 94
market research 33, 134–44
Mass-Observation 121–2, 139
mediate/mediation 81, 87
melodrama 29, 65, 67, 84, 94, 118
mise en scène 92–4
moral panic 119, 151–2
MPAA 9, 10, 13, 44, 54, 137, 171

negotiated reading 86–7, 129, 132
New Wave 47, 79–80
1970s theory 80–7

oppositional reading 86–7, 129, 132

P & A 61, 69, 88
package production 57, 105
pan and scan 52
participant observation 121, 130
passive audiences 123–6
pester power 10
photo effect 107
platform release 62–3, 112
postmodern/postmodernist 23, 83
post-theory 83
primary research 3, 134
Production Code 120–1
production research 134
psychoanalysis 82–3, 106
public sphere 168–70

qualitative research 99, 127, 130, 134–5, 141–2
quantitative research 134

reception (theory) 5, 23, 73, 79, 99, 106, 120, 158
rentals 9, 59, 151
repertoire 104–5
rights 19, 31, 51, 57–9, 65, 69, 113
roadshow 26, 64, 161
Roberts, Julia 110, 112–16
RSS 166

secondary circulation 106–7, 114

secondary research 134–5, 145
self-regulation 59
semiotics/semiology 80–3, 106
slate 11, 57, 62, 110
smart cinema 156–7
soft money 33, 38, 65
specialised cinema 7–29, 39, 42, 60, 64–6, 69–74, 80, 98, 140–5, 153–5, 159, 162, 166–7
spectatorship 5, 79, 83, 172
star image 86, 105–9, 114–16
statutory regulation 59, 126, 151
structuralism 80–5
super cinema 70, 148–9, 154
surrealism 79
synergy/synergistic 10, 50

tentpole 8–12
territory 8, 10, 19, 20, 34–7, 42, 48, 57–8, 109, 135, 137, 151, 162
theatrical (distribution) 9, 14, 25, 44, 50, 53–4, 58–69, 88, 102, 170, 172
turnaround 33
typing 67, 85
UK Film Council 15, 38, 45, 64, 65, 71–2, 137, 139, 142, 155, 167
uses and gratifications model 123, 128

vertical integration 56
video nasties 119, 151
viral marketing 165–6

Washington, Denzel 86, 108–12

wide release 10

window (distribution) 37, 49, 50, 58

Films

(All films are *American* unless otherwise indicated)

A Kind of Loving (UK 1962) 47

A Room with a View (UK 1985) 73

A Very Long Engagement (France 2004) 15

Adieu Philippine (France 1962) 80

Ae Fond Kiss (UK/Bel/Ger/Ital/Spain 2004) 40

Alexander (2004) 35

Alien Autopsy (UK 2006) 76

Amélie (France 2001) 15

American Beauty (1999) 62

Antwone Fisher (2002) 112

Babam Ve Oglum (Turkey 2005) 28

Babymother (UK 1998) 66

Bamboozled (2000) 108

Bandit Queen (UK/India 1994) 51

Bend it Like Beckham (UK/Ger/US 2002) 72

Blade Runner (1982) 23

Boyz N the Hood (1991) 66

Bride and Prejudice (UK/US 2004) 41

Bridget Jones: Edge of Reason (UK/US 2004) 45

Brokeback Mountain (2006) 5, 17, 22, 32, 35, 41, 88–102, 106, 111, 169

Broken Flowers (2005) 36

Bubble (2006) 58

Bullet Boy (UK 2005) 4, 65–8

Cabaret (1972) 49

Calendar Girls (UK 2003) 144

Capote (2005) 102

Cars (2006) 11

Casablanca (1942) 94

Centre Stage (*The Actress*) (Hong Kong 1992) 105

Charlie's Angels (2000) 24

Chicago (2002) 144

City of God (Brazil 2002) 66

Closer (2004) 116

Code Unknown (France 2000) 16

Cosh Boy (UK 1952) 124

Crash (Canada/UK 1996) 123, 130–1

Crash (US/UK/Germany, 2004) 68, 71

Crouching Tiger, Hidden Dragon (Taiwan/Hong Kong/China/US) 14, 19–22, 90, 104

Dance with a Stranger (UK 1985) 112

Dark Water (2005) 14

Darling (UK 1965) 114

Dead Poet's Society (1989) 114

Dil Se (India 1998) 26–7

Dog Day Afternoon (1975) 109–10

Donnie Darko (2001) 23–5, 156

Downfall (Germany 2005) 67

Duel (1972) 49

Easy Rider (1969) 44

El (Mexico 1957) 82

Election (1999) 53, 156

Emmanuelle (France 1974) 16

Emperor of the North Pole (1973) 160

Erin Brockovich (2000) 86–7, 110

Fifty First Dates (2004) 24

Flightplan (2005) 110

Funny Games (Austria 1997) 16

Galaxy Quest (1999) 163

Garfield: A Tale of Two Kitties (2006) 165

Ghost World (UK/Germany/US 2000) 156

Gone with the Wind (1939) 117

Goodnight, and Good Luck (2006) 17

H20dio (Italy 2006) 58

Harry Potter (series) 8, 35, 61, 179

He Got Game (1998) 108

Hero (China 2002) 15, 19–22

Hidden (Caché) (France 2005) 17–19

Hitch (2005) 67

House of Flying Daggers (China/Hong Kong 2004) 15, 19–22

Howard's End (UK 1992) 73

Howl's Moving Castle (Japan 2004) 12, 34

Hud (1963) 92

Hulk (2003) 90

Hustle and Flow (2005) 68

Ice Age (2002) 10

Ice Age 2: The Meltdown (2006) 8–11, 29, 110

Inside Man (2006) 107–12, 168

In the Mood for Love (Hong Kong/France/Thailand, 2000) 21

Jarhead (2005) 90

Jaws (1975) 8, 159

Jean de Florette (France/Italy/Switzerland 1986) 18

Jericho Mile (1978) 49

Johnny Guitar (1954) 96

Kabhi Alvida Naa Kehna (Never Say Goodbye) (India 2006) 28–9

Kabhi Kushie Kabhie Gham (India 2001) 27–8

Kal Ho Naa Ho (India 2003) 46

Kill Bill Vol 2 (2004) 46

Kingdom of Heaven (2005) 35

King Kong (2005) 36

Kuch Kuch Hota Hai (India 1998) 28

Ladies in Lavender (UK 2004) 45

Larry the Cable Guy (2006) 111

Lemming (France 2006) 18

Look at Me (France 2004) 15

Looney Tunes: Back in Action (2003) 143

Lord of the Rings 8, 35, 71, 155, 164

Lonesome Cowboy (1968) 100

Love Actually (UK/US 2003) 46, 144

M:i:III (2006) 11, 62

Malcolm X (1992) 108

Man on Fire (2004) 110

Manon des sources (France/Italy/Switzerland 1986) 18

Miami Vice (2006) 11

Mighty Joe Young (1998) 113

Mix Me a Person (UK 1962) 124

Mo Better Blues (1991) 108

Mona Lisa Smile (2003) 112–16

Monsters Inc. (2001) 40

Morvern Callar (UK 2002) 33

Moulin Rouge (Australia/US 2001) 29, 114

My Beautiful Laundrette (UK 1985) 51

My Darling Clementine (1946) 94

North Country (2005) 18

Oceans 12 (2004) 116

Out of Time (2003) 109

Paper Flowers (India 1959) 105

Peter Pan (2003) 143

Pirates of the Caribbean: Dead Man's Chest (2006) 11

Planet of the Apes (2001) 113

Poseidon (2006) 11

Psycho (1960) 159

Pulse (2006) 14

Raiders of the Lost Ark (1981) 52

Ratcatcher (UK 1997) 33

Red River (1947) 96

Resident Evil: Apocalypse (2004) 45

Ride the High Country (1962) 96

Ringu (Japan 1998) 12–13, 25, 36, 130

Rock Around the Clock (1956) 123

Runaway Bride (1999) 114

Rushmore (1999) 53, 156

Salaam Bombay (India/UK/France 1988) 51

Saturday Night and Sunday Morning (UK 1960) 47

Saw (series) 14

Scream (1996) 13

Sense and Sensibility (UK/US 1995) 90

Shallow Grave (UK 1995) 62

She Hate Me (2004) 108

Shrek (2001) 40

Southlands (2006) 25

Spellbound (1945) 82

Spider-Man (2001) 60, 164

Spirited Away (Japan 2001)
12

Stagecoach (1939) 117

Star Wars (series) 164

Stay Alive (2006) 111

Straw Dogs (UK/US 1971)
132

Sunshine (UK/US 2007) 36

Superman Returns (2006)
11, 36, 161

Sweet Sixteen
(UK/Ger/Spain 2002)
40, 126

Taxi Driver (1976) 82

The Amityville Horror
(2005) 67

The Anderson Tapes (1971)
109

The Avengers (1998) 17

The Battle of the Red Cliff
(China 2008) 22

The Beverley Hillbillies
(1993) 113

The Blair Witch Project
(1999) 44, 165

The Claim
(UK/France/Canada
1999) 36

The Da Vinci Code (2006)
8, 11, 74

The Fountain (2006) 140

The Full Monty (UK/US
1997) 29

The Garden (UK 1990) 51

The Grudge (2005) 14

The Haunted Mansion
(2003) 143

The Incredibles (2004) 11

The Interpreter (2005) 110

The Island (2005) 35

The Killers (1964) 49

The Last Picture Show
(1971) 92

The Last Samurai (2003) 36

*The Life and Times of
Colonel Blimp* (UK 1943)
122

The Longest Yard (1974) 160

The Longest Yard (2005) 35

The Lusty Men (1952) 92

The Matrix (1999) 29

The Misfits (1961) 92

*The Original Kings of
Comedy* (2002) 108

The Passion of the Christ
(2004) 24, 46

The Piano Teacher (France
2001) 16

The Pink Panther (2006) 17

The Promise (China 2005)
22

The Queen (UK 2006) 76

The Ring (2002) 12–14, 25,
36, 60, 130

The Ring Two (2005) 14, 67

The Road to Guantanamo
(UK 2006) 58

*The Rocky Horror Picture
Show* (1975) 161

The Searchers (1956) 93

The Sound of Music (1965)
161

The Wild Bunch (1969) 91

*The Wind That Shakes the
Barley* (UK/Ireland
2006) 42

The Wizard of Oz (1939)
117

Titanic (1997) 43

Toy Story (1995) 11, 155

Training Day (2001) 109

Trainspotting (UK 1996) 62

True Grit (1969) 91

Tsotsi (South Africa/UK
2005) 53

25th Hour (2002) 108

United 93 (France/UK/US
2006) 109

V for Vendetta (2006)
111

Valiant (UK 2005) 67

Van Helsing (2004) 46

Vera (UK 2005) 41

Violent Playground (UK
1958) 124

Walk the Line (2005) 41–2,
111

*Wallace and Gromit: The
Curse of the Were-Rabbit*
(UK 2005) 34, 44

Wedding Crashers (2005)
35

Wimbledon (UK/France
2004) 45

X-Men 2 (2003) 62

X-Men: The Last Stand
(2006) 11

Young Soul Rebels (UK
1991) 66